"Understanding the theology of the reformers means understanding how they have read the Bible. Dennis Ngien's erudite study on Luther's and Calvin's interpretation of the Letter to the Galatians provides us with a thoroughly thoughtful and well-written exploration of how both reformers lifted the treasuries of Paul's writing on the cross and on justification. Seeing both theologians focusing on a theology 'pro nobis,' Ngien shows their message for today's church and theology."

—**VOLKER LEPPIN,**
Yale Divinity School

"Grace and Law in *Galatians* does something original and significant. It is not primarily a study of how Luther and Calvin handled exegetical issues in the text, nor is it primarily a study of how Galatians shaped particular themes in their theology. Rather, it shows us how Paul's letter was an indispensable basis for their understanding and application of the gospel itself. Ngien offers an important resource to all those attempting to understand and apply the gospel."

—**STEPHEN J. CHESTER,**
Wycliffe College

"Dennis Ngien has once again written a fantastic book. Brimming with original insights into Luther's and Calvin's engagement with Galatians, the reader is blessed with a sense of how the gospel enables us to live in Christ and in the neighbour. Ngien's scholarship is outstanding, his prose inviting, and most importantly, his love of the Lord Jesus Christ of whom he writes, overflowing. We are in his debts for providing us with such a book."

—**CHRISTOPHER R. J. HOLMES,**
University of Otago

"While engaging numerous contemporary scholars of Luther and Calvin, the great value of Dennis Ngien's work is he lets both Reformers speak for themselves. Those who seek better to understand the Reformers on the doctrine of justification, the distinction of law and gospel, the nature of the sanctified life, and the assurance of salvation, will find Ngien an illuminating and accessible guide."

—JOHN T. PLESS,
Concordia Theological Seminary

"The history of Lutheran-Reformed polemics has tended to occlude the substantial theological agreement between their founders. Ngien's fresh reading of Luther and Calvin on Paul's Letter to the Galatians is sympathetic, contextual, and pastoral as he explores the Reformers' respective theological nuances on a variety of important themes. Masterfully weaving together primary and secondary sources, Ngien's book is immensely readable, academically-sound, non-combative, and essential reading for all who take the Christian life seriously."

—DENNIS BIELFELDT,
president, Institute of Lutheran Theology

GRACE *and* LAW
in GALATIANS

GRACE *and* LAW *in* GALATIANS

Justification in Luther and Calvin

DENNIS NGIEN

Foreword by Michael Parsons

CASCADE *Books* · Eugene, Oregon

GRACE AND LAW IN GALATIANS
Justification in Luther and Calvin

Cascade Books
An Imprint of Wipf and Stock Publishers
199 W. 8th Ave., Suite 3
Eugene, OR 97401

www.wipfandstock.com

PAPERBACK ISBN: 978-1-6667-1840-9
HARDCOVER ISBN: 978-1-6667-1841-6
EBOOK ISBN: 978-1-6667-1842-3

Cataloguing-in-Publication data:

Names: Ngien, Dennis.

Title: Grace and law in Galatians : justification in Luther and Calvin / Dennis Ngien.

Description: Eugene, OR: Cascade Books, 2023. | Includes bibliographical references and index.

Identifiers: ISBN 978-1-6667-1840-9 (paperback). | ISBN 978-1-6667-1841-6 (hardcover). | ISBN 978-1-6667-1842-3 (ebook).

Subjects: LCSH: Bible.—Galatians—Criticism, interpretation, etc. | Law and gospel. | Paul, the Apostle, Saint—Contributions in theology of law. | Bible.—Epistles of Paul—Theology. | Luther, Martin, 1483–1546—Theology. | Calvin, Jean, 1509–1564—Theology.

Classification: BS2685.52 N44 2023 (print). | BS2685.52 (ebook).

JANUARY 16, 2023 11:03 AM

This book is dedicated to Robert Kolb,
an erudite Reformation scholar, a generous mentor,
and a faithful partner of the gospel.

CONTENTS

FOREWORD

THIS EXCELLENT NEW BOOK by Dennis Ngien reveals as his others have
done his breadth of academic understanding, his pastoral sensitivity, and
his generous spirit in relating to sixteenth-century Reformers seeking
God's way for their own generation—this time through their exposition
of the apostle Paul's letter to the Galatians. It does so by highlighting, on
the one hand, the epistle's teaching elaborated by the Reformers' theology and application, and, on the other hand, their dogmatic doctrine of
justification, centered as it is in Jesus Christ.

The significance of Jesus Christ to the Reformers Martin Luther and
John Calvin cannot be exaggerated. He is as crucial to their theological
reflection and endeavor as he is to their pastoral writing; and, just as clearly,
to their view of evangelical preaching. They exult in and seek to live by
the Lord's grace—his forgiveness, comfort, and salvation. At one point, the
Wittenberg Reformer spells this out as the benevolent work that Christ effects through the preacher toward those in distress. We notice, for example,
in the following quotation the positive verbs associated with the negative
experience of weakness as Christ is said to transform the helpless through
the preached word: "He helps the penitent, comforts the afflicted, recalls
the despairing, raises up the fallen and humiliated, justifies sinners, gives
life to the dying."[1] Significantly, justification, for Luther, begins with and
gains its meaning from Jesus Christ and sits in this tight cluster of benefits bestowed upon those who need the divine grace—the penitent, the
afflicted, the despairing, the fallen and humiliated, sinners, the dying—all,
that is, who have not yet found grace in Jesus Christ. That is, the backdrop
of the Reformers' understanding of justification includes the extreme predicament in which fallen men and women reside outside of Christ.

---

1. *LW* 12:211; WA 40.2:491.

The Genevan Reformer, John Calvin—in many ways a conscious disciple of Luther—speaks this way about justification: "We define justification as follows: the sinner, received into communion with Christ, is reconciled to God by his grace, which cleansed by Christ's blood, he obtains forgiveness of sins, and clothed with Christ's righteousness as if it were his own, he stands confident before the heavenly judgment seat."[2] Again, the emphasis is on the grace of God, the centrality and necessity of Christ, forgiveness and faith in contradiction to the previous predicament of the sinner. To be justified, for Calvin, is to be "accepted, cleansed in him [Christ], to be forgiven, to be clothed with the righteousness of Christ," and to receive "peace and quiet joy" and a clear conscience.[3]

Both Reformers emphatically hold the truth that men and women cannot save or justify themselves—only God can do that. To quote Luther again: "Because we can only be justified and saved through him, it was necessary that he be more than a perfect man. Human power and might can justify and save no one. God alone can do this. Now since the prophet [Isaiah] testifies of Christ, that he will justify all who believe on him, he is testifying that Christ is not only true man, but also true God."[4] Therefore, "whoever strays from this way and does not look for peace in Christ is on the wrong road."[5]

The apostle Paul's letter to the Galatians is primarily about the freedom believers have in Christ. The central, and pivotal, tenet of the epistle is that to which Paul drives from the outset, and from which he moves toward its conclusion: "It is for freedom that Christ has set us free" (5:1). The Reformers' understanding of the doctrine of justification elaborates on this seemingly simple theme: the centrality of Christ in bringing those fettered by sin and law into a wonderful liberty through divine grace alone.

Dennis Ngien, with his usual pastoral wisdom and academic acumen, draws our attention to the Reformers' reading of Galatians, centering on law and grace, on justification, on righteousness, faith, and the work of the Holy Spirit in the Reformers' exposition of this seminal letter. What we learn is how pivotal Pauline theology was to the evangelical faith morphing out from Catholicism and its flawed penitential system in the turbulent sixteenth-century Reformations. We learn, too, how vital the relationship

2. Calvin, *Inst.* 3.17.8.

3. Calvin, *Inst.* 3.13.5.

4. Luther, *Sermons*, 1:450.

5. Luther, *Sermons*, 1:445.

to and experience of Christ was to those leading that revival. And in passing we are fed a feast of good and helpful theology for our own troubled times—a theology centered in Jesus Christ and his grace in justifying those sinners who come to him. I for one am truly grateful for Dennis Ngien's thorough and fascinating Reformational study, which rewards careful reading and reflection.

Michael Parsons
Oxford 2022
Theological Moderator
The Australian College of Theology

Acknowledgments

It had been a privilege to have table talks with the late J. I. Packer, my professor-mentor. Beaming with hope and enthusiasm, Packer once hurled at me this pertinent remark: "Theology is primarily biblical exposition for the people of God"—thus it is not devoid of pastoral and spiritual implications. And in a different context, he exhorted me to be a theologian of both "Bible and tradition." Since then, I have found myself increasingly drawn to the commentaries of the Magisterial Reformers Luther and Calvin, harvesting from them salutary fruits for the souls. This book also comes because of numerous interactions with pastors and leaders, all of whom share Packer's conviction. This comparative study of Luther and Calvin revolves around a few significant themes in their Galatians commentaries, showing how their readings of the biblical texts shape their understanding of the doctrine of justification. It attempts to bring the Reformers' voices to our hearing so that the gospel they proclaim becomes ours, and to cement our gospel-formed identity as God's beloved in the Son in our hearts by the Holy Spirit.

Gratitude must be extended to those who participated in the development of this book. I am immensely indebted to Robert Kolb, an eminent Reformation scholar, who has offered helpful comments, and to whom the book is dedicated. My thanks extend also to Michael Parsons for his stimulating foreword; John M. G. Barclay, Stephen J. Chester, and Jonathan A. Linebaugh, for their erudite scholarship; Volker Leppin, Christopher Holmes, John Pless, Stephen J. Chester, and Dennis Bielfeldt for their generous endorsements; Geoffrey Butler (and a few anonymous friends) for his diligence in proofreading my manuscript; the library staff of Tyndale University for their unwavering efforts in helping authors including myself to soar; and many close friends for praying and rooting for me in all my endeavors. Last and not least, my salutations go to my Ceceilia and Hansel, our boy, for allowing time and space for me to write.

"Glory in nothing but the cross," where the Son of God was given "for us" (Gal 6:14).

Abbreviations

BC	*The Book of Concord: The Confessions of the Evangelical Lutheran Church*. Edited by Robert Kolb and Timothy J. Wengert. Minneapolis: Fortress, 2000
BC (Tappert)	*The Book of Concord: The Confessions of the Evangelical Lutheran Church*. Translated and edited by Theodore G. Tappert. Philadelphia: Fortress, 1959
CNTC	John Calvin. *Calvin's New Testament Commentaries*. Edited by David W. Torrance and Thomas F. Torrance. 12 vols. Grand Rapids: Eerdmans, 1959–1972
CSEL	Corpus Scriptorum Ecclesiasticorum Latinorum
CTS	John Calvin. *Calvin's Commentaries*. 46 vols. Edinburgh: Calvin Translation Society, 1844–1855. Reprint, 22 vols. Grand Rapids: Baker, 1979
Inst.	John Calvin. *Institutes of the Christian Religion*. Edited by John T. McNeil. Translated by Ford Lewis Battles. Library of Christian Classics 20–21. Philadelphia: Westminster, 1960
Inst. (Beveridge)	John Calvin. *Institutes of the Christian Religion*. Translated by Henry Beveridge. 3 vols. Edinburgh: Calvin Translation Society, 1845
LF	Library of Fathers of the Holy Catholic Church: Anterior to the Division of the East and West. Edited by Edward Bouverie Pusey et al. 50 vols. Parker, 1838–1881

LW	Martin Luther. *Luther's Works*. Edited by Jaroslav Pelikan et al. Vols. 1–30. American ed. St. Louis: Concordia, 1955–1973
	Martin Luther. *Luther's Works*. Edited by Helmut T. Lehman. Vols. 31–55. American ed. Philadelphia: Fortress, 1957–1986
	Martin Luther. *Luther's Works*. Edited by Christopher Boyd Brown et al. Vols. 56–82. American ed. New series. St. Louis: Concordia, 2009–
NPNF[1]	*Nicene and Post-Nicene Fathers*, Series 1. Edited by Philip Schaff. 14 vols. London: T&T Clark, 1886–1900
PL	Patrologia Latina. Edited by Jacque-Paul Migne. 217 vols. Paris, 1844–1864
SG	John Calvin. *Sermons on Galatians*. Translated by Kathy Childress. Edinburgh: Banner of Truth, 1997
WA	Martin Luther. *D. Martin Luthers Werke: Kritische Gesamtausgabe*. Part 1, *Schriften*: Vols. 1–56. Weimar: Böhlau, 1883–1929
WA DB	Martin Luther. *D. Martin Luthers Werke: Kritische Gesamtausgabe*. Part 3, *Die Deutsche Bibel*: Vols. 1–12. Weimar: Böhlau, 1883–1929
WA TR	Martin Luther. *D. Martin Luthers Werke: Kritische Gesamtausgabe*. Part 2, *Tischreden*: Vols. 1–6. Weimar: Böhlau, 1883–1929

1

Luther and Calvin in Context

Theological Themes in Galatians

Introduction

The German Reformer Luther was born in 1483 and died in 1546. Calvin the French-Swiss Reformer was born in 1509 and died in 1564. They never met nor dialogued with each other; however, as Wendel and Parker point out, Luther's early writings were known to Calvin during his university period.[1] In 1529, the year when Luther's Marburg Colloquy with Zwingli took place, Calvin was still pursuing law in Orléans and Bourges. By the time Calvin appeared in Basel to work on completing the first edition of his *Institutes* in 1535, Luther was already fifty-two years old, and the preparation of the published version of his 1531 lectures on Galatians was nearing completion. Calvin shows utmost respect toward Luther and, as Wendel saw, "never ceased to render homage to Luther and his work."[2] Wendel cites a passage from Calvin's "Last Warning to Westphal," where he claims that "I would wish that whatever faults may have been mingled among the great virtues of Luther might rather have been buried; and in truth to keep me from touching upon them, more than the great honor and reverence I bear towards the many excellent gifts with

---

1. Wendel, *Calvin*, 19, 38, 41, 131–35; T. H. L. Parker, *John Calvin*, 14, 23, 30. I am indebted to Hesselink's assessment; see Hesselink, "Luther and Calvin," 79n1.

2. Wendel, *Calvin*, 133.

which he was endowed. But to wish to embrace the vices for the virtues, that would indeed be contrary to all good."[3]

Luther produced two major commentaries on Galatians (1519 and 1535); he had lectured on Galatians in 1531, and his editors published the revised commentary in 1535. Together they comprise 604 pages.[4] He also preached a Christmas sermon on Gal 4:1–7 and a new year sermon on Gal 3:23–29,[5] both of which bear the same contents as his commentaries. Luther's *Lectures on Romans* were given in 1515 and 1516, prior to the posting of his ninety-five theses and his break with Rome. His mature thought came later in his 1535 *Lectures on Galatians*, the most representative work written at the peak of his career as a Reformer. By contrast, Calvin's commentary on Galatians, written in 1548, was brief, comprising only 119 pages. In the dedicatory epistle to his commentary on Galatians, he expresses his limitation with modesty: "Of my commentaries I shall only say that perhaps they contain more than it would be modest in me to acknowledge."[6] The translated edition of Calvin's *Sermons on Galatians* appeared in 1997, and it comprises 662 pages. He preached these sermons twice on Sundays in Geneva between November 14, 1557, and May 8, 1558. Childress comments, "The sermons were taken down in shorthand, transcribed and presented to the deacons of the church by Denis Raguenier, a professional scribe hired by the French emigrants in Geneva to do this work. The deacons later had them printed and the proceeds were used for the relief of poor French-speaking refugees."[7] This reflects the commitment the Reformer had toward the ministry of the word for his flock. In total, Calvin's materials on the Galatians amount to 781 pages. The bulk of materials on Galatians make a comparative study of the two Reformers possible and does not present an imbalance in the presentation. Where appropriate, materials from other writings will be used.

---

3. Wendel, *Calvin*, 134, where he quotes the passage from *Calvini Opera*, 9:238; as quoted in Hesselink, "Luther and Calvin," 79n3.

4. *LW* 26–27.

5. *LW* 75:364–96 (Gal 4:1–7); *LW* 76:3–38 (Gal 3:23–29).

6. "The Dedicatory Epistle," in *CNTC* 11:1–2.

7. *SG*, ix.

The Proper Reading of Galatians

The aim of this book is not to defend the Reformers' reading of Galatians against modern biblical scholarship but to read and hear them in their own contexts. Rather than dealing with the history of reception, as Riches has done masterfully,[8] this book focuses on how the Epistle to the Galatians helps shape their understanding of the gospel of justification. This comparative study of Luther and Calvin is far from being exhaustive; it revolves around a few significant themes in their Galatians commentaries, showing how their readings of the biblical texts shape their theologies. The fundamental theological themes that underly their approach include the dialectic of law and gospel, the relationship between active and passive righteousness, faith alone (yet not alone) and its relation to love, the attribution of contraries between Christ and the justified saints, human love and God's love, Christ as gift and example, the creative power of God's word, union with Christ, the economic action of the Son, the role of Holy Spirit in the justified life, faith in Christ and the faith of Christ, uses of the law, true identity as God's gift, flesh and the Spirit, and the "discontinuity"[9] of the old existence from the recreated new one. The Reformers' deliberations on these themes were couched in anti-Catholic polemic; a proper reading of Galatians must therefore consider the intellectual contexts in which their teaching about justification occurs and be understood on that basis. Readers will learn from the Reformers how they apply a text or theological theme homiletically in a pastoral context and appreciate how their understanding of the gospel can shape and nurture the life of faith. It attempts to bring the Reformers' voice within our hearing so that the gospel they proclaim becomes ours, and our gospel-formed identity as God's beloved in the Son is cemented in our hearts by the Holy Spirit.

Galatians was so dear to Luther that he called the epistle "my Kate Von Bora."[10] His exposition highlights the centrality of his theology: that God has reckoned sinner as righteous on account of trust in Christ. The term "the righteousness of God" in Rom 1:17, Kolb notes, refers to "God's essence,"[11] that which defines God. Luther inherits from the medieval tradition the concept of "formal or active righteousness" by which God, who is

8. See Riches, *Galatians through the Centuries*.

9. Hampson, *Christian Contradictions*, 101, where the word "discontinuity" occurs.

10. WA TR 1.69:18–19, no. 146.

11. Kolb, "Luther on Two Kinds," 449.

righteous, judges and condemns sinners.[12] In his *Preface to the Complete Edition of Luther's Latin Writings* (1545), Luther recounts his struggle over the concept of such judging and terrifying righteousness and his renewed vision of God through his reading of Scripture:

> At last, by the mercy of God, meditating day and night, I gave heed to the context of the words, namely, "In it the righteousness of God, as it is written, 'He through faith is righteous shall live.'" There I began to understand that the righteousness of God is that by which the righteous lives by a gift of God, namely by faith. And this is the meaning: the righteousness of God is revealed by the gospel, namely, *the passive righteousness* with which the merciful God justifies us by faith, as it is written, "He who through faith is righteous shall live." Here I felt that I was altogether born again and had entered paradise itself through open gates. There a totally other face of the entire Scripture showed itself to me.[13]

The distinctive understanding of the righteousness of God as a gift, not merit, marks Luther's mature theology.[14] In the preface to his 1535 commentary on Galatians, Luther considers "two kinds of righteousness"—active and passive—as "our theology."[15] That became the key hermeneutical principle for him to unpack the doctrine of justification. The distinction between the two kinds of righteousness is already presupposed in his 1519 commentary on Galatians, where Luther argues that Paul was addressing predominantly the Gentile converts at Galatia who, Luther notes, "had first been taught a sound faith by the apostle, that is, taught to trust in Jesus Christ alone, not in their own righteousness or in the righteousness of the law, [but who] later on . . . were turned away by the false apostles and led to trust in works of legalistic righteousness."[16] Paul's letter must be read in light of that context, where he vigorously instructed and grounded the fallen Galatians in the passive righteousness with which they began their faith, not the righteousness of works in the pre-conversion stage to which they have fallen back (Gal 5:4). Luther realizes the danger of obscuring the distinction between active and passive righteousness in a way that vitiates

---

12. For further discussions, see McGrath, *Luther's Theology of Cross*, 100–106.

13. *LW* 34:337; WA 54:186.

14. See Lohse, *Martin Luther's Theology*, 85–95.

15. "The Argument of St. Paul's Epistle to the Galatians," in *LW* 26:7; WA 40.1:45.

16. *LW* 27:161: WA 2:450.

the gospel of Christ. Prior to the argument of the 1535 commentary on Galatians, Luther pens these sobering words:

> There is a clear and present danger that the devil may take away from us the pure doctrine of faith and may substitute for it the doctrines of works and of human traditions. It is very necessary, therefore, that this doctrine of faith can never be discussed and taught enough. If it is lost and perishes, the whole knowledge of truth, life, and salvation is lost and perishes at the same time. But if it flourishes, everything good flourishes—religion, true worship, the glory of God, and the right knowledge of all things and of all social conditions.[17]

Throughout his commentary, Calvin avers that Paul's struggle was not so much with ceremonies or rites as it was with what truly constitutes the essential contents of the gospel. He writes, "We must always take care of the main articles of the gospel. He who attacks them is a destroyer of the gospel."[18] He exhorts us to begin "right at the beginning"—namely, the "fountain" of grace. The primacy of the righteousness of God as a gift is exalted above human action. How one obtains a righteous standing before God, says Calvin, was Paul's chief concern, and the Galatians commentary was his strenuous response to those who had deviated from the righteousness of faith to the righteousness of works, grace to law, thereby nullifying the gospel of Christ. In the introduction to his Galatians commentary, Calvin offers two important principles that govern his exposition of Paul:

> If this seems far-fetched to anyone, let him consider two things. First, the question [of ceremonies] could not be settled without assuming the general principle that we are justified only by the grace of God; and this excludes not only ceremonies, but other works also. Secondly, Paul was less worried about ceremonies than about the ungodly notion that we obtain salvation by works. Let us observe, therefore, that [Paul] very properly begins right at the beginning. It was necessary to indicate the fountain, so that his readers should know that the controversy was not concerned with some insignificant trifle [like ceremonies or circumcision] but with the important matter of all, the way we obtain salvation.[19]

---

17. *LW* 26:3.
18. *Comm. Gal.* 1:7, in *CNTC* 11:14.
19. "Theme of Paul's Epistle to the Galatians," in *CNTC* 11:6.

Major Theological Themes in Galatians

Both Reformers frame the doctrine of justification within the dialectic of law and gospel, active and passive righteousness. The task of a "real theologian," Luther states, is learning how to "distinguish the Gospel from the Law" without confusing or collapsing them.[20] The two exist in opposition to each other, yet they function together as, to borrow Fink's words, "complementary movements within God's overarching economy of salvation."[21] The law, the agent exposing sin by which we are condemned, is not the final goal; rather, the gospel, the agent of disposing sin by which we are saved, is. It is through the knowledge of our predicament that we are made ready to receive the gospel. Such an understanding has its root in Augustine's *On the Spirit and the Letter*, where he taught that "by the law of works God says: Do what I command! By the law of faith we say to God: Give what you command."[22] They do not contradict each other unless the law is given the soteriological power that only the gospel has. Believers confess they are sinners and have nothing of their own; they renounce establishing their own righteousness and yield themselves to the righteousness that is obtained by faith alone.

The law originates from God, so it is good like God is. It assumes its negative, punitive function when it meets with depraved human nature. The annihilating power of the law is, to use Calvin's term, "accidental"[23]— not intrinsic to its nature but a work it does in response to sin. Dowey writes, "The concept of law here is seen to belong to the revelation of God the creator and to carry no hint of sin or disharmony. It is not something that comes in between God and man, destructive of a personal relation, but is the mode of that revelation. This pure, or positive, or essential idea of the law is always distinguished clearly in Calvin's mind from the second conception, which does stand between God and man."[24] The negative work the law performs is an "alien work," Luther avers; "an action which is alien to God's nature results in a deed belonging to his very nature."[25] The law does the opposite of what the gospel does; it kills us, but the gospel saves.

20. *LW* 26:115; WA 40.1:207.

21. Fink, "Martin Luther's Reading," 35.

22. Augustine, *De Spiritu et Littera* 22, CSEL 60:174, as cited in Fink, "Martin Luther's Reading," 36n46.

23. *Comm. Gal.* 3:10, in *CNTC* 11:53.

24. Dowey, *Knowledge of God*, 225.

25. *LW* 31:44, 51.

Justification occurs within the distinction between the two works: God does an "alien work" of making a person a sinner through the law so that he might do his "proper work" of making her a righteous person through the gospel.[26] Apart from faith, the law works in us only condemnation; in faith, the transition from law to gospel occurs, working salvation in us. To borrow Jüngel's phrase, "God corresponds to himself"[27] in this antithetical unity: that God crushes obstinate people with the law so that he might create in them willful submission by his gospel; the latter is his chief end.

Calvin considers the "third use" of the law as the "principal use" and has a more positive vision of the role it plays in the Christian life. The law, which Calvin regards as a "perpetual rule of a good and holy life,"[28] impels those who are freed from the terror of the law onto the path of sanctification. Conversely, Luther sees the "theological" use of the law as the "principal use," that is, its negative function prepares us to receive grace. Far from being an antinomian, Luther gives the law a legitimate place in the economy of salvation. Both Reformers affirm that truly God-approved works issue from faith in Christ, without which all is sin. But where Calvin lays stress on the law as that which impels us to do good works, Luther holds that the law does not cause anything to happen; good works or love derive their motivation from faith, not from law—though they do remain shaped by the law.

A true theologian knows her audience and knows when to proclaim law or gospel, or Christ as gift or example. Augustine's pair of Christ as *sacramentum* (gift) and Christ as *exemplum* (example) is assumed in the Reformers' exposition. For those who have felt the burden of sins through the law, Christ as Savior and gift must occupy the focus of proclamation, not Christ the example and lawgiver. For those who are smug and callous, Christ as law and example must be announced, lest they turn the gospel into an occasion for the freedom of the flesh. The believer truly feels the struggle or conflict within, pondering whether he is truly God's child. At times he perceives God as an angry, stern judge over him. In such instances, faith must finally prevail, even if it were dim or feeble, or else nothing remains. We must not look subjectively at ourselves for assurance, fixing our gaze on what we are and do, but objectively at Christ, laying hold of who he is and has achieved for us. The economic action of Christ and his abundant

26. *LW* 16:233–34.

27. Jüngel, *God as the Mystery*, 346.

28. *Comm. Gal.* 4:4, in *CNTC* 11:74.

suffering for us strengthens our confidence in combating sin and the temptations that assail us. That God's Son was born of a woman, born under the law, so that we might become the children of God should occupy us in times of temptations. The contraries—law, sin, and death—are rendered powerless over us only once we believe that Christ has undergone them to conquer them for our good.

Faith and love exist, in Pannenberg's phrase, as a "differentiated unity"[29] in the Reformers' understanding of justification by faith. The Reformers reject the scholastics' "faith formed by love" (*fides caritate formata*),[30] arguing that Paul held that "faith alone"[31] justifies; yet justifying faith does not remain alone, for works of love inevitably follow. What they deny is not works per se but a certain doctrine that attributes merit to works, thereby eclipsing the faith alone that justifies, which is, to borrow Linebaugh's phrase, "the grammar of the Gospel."[32] Both Luther and Calvin insert the word "only"[33] into their translations of Paul's letters, though this word, and the similarly meaning "alone," are not in the original Greek texts, to exclude all congruent merit and human deeds from their doctrine of faith. We are justified by no other way except faith "alone." Because we obtain everything freely through faith in Christ, we may now freely live out the command to love God and our neighbor. As Iwand writes, "Human works are borne out of our condition, and we are not born of our works."[34] Our works thus originate from the condition of the person who has been renewed by God's grace; in Cortez's words: "Any role that we play in constituting our own humanity must be subsequent to and always based upon that initial gracious act."[35] Whatever good we might perform ought to be ascribed to divine agency, not transferred to human agency. Both Luther and Calvin are known as theologians of faith; they can also be labeled as "theologians of love."[36] In the commentaries on Galatians, Luther takes

29. Pannenberg, "God of the Philosophers," 33.

30. See Chester, *Reading Paul with Reformers*, 197–201, 265–78, for a fuller account of justifying faith in Luther and Calvin.

31. *LW* 35:189; *Comm. Gal.* 2:16, in *CNTC* 11:39.

32. Linebaugh, "Grammar of the Gospel."

33. See the 1530 translation of Rom 3:28 in Luther, "On Translating: An Open Letter," in *LW* 35:189; *Comm. Gal.* 2:16, in *CNTC* 11:39.

34. Iwand, *Righteousness of Faith*, 62.

35. Cortez, *Christological Anthropology*, 97.

36. For a discussion of the subject of love as intrinsic to Luther's understanding of true faith, see Gritsch, "Martin Luther's Commentary," 110. See also Kärkkäinen, "Evil,

with utmost seriousness the importance of good works and has written much on it, even more than Calvin. This was spirited by perverted notions of good works promulgated by some "fanatics" in Luther's time; it was also spurred by the tendency of evangelical Christians to abuse their freedom. Luther is concerned that the "freedom for which Christ has set us free" (Gal 5:1) be preached, lest the afflicted conscience remains in despair. He, too, is concerned about the abuse of freedom, and thus he stresses the necessity of outward deeds as a consequence of justification.

Faith means more than belief in the objective contents of the Christian faith; it is basically trust that seizes Christ. When Luther and Calvin speak of "faith in Christ," they are speaking of faith as "an instrumental cause" by which we receive Christ and his benefits. The chief cause of justification is God's free mercy, that which renders us righteous as Abraham was. Faith believes against the odds of life and receives God's promise. Paul occasionally uses the phrase *pistis Christou* (e.g., Rom 3:22; Gal 2:16; Phil 3:9), which can be translated as either "the faith of Christ" or "faith in Christ," and Luther and Calvin translate the phrase both ways. As Horrell writes, "The noun *pistis* can mean 'faith' in the sense of belief, or (more often) trust (its usual meaning in Greek of the period), but it can also mean 'faithfulness,' as in Rom 3:3: 'the faithfulness (*pistis*) of God' (KJV has 'the faith of God')."[37] The subjective genitive "the faith *of* Jesus Christ" refers to the gospel itself, or to the faithfulness of God in giving his Son for sin; and the objective genitive "faith *in* Christ" refers to that by which we apprehend Christ.[38] The faith by which we receive Christ is not self-generated and thus is not "of the flesh" (Gal 5:19) but created by the word of God and therefore "of the Spirit" (Gal 5:16). Though faith in Christ is a passive human action, it is not a human achievement or merit. Faith created by God's word, Paulson writes, "takes leave of the old self but flees to Christ, listening only to him and to no one else—especially not one's own self."[39] For the Reformers, the power of faith lies not in itself but in the object it grasps—namely, Jesus

---

Love"; Mannermaa, *Two Kinds of Love*; Kim, *Luther on Faith*, 3, where Luther is labeled as "a theologian of love" no less than of faith. It is Kim's conviction that faith and love constitute, in Kim's phrase, "a thematic pair" that permeates the Epistle of Galatians. In this regard, the same may be said of Calvin, who combines faith and love, with the former causative of the latter.

37. Horrell, *Introduction to the Study*, 108.

38. The two phrases "the faith of Jesus Christ" and "faith in Christ" will also be discussed in chs. 2, 4, and 5.

39. Paulson, *Lutheran Theology*, 124.

Christ, "the Son of God who was given for us." The sacrificial action of God ("faith of Christ") and human reception of faith's object ("faith in Christ"), though distinguished, are one; they fit like conjoined twins.

The person and the work of Christ are one. The virtue of the person of Christ is derived from the goal he came to achieve through his bodily coming (Gal 4:4). This is evident in Luther's explanation of the second article of the *Small Catechism*, where he affirms that soteriology is at the heart of his Christology. He writes, "I believe that Jesus Christ, true God, begotten of the Father in eternity, and also a true human being, born of the Virgin Mary, is my Lord, who has redeemed me, a lost and condemned human being. He has purchased and freed me from all sins, from death, and from the power of the devil."[40] To believe in Christ does not mean intellectually to assent to the dogma that Christ is fully God and fully man, says Luther, "a fact that helps nobody"; it means accepting Christ was sent into the world for our redemption. It is from what Christ does, that is, the office of mediation, that "he receives his name."[41] Congar writes of Luther, "The Incarnation is not only inseparable from the redemptive act; the metaphysical mystery of the hypostatic union is considered solely in the act of salvation of which it forms the very reality."[42] With Luther, Calvin's emphasis is not on how God and humanity are one in Christ, although they are, but on the economic actions of God in Christ for us. In book 2 of the *Institutes*, Edmundson notes, Calvin counsels against dwelling on Christ's essence, that he is fully God and fully man, but exhorts us instead to focus on "his power and his will to save" through which our faith is upheld.[43] Calvin explains, "For it would be of little advantage to know who Christ is, if this second point were not added, what he wishes to be toward us, and for what purpose the Father sent him."[44] Incarnation and redemption, for the Reformers, mutually coinhere; the former receives its meaning and significance from the latter. God in Christ not only assumes our sin to annihilate it but also assumes our sinful person to give us his righteous person as his goal. The essence of the gospel lies in the attribution of contraries, that in becoming a man, the Son of God assumes what belongs to humanity—sin, wrath, and death—to communicate to us what belongs to him—righteousness, mercy,

---

40. "The Small Catechism," in *BC*, 345.

41. WA 16.217:33ff, as quoted in Congar, *Dialogue between Christians*, 374.

42. Congar, *Dialogue between Christians*, 377.

43. Edmondson, *Calvin's Christology*, 87.

44. *Comm. John* 1:49, in *CNTC* 4:43.

and life. Luther and Calvin are in full accord with the Chalcedonian definition of Christ as one person in two natures, which are united unconfused,
unchangeably, indivisibly, and inseparably. The main point of disagreement
among them concerns the usage of the "communication of attributes"
(*communicatio idiomatum*). Luther refers to this mainly in his disputes
with other theologians such as Nestorius and Zwingli. When he engages
in biblical interpretation on Galatians, he, too, comments on this, more so
than Calvin does, in a few places. In their Galatians commentaries, they
endorse the traditional interpretation, that the properties of Christ's two
natures are communicated to the *concretum* of his person. The language of
passion in Scripture such as "God suffers," "God dies," "the blood of God,"
Calvin regards as "improperly" ascribed to God,[45] for suffering is exclusively of Christ's humanity. Though Calvin denies the assertion that God
suffers in Christ, with Luther he nevertheless affirms that the "Son of God"
suffers for us. The Son of God, this person, suffers the death of the cross
in Jesus's humanity. That is, the suffering of humanity is communicated to
Christ the person; thus, it is proper to say God suffers in his humanity, but
not in his divinity. The personal union allows the mutual predication of the
nature's properties, and thus Luther could assert that in Christ, "God died"
and "man Christ created."[46] The properties are mutually communicated to
the person of Christ in the concrete unity of the two natures, not in abstract
separation. Both affirm a real communication between Christ's righteous
person and the creature's sinful person, in which he grants us grace and
eternal life in exchange for sin and death, if only we believe it. To be justified by the law is to be severed from Christ, in which case salvation is lost.
Faith triumphs over law so that it no longer holds us in custody, and over
death so it no longer threatens us. Just as mercy is hidden in wrath, its
opposite, so too blessing is hidden in curse, its contrary. Hidden in Christ,
the blessed curse, is all the fullness of blessings that equip us to conquer the
contraries—sin, wrath, death, and every evil.

Regarding Christology, the evangelical emphasis led the Reformers
to begin with the economic action of the Son. Likewise, in pneumatology,
they started with the economic action of the Holy Spirit; in Swain's phrase,
the "grammar of divine agency."[47] The economic action of the Spirit receives such profound and in-depth attention in Calvin that Warfield labels

45. *Inst.* 2.14.1.
46. *LW* 41:103.
47. Swain, "Heirs through God," 262.

him "the Theologian of the Holy Spirit"[48] as much as he is one of grace, justification, and atonement. The same can be said of Luther, who highly extols the mission of the Holy Spirit in justification and assurance. Prenter places the Holy Spirit at the center of Luther's theology, around which other fundamental tenets of his faith—including justification, grace, and assurance—are understood.[49] Because the Father and the Son are one deity, the fatherly gifts we receive are identical to the Son's gifts; Luther writes, "The same things come both from the Father and the Son."[50] With Luther, Calvin holds that the gift of redemption is "proper to both" the Father and the Son, the one fountain of grace.[51] Just as God acts in Christ to redeem us, so also he acts through the "Spirit of the Son" (Gal 4:6), assuring our hearts that we are God's beloved, just as the Son is. The Triune God acts toward us so that we might be seized by the love revealed in the Son, the identical love that flows between the Father and Son that is impressed upon our hearts by the Holy Spirit. Bayer, a renowned Luther scholar, writes, "The *Spirit* finally is nothing other than the opener and distribution of this self-giving of Christ—and thereby that of the Father as well. We recognize and love God the Father through Jesus Christ in the Holy Spirit."[52] Both the Son and the Spirit work together as mediators: As the Son mediates between God and us, by achieving for us the benefits of expiation and reconciliation, so the Spirit mediates between Christ and us, by applying to us the benefits of Christ's mediatorial activity. A Calvin scholar, Wendel, captures this point well: "The Holy Spirit plays the part of an obligatory mediator between Christ and man, just as the Christ is the mediator between God and man. And in the same way that Jesus Christ is the necessary instrument of redemption, so is the Holy Spirit the no less necessary instrument by means of which this redemption reaches us, in justification and regeneration."[53] Justification is extrinsic in nature and is based on God's word addressing us from outside rather than from within. The alien life of Christ to which we are appointed to live demands that we do not turn inward, trusting in anything within us for assurance, but turn outward and cling to his majestic word for it. The subjective experience of justification has efficacy outside

---

48. Warfield, *Calvin and Augustine*, 21.

49. See Prenter, *Spiritus Creator*.

50. *LW* 26:31; WA 40.1:82.

51. *Comm. Gal.* 1:11, in *CNTC* 11:11.

52. Bayer, *Martin Luther's Theology*, 254.

53. Wendel, *Calvin*, 240.

us, and its reality lies beyond the grasp of human assessment but in the Spirit's cry through the agency of his word.

The Reformers' commentaries on Galatians cover entire soteriological themes including the descent of God in the incarnate Son, and his suffering, burial, and resurrection in which we participate by the Holy Spirit. Augustine writes, "Although just as Father, Son and Holy Spirit are inseparable, so do they work inseparably."[54] With Augustine, the Reformers assert that all three persons work together as one God *ad extra*, bestowing upon us the Father's love through the Son in the Spirit. Yet the acts they perform reveal to us the gift of the Son's natural and filial relation to the Father that God shares with us; and by the Spirit's cry, our hearts can call God "Abba! Father!" As the Father loves the Son, so he loves us in his Son, who is revealed to us by the Spirit. The Trinitarian logic of Paul's gospel can be formulated as such: the economic action of God in Christ through the Holy Spirit stands in the foreground, and it is through these that we are told who God is and what he does for us (*pro nobis*). The God we encounter in his salvific relationship to us in Christ and the Holy Spirit is indeed the Triune God we have from eternity. How God is in and for himself in his immanent life is not the Reformers' preoccupation; rather, they are concerned with how God is for us in his economic action. Both Luther and Calvin stand within the Augustinian tradition that distinguishes the immanent Trinity (God as he is in himself) from the economic Trinity (God as he is for us), as the former is the presupposition of the latter. As Swain explains, "The gospel according to Gal 4:4–7 is that the God who by nature is and acts as Father, Son, and Spirit acts not only in relation to himself but also in relation to us."[55] The missions of the Son and Spirit presuppose the Trinitarian distinctions of persons and their internal relation within God's immanent life. Swain writes, "The named relations of Father, Son, and Spirit are the *presupposition* of the missions, not their *consequence*. The named relations indicate the *agents* of God's monotheistic saving action, not its *effects*."[56] The economic actions of the Triune God in history do not make God Triune; rather, they reveal the God who is in himself eternally Triune.

The Pauline antithesis between "no longer I . . . but Christ" means the justified creature in Christ lives in a paradoxical tension between the two seemingly contradictory modes of existence, yet can by God's verdict make

54. Augustine, *Trinity*, 1:2:7, 70.

55. Swain, "Heirs through God," 266.

56. Swain, "Heirs through God," 266 (emphasis in original).

the movement from the old existence ("no longer I") to the new existence ("but Christ"). The I of the old nature is dead because it is buried with Christ; the I of the new nature is living because Christ lives in it, causing it to live to God. The old I marked by sin, death, and hell gives way to the new I, who is made alive by faith in Christ the crucified, who "loved me and gave himself for me." Luther and Calvin's slant on the "for me" shows that the cross was not a distant event of the past, devoid of any salvific significance for the present. Rather, it happened "for us," as an event that includes us so that we could join with Paul in declaring that we live by the faith whose efficacy is derived from the Son of God. God's entrance into our lives "in Christ" is transformative and is the measure of true personhood. The authentic self is not the self-constituted identity that lives out of its own soteriological resources; it is an excentric self that lives outside itself, not out of anything we bring. As Hampson puts it, "The Christian has a new sense of self, which is not a sense of self as a self-subsisting entity but rather a sense that he lives excentrically to himself."[57] Salvation is wholly accomplished in Christ and needs nothing else; therefore, the new I does not draw what it lacks from Christ and supply the rest through introspection or other humanly devised means of satisfaction. The real self dies to all that lies within but lives "excentrically to himself" by an alien righteousness of Christ, not by circumcision or any special status. Where Christ rules by his grace in the hearts of the faithful, there sin, death, and curse lose their grip on us. But where Christ is not embraced, there these things terrify us and cast us into despair. Without faith, we are deprived of his favor and his gifts, and his victory is not our portion. In Christ, we are made part of his body and are one with him. The distance between God and us is overcome so that we do not see Christ and us as separate from each other but as one person. The self that is seized by Christ no longer lives out of its natural endowments but out of the life of Christ and the benefits he acquired for us. The new I lives in Christ, from whose life flows forth power and hope for its being and well-being. To truly live, the old self must undergo crucifixion with Christ so that it be raised in newness of life. The words of God ("He was given for me") are by which the justified self abandons itself and cleaves to Christ, the very source of self-constitution. God's words are causative of new realities that correspond to them. The old I must undergo the death of self so that it be reconstituted as a new I, as both are the instantiation of God's creative word. Yet the fallen I for whom Christ died and who was

57. Hampson, *Christian Contradictions*, 12.

raised to life is consubstantial with the I of the innocent self of the original creation. The redeemed humanity is of one piece with that of the created state. Christ's redemption does not, to borrow Cortez's word, "replace"[58] our fallen humanity. Instead, it restores it to its original shape, rid of the perversity of self-obsession, and renews it into true life, endowed with the power of living to God. The new identity is bestowed by the gospel, not achieved by human action.

The eternal bliss of communion with God as the creation's objective was lost through Adam's fall but regained by the justifying action of God in Christ. Hence there is nothing for us to do except to extol his grace, just as Paul concludes his epistle ("the grace of the Lord Jesus Christ be with your spirit" [Gal 6:18]) in the same fashion as he begins it ("Grace to you and peace from God our Father and our Lord Jesus Christ" [Gal 1:3]). Luther relishes the explanation of this verse: "Not with wrath of the Law, not the servitude of the Law, which was given through the servant Moses, but grace and truth, which came through Jesus Christ" (John 1:17).[59] This concluding verse, Calvin contends, is intended to highlight the world's negative disposition toward grace: the "ingratitude" the world manifests in its disdain of the abundant riches that Christ's grace brings; and by withdrawing from the cross of Christ, people end up in ruin and damnation. It also aims to create in the believer's heart an openness to the reception of grace. Our hearts must be consecrated, says Calvin, as the "throne and place where grace takes root" so that our faith may not be earthbound, based on creaturely things, but heavenbound, with our hearts lifted upward to God from whom grace pours forth for our benefit.[60] It is this author's intention that by considering the following chapters, readers will be drawn closer to the intimacy of the Father's bosom through Jesus Christ by the Holy Spirit, and that they will "glory in nothing but the cross of Christ" (Gal 6:14).

58. Cortez, *Christological Anthropology*, 95.
59. *LW* 27:407; WA 40.2:616.
60. *SG*, 660.

2

THE DIALECTIC OF LAW AND GOSPEL

Passive and Active Righteousness

THE LAW WAS GIVEN not without purpose, and we are to apply it according to its right intention. The theological function of the law, for both Reformers, is to reveal sin, humble us, and create in us a desire for grace. It causes us to forget all and cleave to the infinite treasure of God's mercy offered in the gospel. A proper use of the law moves one from despair to hope, death to life, and God's wrath to his mercy. The law is deathcausing; the gospel is life-giving. Luther does not negate the role of law in the Christian life, even though he, Althaus writes, "does not use the expression 'the third function of the law.'"[1] In considering the third use as the "principal use," Calvin sees the law play a more positive role in the Christian life. Having been freed from the terrors of the law, the new creature relishes the commandments as God's gift. The law prevents him from wandering from what Calvin calls "the rule of prefect righteousness"[2]—a phrase that does not occur in Luther's writings. Luther sees the "theological use" of the law as the "principal use," considering the emphasis he puts on the old creature, which needs perpetual mortification; Calvin considers the third use of the law as the principal use, respecting the emphasis he puts on the new creature, which needs perpetual renewal. Faith in Christ frees us from the

---

1. Althaus, *Theology of Martin Luther*, 273. See "The Formula of Concord," in *BC*, 502, where Philip Melanchthon incorporates "the third use of the law" as "a sure guide" to the Christian life. The same occurs in *Inst.* 2.7.12n19, where Melanchthon is quoted.

2. *Inst.* 2.8.5.

assaults of the law; it orients all aspects of our lives toward the bidding of the Holy Spirit, through whom Christ lives and reigns in us. Both Luther and Calvin hold that justification is by faith, without human works. However, this in no way excludes good works from the life of a person seized by the grace of Christ. The Reformers frame their doctrine of justification by faith within the paradoxical distinction between law and gospel, the former leading to the latter. We must first be made righteous before we can perform righteous deeds. To reverse the order is to deny the article of faith in Christ, who alone is our righteousness. Righteousness is God's gift, which is received by faith, not achieved by human efforts.

Righteousness: Divine and Human

In the preface to his 1535 commentary on Galatians, Luther declares the core of his theological thinking, which he labels "two kinds of righteousness":

> This is our theology, by which we teach a precise distinction between these two kinds of righteousness, the active and the passive, so that morality and faith, works and grace, secular society and religion may not be confused. Both are necessary, but both must be kept within their limits.[3]

Luther finds confirmation of the distinctive understanding of the passive righteousness of God as a gift in Augustine's *The Spirit and the Letter*, where he, too, interprets it as that by which God makes us righteous.[4] The break with the former idea of active righteousness, that by which God judges us, is apparent in Luther's commentary on Ps 51:14, where he writes, "Therefore remember that the righteousness of God is that by which we are justified, or the gift of the forgiveness of sins. This righteousness in God is wonderful because it makes of God not a righteous judge but a forgiving Father, who wants to use his righteousness not to judge but justify and absolve sinners."[5] Such a vision of God as a Father brings Luther deliverance from the terror that stems from the previous concept of God as a judge.

Luther acknowledges many kinds of righteousness—"political," "ceremonial," "legal," and "works-righteousness"—all of which are forms of

3. *LW* 26:7; WA 40.1:45.

4. *LW* 34:337, where Augustine, *The Spirit and the Letter*, lin. 1, ix, x, 15–16 (PL 44:208–10) is cited.

5. *LW* 12:392; WA 40.2:444.

active righteousness.[6] "But this most excellent, the righteousness of faith, which God imputes to us through Christ without works," Luther says, is "a merely passive righteousness." He further expands:

> For here we work nothing, render nothing to God, we only receive and permit someone else to work in us, namely God. Therefore it is appropriate to call the righteousness of faith or Christian righteousness "passive." This is a righteousness hidden in a mystery, which the world does not understand. In fact, Christians themselves do not adequately understand it or grasp it in the midst of their temptations.[7]

This passive righteousness is alien to us. We could not work or produce it but receive it as a gift given to us by the Father. We cannot create our righteousness but receive it from God, just as the earth cannot produce rain but receives it from above. "As the earth itself does not produce rain and is unable to acquire it by its own strength, worship, and power but receives it only by a heavenly gift from above, so this heavenly righteousness is given to us by God without our work or merit."[8] We do not obtain this divine and eternal righteousness by the performance of works but only through "the free imputation and indescribable gift of God."[9] Luther expands:

> This righteousness is heavenly and passive. We do not have it of ourselves; we receive it from heaven. We do not perform it; we accept it by faith through which we ascend beyond all laws and works. . . . For this righteousness means to do nothing, to share nothing, and to know nothing about the law or about works but to know and believe only this: that Christ has gone to the Father and is now invisible; . . . that he is our high priest, interceding for us and reigning over us and in us through grace.[10]

The distinction between passive and active righteousness corresponds to the distinction taught in his sermon on *Two Kinds of Righteousness* (1519), that is, between the "alien righteousness" we receive by new birth, and "our proper righteousness," "a product of the righteousness of the first type [alien righteousness], actually its fruit and consequence."[11]

6. *LW* 26:4–5; WA 40.1:41.

7. *LW* 26:5; WA 40.1:41.

8. *LW* 26:6; WA 40.1:43.

9. *LW* 26:6; WA 40.1:43.

10. *LW* 26:8; WA 40.1:46.

11. *LW* 31:297–99.

Alien righteousness is "the basis, the cause, the source of all our own actual righteousness";[12] it is given as a remedy to the "original righteousness lost in Adam."[13] The pair of faith and love corresponds to the pair of passive righteousness of faith and the active righteousness of love. Righteousness is passive but is inherently dynamic to produce works of love. Luther states its prolific nature in the preface to his 1535 commentary on Galatians: "When I have this righteousness within me, I descend from heaven like the rain that makes the earth fertile. That is, I come forth into another kingdom, and I perform good works whenever the opportunity arises."[14] The gift of righteous identity expresses outwardly in works of love. In Luther's own words:

> But as the earth does not bring forth fruit unless it has been first watered and made fruitful from above—for the earth cannot judge, renew, and rule the heavens, but the heavens judge, renew, rule, and fortify the earth, so that it may do what the earth has commanded—so also by the righteousness of the law we do nothing even when we do much; we do not fulfill the law even when we fulfill it. Without any merit or any work of our own, we must first become righteous by Christian righteousness, which has nothing to do with the righteousness of the law or with earthly and active righteousness.[15]

Commenting on Gal 3:11, "Now it is evident that no man is justified before God by the Law; for the righteous shall live by faith," Luther quotes Hab 2:4 to support the "exclusive and anti-thetical" nature of faith.[16] He considers righteousness not as a demand to be fulfilled, but as "that by which the righteous lives by a gift of God, namely, by faith. And this is the meaning: the righteousness of God is revealed by the gospel, namely, the passive righteousness with which the merciful God justifies us by faith, as it is written, 'He who through faith is righteous shall live.'"[17] The law and faith are two contrary methods of justification: "If by faith, then not by the Law, because the Law is not by faith."[18] The law does not mix with faith, as per Gal 3:12: "But the law does not rest on faith." Law and promise are

12. *LW* 31:298.
13. *LW* 31:299.
14. *LW* 26:11; WA 40.1:51.
15. *LW* 26:8; WA 40.1:46.
16. *LW* 26:268; WA 40.1:420.
17. *LW* 34:337; WA 54:186.
18. *LW* 26:268; WA 40.1:420.

distinguished, as works are from faith. God's promise is grasped only by faith, not by works.[19] Any conjunction of the law to faith, Luther argues, "extinguishes faith and puts the Law in place of faith."[20] He, too, repudiates the "formed faith"—that is, faith quickened by love—of the scholastics, but affirms "unformed faith," that is, faith alone, as the basis of justification.[21]

Calvin argues by way of syllogism and contradictory premises to flesh out the proper understanding of justification. His text is Gal 3:11, "But that no man is justified by the law":

> If we are justified by faith, then it is not by the law.
> But we are justified by faith.
> Therefore it is not by the law.[22]

Calvin supports the "minor" premise by a passage from Hab 2:4, "The just shall live by his faith," which he quotes in his commentary on Gal 3:11 and Rom 1:17, "For therein is revealed a righteousness of God by faith unto faith. As it is written, 'But the righteous shall live by faith.'"[23] The "major" premise hinges on the different "mode" of justification: by faith or by law. "The law justifies him who fulfils all its commands; faith justifies those who are destitute of the merit of works and rely on Christ alone."[24] Human merits and divine grace are "irreconcilable" opposites;[25] one excludes the other. The law and faith are not opposed to each other, as they both spring from the same God; otherwise, God would deny himself. But the contradiction between them occurs only when the law is granted "the power of justifying,"[26] which is the domain of faith. Calvin avers, "The law is not of faith, that is, it has a method of justifying a man which is completely foreign to faith."[27]

Calvin contends that the preceding clause, "the gospel . . . is the power of God unto salvation" (Rom 1:16), finds its confirmation in the subsequent

---

19. *LW* 26:271; WA 40.1:424.

20. *LW* 26:271; WA 40.1:425.

21. I will discuss the distinction between "unformed" and "formed" in ch. 3.

22. *Comm. Gal.* 3:11, in *CNTC* 11:54.

23. *Comm. Gal.* 3:11, in *CNTC* 11:54; *Comm. Rom.* 1:17, in *CNTC* 8:29.

24. *Comm. Gal.* 3:11, in *CNTC* 11:54.

25. *Comm. Gal.* 3:11, in *CNTC* 11:54.

26. *Comm. Gal.* 3:20, in *CNTC* 11:64.

27. *Comm. Gal.* 3:11, in *CNTC* 11:54.

clause, "For therein is revealed a righteousness of God by faith unto faith."[28] To "seek salvation," Calvin avers, is to "seek righteousness by which we may be reconciled to Him, and obtain that life which consists in His benevolence alone through His being favourable to us. In order that we may be loved by God we must first be righteous, for He hates unrighteousness."[29] The unrighteousness in us provokes God's wrath, and only when sin is forgiven can God love us. Righteousness is to be sought only in the gospel, "the power of God" that delivers us from death. It is bestowed on us as a gift by which we are accepted by God. Calvin argues that "Paul proves the righteousness of faith by the authority of the prophet Habakkuk, who in predicting the destruction of the proud, adds at the same time that the just shall live by his faith."[30] The life the proud have lasts for a moment; by contrast, the life the righteous enjoys is everlasting, as stressed by the future tense of the phrase "shall live." Calvin infers from Habakkuk that faith and the gospel mutually coinhere such that "since the just is said to live by his faith, [Paul] maintains that such a life is also received by the gospel." Calvin writes, "What is the source of that life but the faith which leads us to God, and makes our life depend on Him?"[31] The verb in the future tense ("shall live") points to the life continually governed by "his faith" as the substance by which we continually hide under the protection of God against the storms and trials of life.[32] Then Paul adds "unto faith." This phrase designates the daily progress we make in our faith. The goodness of God we "first taste" is genuine; initially we "see" God's face turned toward us with kindness, says Calvin, "but at a distance."[33] The accent is on a life that does not live by self-reliance but by faith, "the quiet assurance of a conscience that relies on God alone."[34] The more the knowledge of the righteousness of God shines in us as we advance in our faith, the more we grasp God's grace and feel his nearness to us.

28. *Comm. Rom.* 1:16, in *CNTC* 8:27.

29. *Comm. Rom.* 1:17, in *CNTC* 8:27.

30. *Comm. Rom.* 1:17, in *CNTC* 8:28.

31. *Comm. Rom.* 1:17, in *CNTC* 8:29.

32. *Comm. Rom.* 1:17, in *CNTC* 8:29.

33. *Comm. Rom.* 1:17, in *CNTC* 8:28.

34. *Comm. Gal.* 3:11, in *CNTC* 11:54.

Antithetical Unity:
Law and Gospel

The section tackles a few of the Reformers' treatments on Galatians regarding the relationship between law and gospel and its place in their doctrine of justification.

With Jerome, Erasmus asserted that the Antioch dispute in Gal 2:11–14 was not about the different views of salvation that Peter and Paul had; rather, it was a staged disagreement between them—"a valid rhetorical technique" employed to teach the church.[35] But for the Reformers, the public confrontation between them was real, showing how Paul was insistent upon the truth of the gospel against Peter's attempt at Judaizing the Gentiles. The exegetical force of the Antioch incident consists in the ineptitude of the whole law to justify. Paul's chief concern is not so much with customs or ceremonies, but with the mistaken idea that observance of the law can obtain justification. In his 1519 commentary on Gal 2:16, Luther explains at length the two opposing ways of justification. The first is "an external way, by work, on the basis of one's own strength." This kind of righteousness is of human making; it is "acquired by practice . . . and habit," as Aristotle has taught.[36] The second is "an inward way, on the basis of faith and of grace, when a man utterly despairs of his former righteousness [active righteousness]."[37] Aristotle's way is opposed to Christ's and thus must be discarded. The Galatians' error for Luther, Chester argues, was their failure to grasp the distinction between law and gospel, not so much Jewish-Gentile relationships. He rightly observes that

> it is not quite clear whether Luther then believed that Peter's fault was to go back on a decision to eat food forbidden by the law, or simply to eat food approved by the law with Gentiles present or in some sense in a Gentile manner. Yet, by the time of his later *Commentary on Galatians*, Luther argues that Peter had eaten forbidden food, and that from the outset the debate concerned not the customs of different ethnic groups but the contrast between law and gospel.[38]

---

35. For further discussion, see Chester, *Reading Paul with Reformers*, 13–20.

36. *LW* 27:219; *WA* 2:489.

37. *LW* 27:219; *WA* 2:489.

38. Chester, *Reading Paul with Reformers*, 144.

Calvin concedes the linkage between Jewish and Gentile relationships in the body of Christ and the doctrine of justification, viewing the latter as the main point that opens up the Antioch debate.

> Many will be thinking, "What! The issue at stake is the ceremonial law. Why, then, does Paul throw himself right into the middle of the battle by raising issues such as righteousness, man's salvation and the forgiveness of sins? Why does he bring in the whole of the law?" Well, to speak even of one of the ceremonies of the law involves discussing the role and function of the law . . . He (Paul) not only gave his attention to what the Jews believed concerning eating pork . . . he considered why they believed such things. They claimed that the observance of the law was vital to salvation, and this was a yoke upon the conscience that Paul found intolerable. And he saw that they were negating the liberty which the Lord Jesus Christ obtained for us.[39]

Where Luther uses the phrase "faith in Christ," Calvin uses "the faith of Jesus Christ."[40] Concerning Gal 2:16, "A man is not justified by works of the law but through faith in Jesus Christ," Luther observes that "works of the law" generally refers to "whatever is opposed to grace: whatever is not grace is law."[41] "Works" here includes the civil, the ceremonial, and the moral (the Decalogue), and thus the entire law.[42] Luther is at odds with Jerome and Erasmus, who confine Paul's understanding of works to only that of the ceremonial law, excluding the moral law.[43] With Luther, Calvin writes, "The context shows clearly that the moral law is also comprehended."[44] This is so, Calvin explains, especially when Paul "continually" sets the righteousness of the law against the free grace of Christ, the two opposing ways to God.[45] By the phrase "by the faith of Christ," Paul did not intend that "ceremonies or works of any kind are insufficient without the aid of faith."[46] Calvin adds the word "alone" to this verse to underscore an "exclusive" assertion: "Not

---

39. *SG*, 162–64; also quoted in Chester, *Reading Paul with Reformers*, 144.

40. The two phrases "the faith of Jesus Christ" and "faith in Christ" will be discussed further in ch. 5. See also my brief comments in ch. 1.

41. *LW* 26:122; WA 40.1:218.

42. *LW* 26:122; WA 40.1:218.

43. *LW* 26:122; WA 40.1:218.

44. *Comm. Gal.* 2:15, in *CNTC* 11:38.

45. *Comm. Gal.* 2:15, in *CNTC* 11:39.

46. *Comm. Gal.* 2:16, in *CNTC* 11:39.

by works but by the faith of Christ *alone*."[47] Though the word "alone" is not in the original Greek text, Calvin argues the contrast supports the exclusive claim that faith alone justifies us.[48] Luther also inserts the word "only" into his 1530 translation of Rom 3:28. He reasons, "But it is the nature of our German language that in speaking about two things, one which is affirmed, the other denied, we use the word *solum* [only] along with the word *nicht* [not] or *kein* [no]. For example, we say 'the farmer brings *allein* [only] grain and *kein* [no] money'; or 'No, I really have *nicht* [no] money, but *allein* [only] grain.'"[49] The expression "by faith" expels all congruent merit and all human actions that might count toward justification. For Luther, justification "does not allow" any place for works.[50] Likewise, Calvin declares, "We have to ascribe either nothing or everything to faith or to works."[51]

In justification, the law is opposed to faith; whoever seeks to obtain divine favor by merits repudiates the grace of God. Luther gives rigor to Paul's phrase in Gal 2:18, "For if I build up again," and applies it polemically to the false apostles, who insist on circumcision and observance of the law as meriting justification. To build justification on law and human traditions, which Paul had already destroyed, is to demolish the gospel of grace, which Paul had already established. As a rebuttal to his opponents, Luther writes, "Am I now to expel Christ and destroy His kingdom which I planted through the Gospel, and set up the Law once more? . . . In this way I would restore sin and death in place of righteousness and life. For all that the Law does is to manifest sin, cause wrath, and kill."[52] The Papists and fanatical spirits of the time, Luther avows, are "destroyers of the kingdom of Christ and builders of the devil's kingdom, of sin, and of the wrath of God, and eternal death."[53]

The opponents' error for Calvin is not that they deny "Christ, or faith," but that they add a "conjunction" that ceremonies be united to them, making them count toward justification.[54] Hence "Paul opposes to them the

---

47. *Comm. Gal.* 2:16, in *CNTC* 11:39.
48. *Comm. Gal.* 2:16, in *CNTC* 11:39.
49. *LW* 35:189.
50. *LW* 26:137; *WA* 40.1:240.
51. *Comm. Gal.* 2:19, in *CNTC* 11:40.
52. *LW* 26:152; *WA* 40.1:262.
53. *LW* 26:152; *WA* 40.1:263.
54. *Comm. Gal.* 2:16, in *CNTC* 11:39.

grace of Christ alone, and not the moral law."[55] In considering ceremonial service as meritorious, Calvin argues, the Papists have transferred "the glory of salvation" to works.[56] To ascribe "a part of righteousness" to works is to destroy justification by faith alone; he writes, "Of semi-righteousness Paul knew nothing."[57] For this reason, George notes, Calvin rejects the medieval teaching that human beings could earn a congruent merit by taking the "first step toward justification."[58]

The word "flesh" in Gal 2:16 refers to who we are by nature, that we are a miserable and condemned sinner in Adam. All of us are included in the expression "flesh." With David, both Jewish and Gentile people come from "an impure seed" (Ps 51:5) and are not exempted from the depravity of human nature. Calvin regards the scriptural word "uncircumcision" as a predicate of our systemic condition, that we inherit pollution from Adam and fall under God's curse from birth.[59] Circumcision was a sign and testimony of the covenant God made with the Jewish people; this is what sets them apart from unbelievers. Thus Paul could write, "We are Jews and not sinners of the Gentiles" (Gal 2:15). The phrase "Jews by nature" signifies not the old and corrupted nature that requires cleansing by God's sanctifying grace; rather, it refers to the natural blessing the Jewish people inherited from the promise. Calvin cites Rom 11:16 to describe the Jewish people as coming from a "holy root."[60] The Jewish people were marked out as God's children by the sign of circumcision, not because they were superior to others, but simply because of God's free grace. Luther paraphrases Gal 2:15 as this: "We are righteous in as much as we are by nature Jews, not sinners, like the Gentiles."[61] But this righteousness the Jewish people have does not justify, says Luther, for it is "external."[62] Therefore, the Jewish people, like the Gentiles, Luther argues, must relinquish their own righteousness, and seek a righteousness through "faith in Jesus Christ."[63] The righteousness of Christ is freely given to those who are empty and are without any righteousness of

---

55. *Comm. Gal.* 2:16, in *CNTC* 11:39.

56. *Comm. Gal.* 2:16, in *CNTC* 11:39.

57. *Comm. Gal.* 2:16, in *CNTC* 11:39.

58. George, *Galatians*, 201.

59. *SG*, 173.

60. *Comm. Gal.* 2:15, in *CNTC* 11:37.

61. *LW* 27:218; *WA* 2:489.

62. *LW* 26:218; *WA* 2:488.

63. *LW* 27:218; *WA* 2:489.

their own. Calvin writes, "The foundation of free righteousness is when we are stripped of our own righteousness."[64] He cites Rom 3:1–2, where Paul writes of how abundantly blessed the Jewish people have been. But later in Rom 3:9–10, Paul raises the question "What advantage have the Jews?"—to which he replies, "None at all. For we are all under God's curse."[65]

On Gal 2:19, "For I through the law died to the law, that I might live to God," Luther regards as "the most delicious language" the apostle's opposition of "the Law to the Law."[66] Both Luther and Calvin interpret justification as twofold: negatively, it is dying to the law, and positively, living to God. "To die to the law" means to be free from it and not to come under its oppression. There is nothing, Luther opines, "more forceful against justification by the law" than Paul's claim that "I died to the law," meaning, in Luther's words, "'I do not care anything about the Law at all; therefore I am not justified by it.'"[67] The law dares not set the standard for becoming God's child and enjoying his favor. Similarly, Calvin puts it forcefully: "To die to the law is to renounce it and to be freed from its dominion, so that we have no confidence in it, and it does not hold us captive under the yoke of slavery."[68] Those who attempt to justify themselves through the law misunderstand or misuse it; they are sinners and remain such, and therefore come under the punitive function of the law, that is, curse and damnation. The "true role" of the law, Calvin says, is to "kill us." Thus he avers, "Those who live to the law have never felt the power of the law or even tasted what it is all about; for the law, when truly understood, makes us die to itself."[69] Calvin further explains how Paul was dead through the law: "I can have no life, I can have no assurance of salvation, I can have no comfort, or rest, or happiness. In short, there is nothing in the law to draw me closer to God. . . . Indeed, it sends me into the depths of hell. This would have been my portion if I had remained under the law."[70] While the gospel has its own efficacy to bless and save, the law possesses its own power to curse and kill. "Hence it follows that the death brought about by the law is truly deadly. With it is contrasted another kind of death, in the life-giving fellowship of

---

64. *Comm. Gal.* 2:16, in *CNTC* 11:40.

65. *SG*, 174.

66. *LW* 26:155; *WA* 40.1:255.

67. *LW* 26:157; *WA* 40.1:270.

68. *Comm. Gal.* 2:19, in *CNTC* 11:42.

69. *Comm. Gal.* 2:19, in *CNTC* 11:41.

70. *SG*, 195.

Christ."[71] Similarly, Luther writes, "Thus against my death, which binds me, I have another death, that is life, which makes me alive in Christ."[72] Here Luther opposes "the law of Moses" that binds us to "the law of grace" that frees me. To live to Christ means to be placed "under another Law, namely the Law of grace, which rules over sin and the Law."[73] The law of grace that saves kills the law that condemns. Grace liberates us from "the bonds" of our death and abolishes death with the "same bonds" so that it has no power over us. Luther avers, "Thus death, which bound me, is now bound itself; death, which killed me, is now killed itself through death, that is, through life itself."[74] The law that kills is now killed by grace that kindles life.

Both Reformers affirm the doctrine of total depravity, in which all are destitute of the inherent power of keeping the law perfectly. This was said contrary to the "Papists," whose doctrine that humans possess some causal power to keep the law Calvin regards as "detestable."[75] Calvin again uses the contrast to exclude all merit of works from justification. "For faith, inasmuch as it contains the free goodness of God, Christ with all his blessings, the testimony of our adoption which is given in the Gospel, is universally contrasted to the law, the merit of works and human worth."[76] The understanding emerges again in their interpretation of Gal 3:2–6. There Luther maintains that "there can be no middle ground" between the word of the gospel or the law.[77] Calvin also holds one way to righteousness: faith.[78] Abraham was justified by faith, because he trusted the word of God's promise, despite contrary to all evidence and experience. Righteousness was reckoned to Abraham, who had no righteousness of his own. Calvin says, "Faith therefore has a relation and respect to such a Word of God as may enable men to rest and trust in God."[79] Justification occurs by "imputation," not by an infusion into us by "habit or quality."[80] The righteousness we obtain by faith, Calvin avers, "is not a quality inherent in us but the pure gift of

---

71. *Comm. Gal.* 2:19, in *CNTC* 11:42.

72. *LW* 26:163; *WA* 40.1:278.

73. *LW* 26:158; *WA* 40.1:271.

74. *LW* 26:163; *WA* 40.1:278.

75. *Comm. Gal.* 3:10, in *CNTC* 11:53.

76. *Comm. Gal.* 3:6, in *CNTC* 11:50–51.

77. *LW* 26:203; *WA* 40.1:329.

78. *Comm. Gal.* 3:6, in *CNTC* 11:50.

79. *Comm. Gal.* 3:6, in *CNTC* 11:50.

80. *Comm. Gal.* 3:6, in *CNTC* 11:50.

God and is possessed by faith only."[81] The "principal cause" of justification, he continues, is the mercy of God; the "instrumental cause" is faith, which grasps the pure gift of God's righteousness.[82]

The law, in and of itself, is not negative or destructive, even when used by the devil in a demonic way. Only when the law encounters sin does it become negative. Calvin expressly says, "Hence we conclude that it is accidental that the law should curse, though at the same time perpetual and inseparable. The blessing which it offers us is excluded by our depravity, so that only the curse remains."[83] In this connection, Luther also is cognizant of the nature of the law, as in Rom 7:12, "So the law is holy, and the commandment is holy, just and good." The law's negative function is consequential upon sin (cf. Rom 7:12–16); as Paul said, "Did that which is good bring death to me? By no means!" (Rom. 7:13).[84] Due to depravity, the law assumes the negative role of cursing rather than consoling. But this does not mean the law serves no other purpose than causing death; Luther writes, "For the Law is a Word that shows life and drives us toward it."[85] Its "chief use and end" is "to reveal death, in order that the nature and enormity of sin might thus become apparent."[86] The law truly condemns us, not so that we may remain in condemnation, but that we may be "terrified and humbled and thus fear God."[87] "Except for faith," Luther thus writes, "the law is the best, the greatest and the loveliest among the physical blessings of the world."[88]

Luther interprets Gal 3:10 in the light of Rom 2:13, "It is not the hearers of the law who are righteous before God but the doers of the law will be justified." Luther uses the language of the contrary to reflect the actual contents of the distinction between faith and law. Relying on works of the law and trusting in Christ are "contraries."[89] To "do the Law," for Luther, "is first to believe and so, through faith, to keep the Law."[90] Through the

81. *Comm. Gal.* 3:6, in *CNTC* 11:50.

82. *Comm. Gal.* 3:6, in *CNTC* 11:50.

83. *Comm. Gal.* 3:10, in *CNTC* 11:53.

84. *LW* 26:335; WA 40.1:516.

85. *LW* 26:335; WA 40.1:516.

86. *LW* 26:335; WA 40.1:516.

87. *LW* 26:335; WA 40.1:516. .

88. *LW* 26:251; WA 40.1:396.

89. *LW* 26:253; WA 40.1:398.

90. *LW* 26:255; WA 40.1:400.

illumination of the Holy Spirit, we "begin to keep the Law, to love God and our neighbor. . . . This is really keeping the Law; otherwise the Law remains permanently unkept."[91] Such perspective is intrinsically tied to Luther's understanding of the first table of the Decalogue, especially in reference to the first commandment that teaches God must be "worshipped by believing and fearing Him."[92] It reinforces the spiritual sense of "to do," which is inconceivable apart from "hearing with faith, that is, through the promise."[93] Luther identifies two classes of the doers of the law: one uses the law diabolically to achieve justification; the other uses it properly, by believing, which then results in keeping the law. The first refers to those who seek justification through performing the law; the second refers to those who trust completely in God's mercy for justification. These two classes do not coincide.

The Papists, Calvin argues, have misinterpreted the following passage—"For not the hearers of the law are just before God, but the doers of the law shall be justified" (Rom 2:13)—and converted salvation into a "contract God made with us, and that contract is the law."[94] "To do the law," Calvin writes, requires that we fulfill the law not only "in part" but in "everything that belongs to righteousness."[95] But none can fulfill the law's demands perfectly; every person is by nature removed from righteousness unless reckoned as such by God.

> By nature, we are completely hostile to God's righteous standards. Now that he has regenerated by his Holy Spirit, we are entirely indebted to him; every good thing we possess we have received from his hand, and he simply rewards his own gifts in us. Can we, therefore, speak of merit? No. Indeed, we must go further and say that even though our Lord deigns to crown our works when they are good in his sight, they can only be partly good, for there will always be enough sin mixed in with them to condemn us. Thus, we are stripped of all confidence in our own righteousness, because our works have insufficient worth in the eyes of God. . . . That is why we need to consider the second aspect to the solution . . . which is "living by faith."[96]

91. *LW* 26:255; WA 40.1:401.
92. *LW* 26:253; WA 40.1:399.
93. *LW* 26:253; WA 40.1:399.
94. *SG*, 273.
95. *Comm. Gal.* 3:12, in *CNTC* 11:55.
96. *SG*, 274.

The inefficacy of the law reveals our need for a righteousness beyond ourselves and leads us to the righteousness that faith offers.[97] Calvin contrasts the language of law with the language of faith; each tries to win God's approval or attain righteousness. The former says, "We must obey and observe all his commandments"; the latter says, "[We] rest entirely upon God's Word, allowing it to dwell in [our] heart and upon [our] life."[98] Law and faith are incompatible and can in no wise be conjoined; they are like "fire and water."[99] On Gal 3:10, "For all those who rely on works of the law are under a curse," Calvin, like Luther, argues from "contradictions," that "the same fountain does not yield both hot and cold."[100] Calvin frames his thinking around a syllogism:

> Whoever has come short in any part of the law is cursed.
> All are held chargeable of this guilt.
> Therefore all are cursed.[101]

Whoever wishes to seek justification in the works of the law subjects themselves to the curse. Deviation from any part of the law faces condemnation. To seek justification by works is to forfeit the righteousness of faith; the one excludes the other.

In Gal 3:19, the apostle asks, "Why then the law?" The answer: "Because of transgressions it was added." From this, Luther derives the "primary purpose of the Law of Moses" and "the true function and chief and proper use of the Law": to highlight our sinfulness and the miserable condition under God's wrath and judgment.[102] "Through the law sin is not only disclosed and recognized," Luther writes, "but that through this disclosure sin is increased, inflated, inflamed and magnified."[103] He finds support of his interpretation in Rom 7:13, "It was sin, working death in me through what is good, in order that sin might be shown to be sin, and through the commandment might become sinful beyond measure."[104] Negatively, the law functions like "a hammer" that condemns a sinner to

---

97. *SG*, 275.

98. *SG*, 275.

99. *SG*, 275.

100. *Comm. Gal.* 3:10, in *CNTC* 11:53.

101. *Comm. Gal.* 3:10, in *CNTC* 11:53.

102. *LW* 26:309; *WA* 40.1:481.

103. *LW* 26:314; *WA* 40.1:487.

104. *LW* 26:314; *WA* 40.1:487.

death. However, the law has value, as it allows grace to have access to the one who has been crushed by the hammer.[105] By crushing sinners via the law, God created them as the object of his mercy. "Therefore the Law is a minister and a preparation for grace."[106] God performs his "natural and proper work" of justifying via the "alien work" of damning, says Luther; "an action which is alien to God's nature results in a deed belonging to his very nature."[107] This befits the paradoxical nature of God, "the almighty Creator who makes everything out of nothing," to make sinners into saints.[108] The law's "true use"[109] is to lead the afflicted conscience to grace. "Therefore," Luther concludes, "the Law with its function does contribute to justification—not because it justifies, but because it impels one to the promise of grace and makes it sweet and desirable."[110]

On Gal 3:21, "Is the law, then, against the promises of God? God forbid," Luther writes, "Although the law discloses and increases sin, it is still not against the promises of God but is, in fact, for them. For in its true and proper work and purpose it humbles man and prepares him—if he uses the Law correctly—to yearn and seek for grace."[111] Ebeling notes, "The hopelessness of their situation, their subjection to the power of sin, is made all the more hopeless by the law."[112] The law strips us of everything in us, Calvin writes, so that

> naked and empty-handed, [we] flee to his mercy, repose entirely in it, hide deep within it, and seize upon it alone for righteousness and merit. For God's mercy is revealed in Christ to all who seek and wait upon it with true faith. In the precepts of the law, God is but the rewarder of perfect righteousness, which all of us lack, and conversely, the severe judge of evil deeds. But in Christ his face shines, full of grace and gentleness, even upon us poor and unworthy sinners.[113]

105. *LW* 26:314; WA 40.1:488.
106. *LW* 26:314; WA 40.1:488.
107. *LW* 26:314; WA 40.1:488; *LW* 2:134n3; 31:51.
108. *LW* 26:314; WA 40.1:488.
109. *LW* 26:315; WA 40.1:490.
110. *LW* 26:315; WA 40.1:490.
111. *LW* 26:328; WA 40.1:508.
112. Ebeling, *Truth of the Gospel*, 145.
113. *Inst.* 2.7.8.

Luther does not concede any contradiction between the law and the gospel, for both proceed from the same God, unless one misuses the law to attain righteousness. Similarly, Calvin avows, "Whoever alleges any contradiction between them blasphemes against God."[114] Contradiction occurs if the law possesses the soteriological power only the gospel has. There are not "two contrary roads" toward justification, but only one, that being crushed under the weight of the law we flee to Christ in whom is found the consolation of the gospel.[115] In stripping soteriological power from the law, Paul eliminates the contradiction. "I would admit," Calvin paraphrases, "that righteousness is obtained by the law if salvation were found in it."[116] But this is not so, as the next verse reads "the Scripture hath shut up all things under sin" (Gal 3:22). By "Scripture," Paul means "the law itself," which consigns all to the opposites of righteousness and life—namely, sin and death. Those who seek righteousness in the law incur nothing but curse and damnation. Not just "all men"—Paul used the all-embracing phrase "all things," which includes not only people but everything they possess.[117] All are nullified, removed from life, unless they cling to the "promise by faith."[118] For both Luther and Calvin, consolation is found in condemnation, its opposite. Calvin writes, "Whenever we hear ourselves condemned in Scripture, there is help provided for us in Christ if we betake ourselves to Him."[119] The voice of condemnation we hear in the law is not the final word; rather, it is God's ordained means for placing us under a death-causing sentence whereby we rely not on our works but on God alone for deliverance. The paradox consists in the fact that "God so often pronounce[s] that we are lost," says Calvin, so "that we may not perish eternally but may be struck and confounded by such a horrible sentence and by faith seek Christ," our only hope.[120]

Calvin's rendering of Gal 3:24 is akin to Luther's. The law functions like a "mirror," which displays the righteousness of God through which we are exposed of our unrighteousness.[121] We, too, recognize that righteousness

114. *Comm. Gal.* 3:21, in *CNTC* 11:64.
115. *Comm. Gal.* 3:21, in *CNTC* 11:64.
116. *Comm. Gal.* 3:21, in *CNTC* 11:64.
117. *Comm. Gal.* 3:22, in *CNTC* 11:64.
118. *Comm. Gal.* 3:22, in *CNTC* 11:65.
119. *Comm. Gal.* 3:22, in *CNTC* 11:64.
120. *Comm. Gal.* 3:22, in *CNTC* 11:64.
121. *SG*, 314.

is not in us and must be sought outside us. The law condemns us unless we seek remedy in the gospel. Calvin avers, "The threatenings [of the law] urged and pressed them to seek refuge from the wrath and curse of God. Indeed, it gave them no rest till they were constrained to seek the grace of Christ [gospel]."[122] Calvin concludes, "The whole law, in short, was nothing but a manifold variety of exercises in which the worshippers were led by the hand to Christ."[123] The law does not justify, but it is not superfluous. The law was "added" to the promise (Gal 3:19), says Calvin, but not because the promise lacks the power to save and has to be supplemented by the law. The word "added" serves to convict us that we, by our sinful or fallen nature, treat God's goodness with contempt, and that God hammers us harshly through the law so we might trust in his promise. Calvin writes, "We virtually constrain him to use force in order to humble us; only when our wills are thus inclined by force will we seek his grace in the Lord Jesus Christ."[124] The law thus, Calvin claims, "is the true preparation of Christ."[125] Once the transposition from the law to the gospel by faith occurs, its temporary nature of condemning ceases. Thus Gal 3:25 says, "But now that faith has come, we are no longer under a custodian," that is, under the law.

The image of the custodian allows Luther to teach the preparatory use of the law. The custodian educates, drives, and disciplines his pupils not to keep them in custody forever, but to prepare them to "freely enjoy their liberty and their inheritance" without any custodial constraint.[126] Likewise, "those who are frightened and crushed by the Law should know that these terrors and blows will not be permanent, but that by them they are being prepared for the coming of Christ and the freedom of the Spirit."[127] The metaphor of the law as "our schoolmaster" in Gal 3:24 allows Calvin to describe the preparatory function of the law; he writes, "The grammarian trains a boy and then hands him over to someone else who polishes him in the higher disciplines." Likewise, the law functions as the grammarian who educated pupils to prepare them for "the theology of faith for their completion."[128] Faith has abolished not the law's contents but its

---

122. *Comm. Gal.* 3:24, in *CNTC* 11:66.

123. *Comm. Gal.* 3:24, in *CNTC* 11:67.

124. *SG*, 316.

125. *Comm. Gal.* 3:18, in *CNTC* 11:60.

126. *LW* 26:347; *WA* 40.1:532.

127. *LW* 26:347; *WA* 40.1:532.

128. *Comm. Gal.* 3:24, in *CNTC* 11:66.

condemnatory function. What is ended is not the law itself but its time of custody. Luther writes, "The time of Law is not forever; but it has an end, which is Christ. But the time of grace is forever; for Christ, having died once for all, will never die again (Rom. 6:9-10). He is eternal; therefore the time of grace is eternal also."[129]

The Allegory of Hagar and Sarah: Children of the Flesh and Promise

In Gal 4:21-26, Luther makes use of the allegory of Abraham and Sarah in the Genesis account to instruct people of the distinction between two covenants, law and promise.[130] Paul applied allegories, Luther writes, "to the teaching of faith, grace and Christ, not to the Law and works, as Origen and Jerome did."[131] Of the two sons of Abraham, one of whom represents the covenant of slavery, and the other the covenant of freedom. God promised Abraham a son through whom would proceed manifold offspring. Childless, the elderly Abraham and his wife worked out their plan that Abraham were to bear a son named Ishmael through his servant, Hagar. However, Isaac was born to Abraham and Sarah. Of Ishmael, Luther writes, "There was no statement from God that preceded, as there was when Sarah gave birth to Isaac, but only the statement of Sarah, it is abundantly clear that Ishmael was Abraham's son only according to the flesh and without the Word."[132] What was lacking in Ishmael's birth was the word of promise, so he, like other children, was a natural son, "according to the flesh." Unlike Ishmael, Isaac's birth has the word of promise in Gen 17:19, "Sarah your wife shall bear your son, and you shall call his name Isaac." Luther discerns a significance in God's naming: not only does God name Isaac, crediting him as the son of "the promise," but God also names Sarah, granting her the honor of being "the mother of the promised son."[133] The difference between the old and new covenants parallels that between Hagar as Mount Sinai and Sarah as the Jerusalem above. The law given on Mount Sinai could be obeyed but not beget new life; the promise given through the word must be

129. *LW* 26:342; WA 40.1:526.

130. See Maschke, "Authority of Scripture," where he argues that Luther has not abandoned the use of allegory to illustrate theological arguments of the gospel.

131. *LW* 26:433; WA 40.1:652.

132. *LW* 26:435; WA 40.1:655.

133. *LW* 26:435; WA 40.1:655.

believed, and new life emerges out of it. The world is inclined to trust in the works of the law, not in the gospel. People of every age perceive righteousness only through the law. Luther writes, "Therefore if they follow the Law and perform its outward works, they think they are righteous. All such men are slaves and not free men, because they are sons of Hagar, who gives birth to slavery. . . . Therefore, they remain under the curse of the Law, under sin, death, and the power of the devil, under the wrath and judgment of God."[134] Sarah, "the free woman," that is, "the true church," is seemingly barren.[135] The gospel she preaches is not as appealing as is the teaching about the law and works. It attracts fewer adherents and has apparently little success. Despite contrary appearances, the church of Christ alone is prolific, giving birth to children and heirs because of the efficacy of the word.[136] The gospel frees us from the curse of the law and every other vice, not through the law and works, but through Christ. Therefore, the Jerusalem stated above—that is, the church—is free from the rigor of the law and works. Just as she is a free mother, not subject to law, sin, or death, so are the children begotten of her. Isaac, born of God's promise, receives the inheritance from his father, apart from the law or works; likewise, we are born of the word as heirs by Sarah, without the law or works.Calvin's exposition of the two covenants does not differ from Luther's except for the different categories he supplies. The two sons are born of Abraham according to the flesh. The difference lies in that Ishmael's birth was ordinary, "nothing beyond nature," but Isaac's birth was miraculous, based on "the promise of grace."[137] As in Abraham's house there are two mothers, so it is in the church: the first mother is Sinai and the second is Jerusalem. Calvin notes, "Doctrine is the mother by whom God begets us. It is twofold, legal and evangelical. The legal bears children to bondage; hence the simile of it is Hagar. But Sarah represents the second, which bears the children of freedom."[138] The legal and evangelical covenants represent two mothers from whom two kinds of children proceed. Children born out of the legal covenant, or the first mother, Hagar, are slaves; those born out of the evangelical covenant, or the second mother, Sarah, are free people. The church consists of sons of Abraham, born only of heavenly grace. God has invested the church with "a title of wonderful

134. *LW* 26:442–43; *WA* 40.1:666.
135. *LW* 26:443; *WA* 40.1:667.
136. *LW* 26:443; *WA* 40.1:667.
137. *Comm. Gal.* 4:23, in *CNTC* 11:85.
138. *Comm. Gal.* 4:24, in *CNTC* 11:86.

and highest honor," calling her "the mother of all believers."[139] God governs us through the "incorruptible seed"[word] he deposited in the church by which "she forms us, cherishes us in her womb and brings us to light."[140] Calvin quotes Isa 59:21, "My words which I have put in thy mouth, shall not depart out of thy mouth, nor out of the mouth of thy seed, nor out of the mouth of thy seed's seed, saith the Lord, from henceforth and forever."[141] Whoever does not have the church as their mother and does not want to be her son, says Calvin, cannot have "God as his Father."[142] His true church and her maternal care are God's ordained means by which God's people are born and brought to maturity. Calvin quotes Isa 54, where the prophet proclaims that the barren woman will become fertile, to speak of the prolific nature of the church. Just as the barren woman is made fruitful, "not by any preparation of hers but by the free blessing of God," so too, numerous children will emerge from all nations and become part of the church purely by God's promise.[143] "Through the gospel," says Calvin, "God has become our Father, and has declared that an inheritance awaits us, bought not by ourselves or any other mortal creature, but by Jesus Christ."[144]

Luther, in discussing the two covenants, contrasts the "physical promises" of the law with the "spiritual promises" of the gospel—namely, Christ and his kingdom.[145] The old covenant (law) has its own promises, which by nature are "conditional." It does not promise life freely; it bestows life only if we can keep the law. Otherwise, it leads us into despair and damnation.[146] Similarly, Calvin affirms that "the law has its promises but . . . they all have conditions. The promise . . . abolishes all human pride, casts man down and reveals that he is lost. The only answer, therefore, is in the Lord Jesus Christ."[147] The new covenant (gospel) has its own promises, too, which by nature are unconditional. Neither do their promises "demand anything of us" or "depend upon our worthiness as a condition."[148] Instead, they

139. *Comm. Gal.* 4:26, in *CNTC* 11:88.

140. *Comm. Gal.* 4:26, in *CNTC* 11:88.

141. *SG*, 446.

142. *Comm. Gal.* 4:26, in *CNTC* 11:88.

143. *Comm. Gal.* 4:27, in *CNTC* 11:88.

144. *SG*, 451.

145. *LW* 26:437; *WA* 40.1:658.

146. *LW* 26:437; *WA* 40.1:658.

147. *SG*, 451.

148. *LW* 26:437; *WA* 40.1:658.

unconditionally promise forgiveness of sin, grace, and righteousness. Ishmael was born of the slave, with no "promise" of deliverance from God; the law was given, vacuous of grace, and the old covenant was established with no promise of life attached. Luther avers, "For the law did not have promises added to it about Christ and His blessings, about deliverance from the curse of the Law, sin, death."[149] However, this sharp opposition between law and promise for Calvin is to be ascribed to the "bare law in a narrow sense," that is, law conceived apart from grace.[150] What Paul opposes is not the law per se but bare law—namely, the law as it meets the sinner. Calvin writes, "Those who cleave to the bare law [for justification] and do not know it as a schoolmaster to bring them to Christ, but rather make it a barrier against coming to him, are the Ishmaelites born to slavery."[151] The law does not bestow sonship, which only the promise does. As Gal 4:18 says, "Now we, brethren, as Isaac was, are the children of promise." By turning back to the law and works, the Galatians revert from sonship to slavery.

The Third Use of the Law: The Place of Law for Believers

When faith comes, we are no longer under the law's dominion. This in no way means the law is abolished and denied a legitimate place in the life of the Christian. It is here that Calvin's "third and principal use of the law" comes into focus.[152]

> The law, insofar as it is a rule of life, is a bridle which keeps us in the fear of the Lord, a spur to correct the slackness of our flesh, in short, so far as it is profitable for teaching, correcting, reproving, that believers may be instructed in every good work, is as much in force as ever, and remains intact.[153]

The recurring phrase "a rule of life" in Calvin, though not in Luther, underscores the normative function of the law in the Christian life. The principal use of the law pertains to the believers who live according to the

149. *LW* 26:437; WA 40.1:658.
150. *Inst.* 2.7.2.
151. *Comm. Gal.* 4:24, in *CNTC* 11:86.
152. *Inst.* 2.7.12.
153. *Comm. Gal.* 3:25, in *CNTC* 11:67.

bidding of the Holy Spirit.[154] The chief purpose of the law, says Calvin, is "the fulfillment of righteousness to form human life to the archetype of divine purity. For God has so depicted his character in the law that if any man carries out in deeds whatever is enjoined there, he will express the image of God, as it were, in his own life."[155] When we are set free from the negative power of the law, the law is not to be relegated to an addendum. Calvin writes, "Moreover, we are not so exempted from the law by Christ's benefit that we no longer owe any obedience to the teaching of the law and may do what we please. For it is the perpetual rule of a good and holy life."[156]

Luther and Calvin vary in their handling of Gal 3:19. Calvin is with Luther in stating that the law includes "the moral law."[157] But for Calvin, the peculiar office of Moses is broader than just moral law; it also includes "many promises concerning the free mercy of God and Christ which belong to faith."[158] Here Paul speaks of the old covenant, which, Calvin avers, consists in "prescribing a rule of life and ceremonies to be observed in the worship of God and in adding promises and threats to them."[159] These promises are, says Calvin, "accidental and quite outside the comparison between the law and the doctrine of grace."[160] Hesselink recognizes that, in Calvin, the word "accidental" here takes on a meaning different from the former usage: "There the contrast was between an original and accidental function of the law; here it is between Moses' proper role as a lawgiver and the 'accidental' inclusion of promises of grace."[161]

Law and grace originally do not exist as an antithesis. Just as the gospel is filled with grace, Calvin avers, so is the law "graced with the covenant of free adoption."[162] Not only did David grasp "the precepts [commands], but its accompanying promise of grace" as well.[163] To borrow Zachman's phrase, "the law in the broad sense"[164] for Calvin refers to "the Ten

---

154. *Inst.* 2.7.12.

155. *Inst.* 2.8.51.

156. *Comm. Gal.* 4:4, in *CNTC* 11:74.

157. *Comm. Gal.* 3:19, in *CNTC* 11:60.

158. *Comm. Gal.* 3:19, in *CNTC* 11:60.

159. *Comm. Gal.* 3:19, in *CNTC* 11:60, 65.

160. *Comm. Gal.* 3:19, in *CNTC* 11:60.

161. Hesselink, "Luther and Calvin," 74.

162. *Inst.* 2.7.2.

163. *Inst.* 2.7.12.

164. Zachman, *Assurance of Faith,* 145.

Commandments [that] were given within the covenant of free adoption in Christ, and cannot be understood apart from that context."[165] "Bare law in the narrow sense,"[166] that is, law abstracted from Christ, is no vessel of grace but a "dead letter" that kills.[167] Calvin says, "What is the law without Christ but a dead letter?"[168] The law separated from Christ is death-causing; with Christ, it is life-giving. For Luther, the law is never life-bestowing, though it is life-informing for the person of faith. The Creator, not the righteous deeds of Adam and Eve, governed and sustained their well-being, *shalom*. However, when people use the law improperly to acquire justification, Paul does not shy away from opposing it to the gospel. In his *Institutes*, Calvin argues that Paul "was sometimes compelled to take the bare law in a narrow sense" to repudiate "perverse teachers" who misused the law to merit righteousness.[169] Paul did not "oppose the law itself to the grace of adoption," Zachman rightly notes, but "bare law" itself.[170] The negative language of both Reformers achieves the same purpose—namely, to condemn. Hesselink discerned that in Calvin, "the original intent of the law" is set opposite to its "accidental function due to sin"; in Luther, the "spiritual intent" of the law is opposed to its diabolical use by "the self-righteous."[171]

The law, which no longer frightens our conscience, is not abrogated, but continues and is deemed, as Calvin puts it, the "best instrument" of conformity to the commands of God.[172] "Where the Spirit reigns," Calvin avers, "the law no longer has any dominion."[173] Christians under the Spirit of grace relish the law, for its curse is past, and it no longer frightens them.[174] Having been freed from the punitive function of the law, the Christian finds pleasure in the law and seeks correspondence with its righteousness. Calvin writes, "By mouldering our hearts to His righteousness, the Lord delivers

165. *Comm. Ezek.* 20:12, in CTS 12:299.

166. *Inst.* 2.7.2.

167. *Comm. 2 Cor.* 3:6, in CNTC 10:42.

168. *Comm. Phil.* 3:16, in CNTC 11:271.

169. *Inst.* 2.7.2. See Zachman, *Assurance of Faith*, 145, where he quotes the same text from Calvin's *Institutes* to hold that "Paul, according to Calvin, will oppose the law in the narrow sense to the covenant of grace only to argue against justification by works of the law, and not to oppose the law itself to the grace of adoption."

170. Zachman, *Assurance of Faith*, 145.

171. Hesselink, "Luther and Calvin," 74.

172. *Inst.* 2.7.12.

173. *Comm. Gal.* 5:26, in CNTC 11:106.

174. *Inst.* 2.7.7.

us from the severity of the law, so that He does not deal with us according to its covenant nor does He bind our consciences under its condemnation. Yet the law continues to perform its office of teaching and exhorting."[175]

As part of his explanation of Gal 3:19, Calvin reminds his readers that "the law has many uses, but Paul confines himself to one which serves his present purpose. He did not intend to inquire in how many ways the law is of advantage to men."[176] Then Calvin issues a caution, Hesselink notes,[177] which must not be taken as an attack on Luther:

> Readers must be put on their guard on this matter; for I see many make the mistake of acknowledging no other use of law than what is expressed here [its negative function]. But elsewhere Paul himself applies the precepts of the law to teaching and exhortation (2 Tim. 3:16). Therefore this definition of the use of the law is not complete and those who acknowledge nothing else in the law are wrong.[178]

The "many" here does not necessarily include Luther but "probably," Battles argues, refers to "the libertine sect" and "the Antinomian," especially John Agricola, who parted with Luther, rejecting Moses and the two tables of the law.[179] In his exposition of Gal 3:12, Luther acknowledges how the law can be used both "politically and theologically."[180] As part of his explanation of Gal 3:25, he expressly writes, "Its civil use is good and necessary, but its theological use is the most important and the highest," as it humbles us, causing us to yearn for the sweetness of God's grace.[181] Hesselink writes, "Thus the differences [between Luther and Calvin] are there, reflecting their dogmatic presuppositions, but they are fundamentally one in understanding the message of Galatians."[182] While Luther's focus is on the old creature as a sinner who must undergo a perpetual death by the "theological" use of the law, Calvin's focus is on the new creature in Christ who must undergo perpetual renewal by the "third use" of the law. Having been liberated from the custody of the law, Luther writes, "We live securely

---

175. *Comm. Gal.* 5:24, in *CNTC* 11:106.

176. *Comm. Gal.* 3:19, in *CNTC* 11:61.

177. Hesselink, "Luther and Calvin," 74.

178. *Comm. Gal.* 3:19, in *CNTC* 11:61.

179. See *Inst.* 2.7.13n20; also cited in Hesselink, "Luther and Calvin," 81n49a.

180. *LW* 26:274; *WA* 40.1:428.

181. *LW* 26:348; *WA* 40.1:533; cf. *LW* 26:329; *WA* 40.1:508.

182. Hesselink, "Luther and Calvin," 78.

and happily with Christ, who reigns sweetly in us by the Holy Spirit."[183] But our faith is not perfect; it hinders us from apprehending Christ perfectly. The imperfection of faith is not due to any deficiency in Christ, who has no lack, but in us, who still struggle with the old flesh. Commenting on Rom 7:23, "But the law in our members is at war with the law of our mind," Luther writes, "We are partly free of the Law and partly under the Law. With Paul we serve the Law of God with our mind, but with our flesh we serve the law of sin."[184] The flesh has to be crushed by the word of the law so that it does not reign; faith has to be created through the word of the gospel so that it grasps Christ. Luther writes, "When faith is present, our custodian, with his gloomy and grievous task, is also forced to yield."[185] The punitive and accusatory function of the law recurs in his commentary on Gal 4:3, where he avers, "Even in its best use, therefore, the Law can only produce a knowledge of sin and the terror of death."[186] It could produce only "the elements of this world,"[187] including sin, death, and other vices, the opposite of heavenly things such as righteousness, life, and other virtues. The negative aspect of the law remains the principal and dominant usage. Yet hidden in this negative is the positive, that the law makes God's grace "very sweet," says Luther, "and His gift precious beyond telling."[188] Luther thus exults in superlatives: the "best use" of the law, though negative, is the "highest and greatest" one, as it causes us to cleave to Christ, the "sweetest" mediator.[189]

Luther's accent on the negative use of the law is not to be taken as a negation of the positive role of the law. Far from being an antinomian, he declares, "The law is to be retained so that the saints might know what sort of works God requires and in what things they should practise obeying God."[190] The Christian not only does battle with residual sin, she also needs guidance in good works. Luther states this clearly in his *Bondage of the Will*: "Those who have obtained mercy and have been justified already [are] to be energetic in bringing forth the fruits of the Spirit and of the righteousness given them, to exercise themselves in love and good works, and boldly to

183. *LW* 26:349; WA 40.1:534.

184. *LW* 26:349; WA 40.1:535.

185. *LW* 26:351; WA 40.1:538.

186. *LW* 26:363; WA 40.1:554–55.

187. *LW* 26:365; WA 40.1:558.

188. *LW* 26:329; WA 40.1:509.

189. *LW* 26:329; WA 40.1:509.

190. WA 39.1:485, as cited in Althaus, *Theology of Martin Luther*, 272.

bear the cross and all the other tribulations of this world."[191] Because we are "called to freedom" (Gal 5:13) through faith in Christ, we can now freely live out the command to love God and our neighbor. The commandments not only serve as a "mirror" in which we see our sin, but, as Althaus wrote of Luther, "beyond this as instruction about 'good works' God wants. Such instruction is necessary and wholesome for the Christian."[192] On Gal 5:14, where he discusses the relationship between the first table and second table of the law, Calvin shares the same position as Luther: "Love to men springs only from the fear and love of God."[193] In matters of importance, "piety towards God" is prior to "the love of neighbor."[194] The love of neighbor stems from faith in God, as fruit from root.[195]

Both Reformers concur that good works proceed from faith in God, as effect from cause. However, there is a subtle difference in *emphasis* in the Reformers with respect to the motivation of good works. The impetus to do good works for Luther lies in trust when we hear God declare, "You are forgiven and thus my righteous child."[196] "True and living faith," Luther asserts, "arouses and motivates good works through love."[197] The law itself cannot cause things to happen; it does not motivate us to please God, which faith alone exhausts. Truly God-pleasing conformity to the commands of God proceeds from faith but is instructed by the law. For Calvin, the Christian law is a "perpetual rule of a good and holy life";[198] it guides us and keeps us safe on the path of sanctification. "Principally," he asserts, the law impels us to obey and "urges" us on to perform God-approved services.[199] The "third use" of the law is thus "a better and more excellent use,"[200] through which the saints attain the goal toward which their efforts press forward. As Dowey says, "Once the legal curse is removed and so long as all justification by works of any kind is banished, the law can return to its original and

191. Luther, *Bondage of the Will*, 180.

192. Althaus, *Theology of Martin Luther*, 272.

193. *Comm. Gal.* 5:14, in *CNTC* 11:101.

194. *Comm. Gal.* 5:14, in *CNTC* 11:100–01.

195. The next chapter will deal with the relation between faith and love, with its emphasis on the prolific nature of faith in the production of good works.

196. *LW* 31:300–301.

197. *LW* 27:30; *WA* 40.2:37.

198. *Comm. Gal.* 4:4, in *CNTC* 11:74.

199. *Inst.* 2.7.12.

200. *Inst.* 2.7.13.

proper role of being an articulation of the love of God and thus is helpful in the Christian life."[201] Because Christians are free from all negativities of the law—its terror, oppression, and burden—Calvin avows that "the teaching of the law will not only be tolerable, but even pleasing and agreeable; and we must not refuse the bridle which restrains us *gently*, but does not drive us further than is expedient."[202] The law, a gentle bridle, restrains the desires of the flesh and arouses the faithful to love God.

Concluding Reflections

The Reformers' emphasis on faith alone is integral to their doctrine of grace alone. In this they radicalize God's action, negating all other activity as intrinsic to their distinctive understanding of justification by faith. All of salvation is God's gift, unilaterally offered to us, which we only receive by faith—and nothing else. "The dialectic between law and gospel," Fink notes, "would seem to rule out any notion of human beings offering back to God."[203] Such an assertion, he recognizes rightly, needs some clarification.[204] The idea of humans offering back to God does not seem to bear any relation to the God whose deity is nothing but giving. For Luther, the law "demands" something of us; the gospel "grants freely." Both are contrary doctrines, just as "receiving and offering" are irreconcilable opposites. He writes, "Now demanding and granting, receiving and offering, are exact opposites and cannot exist together. For that which is granted, I receive; but that which I grant, I do not receive but offer to someone else."[205] The gospel for Luther is "a gift and offers a gift," freely given; it thus befits the character of the gift not to "demand anything."[206] It simply "commands us to hold out our hands and to receive what is being offered."[207] The receptive character of faith, Bayer writes, is itself the "counter-gift" offered to God in response to the gift received.[208] Without faith, God is robbed of his majesty. Faith,

201. Dowey, "Law," 151.

202. *Comm. Acts* 15:10, in *CNTC* 7:41 (emphasis added).

203. Fink, "Martin Luther's Reading," 47.

204. Fink, "Martin Luther's Reading," 47. For further discussion, see Hamm, "Luther's Revolutionary Theology."

205. *LW* 26:208; *WA* 40.1:337; also quoted in Fink, "Martin Luther's Reading," 47.

206. *LW* 26:209; *WA* 40.1:337.

207. *LW* 26:208; *WA* 40.1:337.

208. Bayer, "Ethics of Gift," 458.

though passive, is inherently causative or, in Luther's word, "omnipotent"; its "power" manifests itself by outward effects such as attributing glory to him and his majesty.[209] This reciprocal offering, says Luther, is "the supreme worship, the supreme allegiance, the supreme obedience, and the supreme sacrifice"[210] the recipients render to God, whose sole purpose is to benefit us, not to gain from us.[211] The passive act of attribution for Luther is "the highest thing" that we can offer back to the God of the first commandment and the first article of the Creed, thereby acknowledging God as "the Author and Donor of every good."[212] In so doing, Luther avers, faith "consummates the Deity"; it creates God "not in the substance of God but in us."[213]

Luther is wary of any understanding of faith as a meritorious work. He writes, "Faith then is not a work, since it looks only toward the promise. The promise, however, is a kind of gift, that we bring nothing to faith, because the promise came earlier and because reason turns away from faith. It is up to God alone to give the faith contrary to nature and ability to believe contrary to reason. That I love God is the work of God alone."[214] God's promise always comes before our trusting the promise, and it stands even if we shun it. For Luther, it remains a mystery how we can resist the promise once it has been delivered, a theodical question that escapes comprehension.

With Luther, Calvin highlights Abraham's faith as the condition of possibility of true worship: "No greater worship can be given to God than by sealing His truth by our faith. On the other hand, no greater insult can be shown to Him than by rejecting the grace which He offers us, or by detracting from the authority of His Word. For this reason, the main thing in the worship of God is to embrace His promises with obedience."[215] Faith as the passive reception of God's promise is itself a gift we offer back to God as a worshipful response to his prior gift. "God's categorical giving," Bayer avers, "does not exclude the counter-gift of the creature, but rather empowers the creature to this counter-gift as a response."[216] Is faith another form of works-righteousness? Not so, for even our response is a gifted kind, one that

---

209. *LW* 26:227; WA 40.1:360.

210. *LW* 26:227; WA 40.1:360.

211. *LW* 26:227; WA 40.1:360.

212. *LW* 26:227; WA 40.1:360.

213. *LW* 26:227; WA 40.1:360.

214. *LW* 34.160.

215. *Comm. Rom.* 4:20, in *CNTC* 8:99.

216. Bayer, "Ethics of Gift," 458; also quoted in Barclay, *Paul and the Gift*, 114n89.

is implanted by the love of the cross: "He gave himself for me." Faith does not achieve justification; it simply receives God's justifying verdict through Christ. Hence all ground for boasting is eliminated. Calvin contends, "If Abraham is justified because he embraces the goodness of God, by faith, it follows that he has no cause for glorying, since he brings nothing of his own except the acknowledgement of his own misery which seeks for mercy."[217]

In his sermon on Gal 2:15–16, Calvin does not deny the concept of gift as unilateral; he uses it to exclude human merits from justification. To make this point, Calvin compares a rich man with a poor man:[218]

> [There] are two men seeking food and shelter. One has money and wishes to be treated in accordance with his means. They both ask for something to eat, but the second man is poor and does not have a penny, so he begs for alms. They both have something in common, for they both seek food, but the first has money with which to satisfy his host. Thus, after eating and drinking well and being courteously entertained, the host, for his part, will be happy to receive his payment, no longer thinking that his guest is in any way indebted to him. Why? Well, he has been satisfied and has even gained from it. But the life of the poor man who asks for alms depends upon the one who can provide him with food and shelter, for he can give him nothing in return. In the same way, if we seek to be justified by the law we must deserve that justification; for then God will receive from us and we from him in a reciprocal manner.[219]

Calvin raises a question, "Is such a thing possible?" Could justification be reciprocal—that is, does God receive something from us even as we receive something from him? "Not at all" is his reply. "We cannot obtain righteousness by the law, and . . . if we believe we can make God our debtor, we will only provoke his wrath."[220] We can come only as poor beggars, with no capacity of reciprocal benefit for God except to cling to God for the fulfillment of our needs. Faith does not bring anything of itself, but simply receives what God has offered. Calvin writes, "Not as if faith were a virtue proceeding from us, but we must come humbly, confessing that we cannot obtain salvation except as a free gift."[221] The nature of the gift does not

217. *Comm. Rom.* 4:3, in *CNTC* 8:83.
218. *SG*, 177.
219. *SG*, 177.
220. *SG*, 177.
221. *SG*, 177.

require anything from us but elicits a humble reception from us, an action that does not deprive God of his majesty.

"The passive receptivity of faith"[222] highlights God's causative action in a such a way that expels human merits from the doctrine of justification. We stand before God not as an active but a passive person, receiving from him all his gifts, totally underserved but freely given. Whoever tries to achieve sonship by their own efforts, says Luther, are slaves, from whom all inheritance is withheld.[223] Likewise, for Calvin, inheritance is excluded from those who attempt to obtain sonship by their own merits by which they lapse into slavery.[224] He writes, "Thus, we obtain this deliverance only through the seed [the word] which brings regeneration and complete liberty."[225] The children of God are accounted righteous on account of God's promise that grants us eternal life. Their status as sons is given by new birth, not by human efforts. To borrow Calvin's categories, the "legal" birth, which proceeds from the righteousness of the law, does not make us the beneficiaries of God's inheritance—only the "evangelical" birth, wrought by the righteousness of faith, does this. Not legal birth, or that of the law, but evangelical birth, that of the gospel, is the cause of justification. Correspondingly, not "legal repentance" but "evangelical repentance" promises deliverance from the misery of sin and terror of God's wrath. Of their difference, Calvin speaks of "legal repentance; or that by which the sinner, stung with a sense of his sin, and overwhelmed with fear of the divine anger, remains in that state of perturbation, unable to escape from it . . . [and of] Evangelical repentance; or that by which the sinner, though grievously downcast in himself, yet looks up and sees in Christ the cure of his wound, the solace of his terror; the haven of rest from his misery."[226]

---

222. See Kim, *Luther on Faith*, 139, where the phrase "the passive receptivity of faith" appears.

223. *LW* 26:449; WA 40.1:675.

224. *SG*, 442.

225. *SG*, 442.

226. *Inst.* 3.3.4 (Beveridge).

3

Faith Alone, Yet not Alone

Faith as the Causative Agency of Love

The distinctive form of the Christian life for Luther and Calvin is two-fold: inwardly, faith before God, and outwardly, love before people—and the two are never separated. The claim that the Reformers, in their over-emphasis on the doctrine of justification, have not given due attention to—or even denigrated—works is a misnomer. Certain traditions[1] may be guilty of that, but not Luther and Calvin, who are not only theologians of "faith," but also theologians of "love."[2] Paul indeed was promoting works, the Reformers contend—not the kind of works that merits justification, but rather the kind that proceeds from it. Luther writes, "Therefore, faith remains the agent, love remains the act."[3] Faith is the causative agency of love; love is the resultant fruit of a true faith. Faith, to borrow Chalmers's phrase, is "the expulsive power of a new affection."[4] Faith is "expulsive," as it expels works or other self-chosen forms of duties from

---

1. See Barclay, *Obeying the Truth*, 7, where he attributes to the "Lutheran" tradition the neglect of Paul's ethical admonitions in Gal 5 and 6 because of their overemphasis on doctrinal teaching.

2. Kim, *Luther on Faith*, 3. According to Kim, there have been three misconceptions of the relation of faith and love in Luther's theology: first, Luther has "little or no teaching on love or sanctification"; second, "sanctification is reducible to his teaching on justification by faith"; and third, his thoughts on the subject are "self-contradictory" (Kim, *Luther on Faith*, 4–5).

3. WA 17:98; 11:25, as cited in Wannenwetsch, "Luther's Moral Theology," 128.

4. Chalmers, *Expulsive Power*.

the doctrine of justification; it is "power" or, in Luther's word, "energy"[5] transforming our existence, with love as its outcome. Following Erasmus, Luther conceives of faith as that "which is powerfully active, not one that snores once it has been 'acquired.' . . . It is powerfully active through love."[6] Faith and love are of one piece.

Earlier in his commentary on Gal 2:16, Luther states Paul's doctrine of faith: "By faith alone, not by faith formed by love, are we justified. . . . This faith justifies without love and before love."[7] After Paul had instructed faith, Luther claims, he ends with, in Kim's words, a "transitional point" that leads to the theme of love.[8] This is stated in his comment on Gal 4:9: "This is the conclusion of Paul's argument: From here until the end of the epistle he will not argue very much but will set forth commandments about morality."[9] Later in his comment on Gal 5:12, Luther again indicates, "For the apostle makes it a habit, after the teaching of faith and the instruction of consciences, to introduce some commandments about morals, by which he exhorts the believers to practice the duties of godliness toward one another."[10] Ethical concerns and admonitions are not viewed as, to borrow Kamell's phrase, "an addendum"[11] but as constitutive of Paul's soteriology in which justification and sanctification are joined together. With Luther, Calvin asserts, "It is not our doctrine that the faith which justifies is alone. We maintain that it is always joined with good works. But we contend that faith avails by itself for justification."[12] The main impetus behind Paul's attack on "the works of the law," Barclay notes, is not to dismiss works altogether from

---

5. *LW* 27:336; WA 2:567.

6. *LW* 27:336; WA 2:567.

7. *LW* 26:137; WA 40.1:239.

8. Kim, *Luther on Faith*, 65.

9. *LW* 26:394; WA 40.1:600; also quoted in Kim, *Luther on Faith*, 65.

10. *LW* 27:47; WA 40.2:58; also quoted in Kim, *Luther on Faith*, 65.

11. See Kamell, "Life in the Spirit," 362, where she summarizes different readings of Galatians: "Luther's concern to avoid linking justification with works led him to introduce the last two chapters of Galatians in his commentary as 'all kinds of admonitions and precepts' that came from 'after [Paul] had taught faith and instructed the conscience.' He conceived of these injunctions not as of soteriological import but as an addendum to prevent Christians from being seen as 'enemies of decency and of public peace.'" In contrast, she continues, Gordon Fee and Frank Matera argue that Gal 5–6 "actually form the climax of Paul's argument," which combines faith and love as part of Paul's doctrine of salvation.

12. *Comm. Gal.* 5:6, in *CNTC* 11:96.

the Christian life, but to ground works properly in faith.[13] The Reformers disavow any antipathy toward works as part of their doctrine of faith. Love does not grant efficacy to faith; rather, it flows from faith, as fruit is from a tree. The faith that justifies us is not formed by love but operates through love, its instrument. Justification by faith alone is no basis for ethical passivity, for to grasp Christ as our expiator is to grasp him as our example, the former grounding the latter. Faith is dynamically transformative, freeing the human will to love so that through their works, people are not seeking good for themselves but bestowing good on others. This understanding of love flows out of the cross, in which God's love is revealed in the opposite of human love. God's love seeks to create *ex nihilo*, bestowing good on objects not worthy in themselves; human love seeks to gain good from objects worthy in themselves. Apart from the faith (Rom 14:23) the Holy Spirit works in us, no good we do can be considered good. Faith constitutes the ground of all good works we do willingly and cheerfully, entirely free of the reciprocal yoke. Whoever is reconstituted by faith, says Luther, "knows all things, can do all things, ventures everything that needs to be done, and does everything gladly and willingly, not that he may gather merits and good works, but it is a pleasure for him to please God in doing these things. He simply serves God with no thought of reward, content that his service pleases God."[14] Similarly, "bare faith" suffices to obtain righteousness, Calvin claims, "without pomp of ceremonies but is satisfied with the spiritual worship of God";[15] and yet to be justified by faith does not mean to be "set free from good works," for faith, Calvin says, is not "idle."[16] Godfrey provides a crisp summary of Calvin's view: "True faith is living and fruitful. It certainly produces a Christian life of love and good works, but the love and good works are not part of justification. Faith alone justifies, but true faith is never alone in the justified."[17]

---

13. Barclay, *Obeying the Truth*, 6–7.

14. *LW* 44:27.

15. *Comm. Gal.* 5:6, in *CNTC* 11:95.

16. *Comm. Gal.* 3:12, in *CNTC* 11:54.

17. Godfrey, "Calvin and the Council," 125.

Faith and Love:
"Faith Working through Love"

For the scholastics, faith alone is dead; love supplies life to faith, rendering it effective. Aquinas asserts, "When unformed faith becomes formed, it is not the faith itself that is changed, but the soul, the subject of faith; at one instant it has faith without charity, and at the next, faith with charity."[18] From this comes two kinds of faith: one "formed" or animated by love, which possesses the capability of congruous meriting of justification; the other "unformed" by love, which possesses no power of meriting grace.[19] Fink explains:

> Medieval theologians . . . had reconciled Paul's language of justifi-
> cation by faith with the love command of Christ by a metaphysi-
> cal distinction in causation. Faith was seen as the material cause
> of salvation; love as the formal cause. This love, infused by God's
> grace, is thus the *forma*, the divine reality which "(in)forms" faith,
> giving it tangible reality. Love thus changes from a "dead," formless
> void to something living and active, a "colorful" knowing.[20]

Earlier in 1519, Luther takes the phrase "faith working through love" (Gal 5:6) as Paul's aim to demonstrate the reality of faith; true faith exists if it were conjoined to love.

> Therefore he who hears the Word of God sincerely and clings to
> Him in faith is at once also clothed with the Spirit of love, as Paul
> has said above, "Did you receive the Spirit by works of the law,
> or by hearing with faith" (Galatians 3:2)? For if you hear Christ
> sincerely, it is impossible for you not to love Him forthwith, since
> He has done and borne so much for you.[21]

The substance of his view recurs with greater vigor later in his Galatians commentary of 1535, where Luther repudiates his opponents' view
that unformed faith is one without any causal power to justify unless formed
by love: "Who could stand for the teaching that faith, the gift of God that is

18. Aquinas, *Summa theologiae* 31:131 (IIa-IIae, q.65, a.4, ad.4), as quoted in Chester, *Reading Paul with Reformers*, 86.

19. For a detailed understanding of the two kinds of faith, see "The Canons and Dogmatic Decrees of the Council of Trent," in Schaff, *Greek and Latin Creeds*, sixth session,
chs. 8, 11.

20. Fink, "Martin Luther's Reading," 45.

21. *LW* 27:336; *WA* 2:566.

infused in the heart by the Holy Spirit, can coexist with mortal sin . . . ? To believe this way about infused faith is to admit openly that they understand nothing about faith."[22] He appeals to the perspicuity of Paul's words.

> Paul does not make faith unformed here, as though it were a shapeless chaos without the power to be or to do anything; but he attributes the working itself to faith rather than to love. . . . He does not say "Love is effective." No, he says: "Faith is effective." He does not say: "Love works." No, he says: "Faith works." He makes love the tool through which faith works.[23]

As an elucidation of Luther's view, Chester draws a distinction between two assertions. First, faith is "active through love," a "middle" participle; and second, faith is "made effective through love," a "passive" participle. He writes:

> Although Luther does not say so, these points clearly rely on taking the participle *energoumene* as middle rather than passive. If passive it could be taken as saying that faith "is made effective through love." Yet while some patristic writers do take the participle as passive the majority of commentators in all eras, including most pertinently the Latin of the Vulgate itself, and therefore also many medieval advocates of the doctrine of faith formed by love, take it as middle. Luther's argument is that when the participle is so taken as middle in voice, Paul's words do not easily speak of faith as something passive or unformed but as something active and working.[24]

The phrase "faith working through love" in Gal 5:6, Luther argues, has allowed the sophists to "transfer justification from faith and attribute it solely to love," propounding that Paul was espousing this: "Faith does not justify; in fact, it is nothing unless love the worker is added, which forms faith."[25] Luther takes pains to clarify that Paul's phrase does not refer to "'faith, which justifies through love,'" or "'faith, which makes acceptable through love,'" or "'Love makes one acceptable.'"[26] Rather, Paul taught that

22. *LW* 27:28; WA 40.2:35.

23. *LW* 27:28; WA 40.2:35.

24. Chester, "Faith Working through Love," 44. See also Riches, *Galatians through the Centuries*, 262; Schreiner, *Galatians*, 317, who construes the participle "working" as a middle.

25. *LW* 27:28; WA 40.2:34.

26. *LW* 27:28; WA 40.2:35.

"works are done on the basis of faith through love, not that a man is justified through love."[27] The force of Luther's argument centers on the word
"working," which describes faith as "'working through love'" rather than
"justify[ing] through love."[28] Confusion arises, Luther continues, when
the sophists identify working with justifying; they also confuse works
with righteousness, as works "are not righteousness, but . . . are done by
righteousness."[29] "Working," Luther avers, is predicated of faith, not of love.
A genuine faith is not an "unformed" or "shapeless chaos"; rather, it is "an
effective and active" thing, possessed of the efficacy of being or doing.[30]
Faith, not love, is a causal agent; it, not love, works. It works through the vehicle of love. Love is a "tool" through which faith performs its acts.[31] A tool
has no intrinsic power to accomplish anything; its power to act is received
from the one who employs it. Faith of the "true and living" kind, Luther
asserts, "arouses and motivates good works through love." He further clarifies: "'He does not truly believe if works of love do not follow his faith.'"[32]
Luther's stance stands in contradiction with that of medieval exegesis in
which the unformed faith, which lacks vitality, must be quickened by love
to make true faith. Faith, for him, is not "an idle quality or an empty husk
in the heart" until love comes; it is "'a sure trust and firm acceptance in the
heart' [that grasps Christ]. . . . Therefore our 'formal righteousness' is not
a love that informs faith; but it is faith itself, a cloud in the hearts, that is,
trust in a thing we do not see, in Christ, who is present especially when He
cannot be seen."[33]

The immediate context of this passage, Luther argues, does not
pertain to the question of what faith is, which was already dealt with in
Galatians's preceding chapters. Rather, here, he argues, "Paul is describing
the whole of the Christian life in this passage: inwardly it is faith toward
God, and outwardly it is love or works towards one neighbor. Thus a man
is a Christian in a total sense: inwardly through faith in the sight of God,
who does not need our works; outwardly in the sight of men, who do not

27. *LW* 27:28; WA 40.2:35.

28. *LW* 27:28; WA 40.2:35.

29. *LW* 27:29; WA 40.2:35. See n25, citing Aristotle: "There is a difference between . . .
the act of justice and what is just." Cf. *Nicomachean Ethics*, 5:7.

30. *LW* 27:29; WA 40.2:35.

31. *LW* 27:29; WA 40.2:36.

32. *LW*27:30; WA 40.2:37.

33. *LW* 26:129; WA 40.1:229.

derive any benefit from faith but do derive benefit from works or from our love."[34] Luther counsels against confusing what precedes—namely, faith—with what follows, that is, works. The works of love produced by faith do not avail before God in relation to justification, but they are of help in the believers' relation to their neighbors by love. The Christian life is characterized by a living faith, which Luther understands as an "internal" power, "the impulse and motivation" of love, its "external function."[35] He illustrates the effective nature of faith by the parable of the tree and its fruits: "First there must be a tree, then the fruit. For apples do not make a tree, but a tree make apples. So faith first makes the person, who afterwards performs works."[36] The antecedent claim is that faith alone justifies; the subsequent claim is that justifying faith is never alone. Works follow faith, as fruit from a tree. Luther writes, "It is true faith toward God, which loves and helps the neighbor."[37] The inclusion of works in his understanding of justifying faith, Luther notes, enables Paul to meet two groups of people: "the Jews and the works righteous," who deny that faith alone, abstracted from works, justifies; and "the idle and the sluggish," who rationalize that since faith alone justifies, mere belief suffices, leading them to show disdain for good works.[38]

Like Luther, Calvin's comments on Gal 5:6 were set against the Papists. He contends they twisted the meaning of this verse to mean this: "If the faith that justifies us be that which works by love, faith alone does not justify." Against such "vain babbling," Calvin writes:

> It is not our doctrine that the faith which justifies is alone. We maintain that it is always joined with good works. But we contend that faith avails by itself for justification. The Papists . . . tear faith to pieces, sometimes making it *informis* [unformed] and empty of love, and sometimes *formata* [formed]. But we deny that true faith can be separated from the Spirit of regeneration. When we debate justification, however, we exclude all works.[39]

The present passage, Calvin continues, "does not dispute whether love cooperates with faith in justifying"; but, in addressing idle Christians, Paul

34. *LW* 27:30; WA 40.2:37.
35. *LW* 27:30; WA 40.2:38.
36. *LW* 26:255; WA 40.2:402.
37. *LW* 27:31; WA 40.2:38.
38. *LW* 27:30; WA 40.2:37.
39. *Comm. Gal.* 5:6, in *CNTC* 11:96.

joins faith to love, "the true exercises of believers."[40] He adamantly declares the performative character of true faith, that which truly works through love. When justification is in view, he does not allow any inclusion of love or of works, "but resolutely holds onto the exclusive adverb."[41]

Faith and Union with Christ: Justification and Sanctification

In his comments on Gal 2:16, Luther writes against the medieval concept of "faith formed by love" (*fides caritate formata*) and offers a Christocentric understanding of faith, focusing on Christ whom faith grasps.

> Where they [scholastics] speak of love, we speak of faith. And while they say that faith is the mere outline but love is its living colors and completion, we say in opposition that faith takes hold of Christ and that He is the form that adorns and informs faith as color does the wall . . . It takes hold of Christ in such a way that Christ is the object of faith, or rather not the object but, so to speak, the One who is present in the faith itself. Thus faith is a sort of knowledge or darkness that nothing can see. Yet the Christ of whom faith takes hold is sitting in this darkness as God sat in the midst of the darkness on Sinai and in the temple.[42]

Earlier in his exegesis of Gal 2:16–17, Luther argues that Paul teaches faith alone justifies. "Faith justifies because it takes hold of and possesses this treasure, the present Christ."[43] Herein lies the christological framework in which faith places the believer "in Christ" (Gal 5:6), to receive from him all the benefits. If faith has to become a formed faith by human action in order to justify, Allen agues, that would have "diminish[ed] the Christ-centered basis of justification."[44] Contrary to the sophists who teach that "love forms and trains faith," Luther insists it is "Christ who forms faith and trains faith or who is the form of faith."[45] The Christ whom faith seizes, says Luther, is "the true Christian righteousness. Here there is no work of

40. *Comm. Gal.* 5:6, in *CNTC* 11:96.
41. *Comm. Gal.* 5:6, in *CNTC* 11:96.
42. *LW* 26:129–30; *WA* 40.1:229.
43. *LW* 26:130; *WA* 40.1:229.
44. Allen, *Justification and the Gospel*, 110.
45. *LW* 26:130; *WA* 40.1:229.

the Law, no love."[46] However, at Gal 5:6, Paul's emphasis shifts, as he dwells on the unity of faith and love, just as "heat and light" are inseparable from "fire."[47] As Luther states in his *Preface to Romans* (1522), "It is impossible for [faith] not to be doing good works incessantly. It does not ask whether good works are to be done, but before the question is asked, it has already done them and is constantly doing them."[48] Chester writes, "Yet the faith spoken of is the same faith in both contexts. It is faith in which Christ is present and it is because of that presence that faith is able to work through love."[49] The christological phrase "in Christ" accentuates that the Christ present in faith is "the impulse" of works of love.[50] Luther affirms, "Whatever there is in us besides Him—whether it be intellect or will, activity or passivity, etc.—is flesh, not Spirit."[51]

Erasmus had paved the way for both the Wittenbergers and Genevans to understand faith as trust and not as the mere acknowledgment of facts, as in medieval usage. His philological work yielded several meanings of the term "faith." Commenting on "from faith to faith" (Rom 1:17), Erasmus writes:

> But sacred literature frequently uses these words loosely, for it often uses *fides* [faith] for *fiducia* [trust] in God almost in the sense of hope; sometimes for the belief or conviction by which we assent to the things handed down to us about God—by which even the demons believe. Sometimes the word faith [*fides*] embraces all these meanings: that assent to the truth both of the historical record and of the promises, and the trust [*fiducia*] that arises from his omnipotent goodness, not without the hope, that is, the expectation, of the promises.[52]

Melanchthon reinforces Erasmus's observation, Kolb notes, that the word faith (*pistis*) means more than what has been taught by the scholastic theologians. He was instrumental in convincing Luther, Kolb continues,

46. *LW* 26:130; WA 40.1:229.
47. *LW* 35:371.
48. *LW* 35:370.
49. Chester, "Faith Working through Love," 47.
50. *LW* 27:30; WA 40.2:38.
51. *LW* 27:25; WA 40.2:30.

52. See Erasmus, *Annotations on the New Testament: Acts–Romans–I and II Corinthians*, 345, in *Collected Works of Erasmus* (Toronto: University of Toronto Press, 1974–), 56:43–44, as cited in Chester, *Reading Paul with Reformers*, 156–57n65.

that faith refers to "the trust that clings to an object, particularly a person."[53] For his part, in his sermon on Gal 5:6, Calvin takes issue with the Papists' view of faith as simply a matter of historical knowledge, which is "not yet complete" but "needs to be established" by love. Against such view, he rebuts:

> But when the Scriptures speak of faith, they mean the knowledge which has been granted to us by the Holy Spirit, not an idea that simply flutters around in our head. It is sealed upon our hearts, which demonstrates that a miraculous work of God . . . had taken place within us before we could be illumined and established in the faith . . . Furthermore, it is not enough to have a vague knowledge of the fact that Jesus Christ is the Redeemer. Faith means that each of us knows him to be our Redeemer. Is this possible unless the Lord Jesus lives and reigns within us, causing his love to burn within us, that we might give ourselves solely to him?[54]

In his commentary on Gal 3:13, Luther understands faith as "nothing else but the truth of the heart, that is, the right knowledge of the heart about God."[55] And yet "the knowledge of Christ and faith is not a human work but a divine gift."[56] Reason cannot yield a true knowledge of God; only faith could. Luther notes that Abraham's faith is efficacious enough to kill reason, "the greatest and most invincible enemy of God,"[57] by trusting in the word of God in which a son was promised to him. Faith justifies, as in Abraham, because it embraces God's promises, and in doing so, it acknowledges God to be truthful, thereby rendering God honor that is rightly due him. Faith for Calvin is not about an intellectual conviction of the truth, which is inept in obtaining righteousness; he writes, "Faith therefore has a relation and respect to such a Word of God as may enable men to rest and trust in God."[58] Faith understood as "trust" appears in Calvin's exposition of Rom 4:20, where he regards Abraham's faith as a fragrance of praise to God. "No greater worship can be given to God than by sealing His truth by our faith. On the other hand, no greater insult can be shown to Him than by rejecting the grace which He offers us, or by detracting

53. Kolb, *Luther's Treatise*, 46.

54. *SG*, 485–86.

55. *LW* 26:238; WA 40.1:377.

56. *LW* 26:238; WA 40.1:377.

57. *LW* 26:229; WA 40.1:362.

58. *Comm. Gal.* 3:6, in *CNTC* 11:50.

from the authority of His Word. True religion begins with faith."[59] Abraham believes against reason and experience and receives God's promise apart from any prior worth or works. Commenting on Gen 15:6, Luther writes, "In this passage, no mention is made of any preparation for grace, of any faith formed through works, or of any preceding disposition. This, however, is mentioned: Abraham was in the midst of sins, doubts, and fears, and was exceedingly troubled in spirit."[60] And yet Abraham's faith pleased God, Calvin explains, "because by it he embraced the promise of God"; and "because hence Abram obtained righteousness in the sight of God, and that by imputation."[61] Abraham was justified by the promise of a blessing given 430 years before the law appeared; as Paul states in Rom 4:17, "I have made you the father of many nations—in the presence of the God in whom you have believed." The promise of salvation emanates from a covenantal God and is efficacious without reference to the law. The promise of God is no empty solicitude but intrinsically creative; it has "established" Abraham as the father of many nations, a reality that corresponds to the causative nature of the promise.[62] Righteousness is reckoned to Abraham through faith, not through the law, which came much later. With this, the Galatians err in seeking righteousness through the law.

The promise is of no use unless received by faith. Paul vigorously impresses upon us that "Abraham believed, and it was reckoned to him as righteousness" (Gal 3:6) to accentuate the receptive character of faith. With Calvin, Luther speaks of the "omnipotent" power of faith, which by grasping the promises of God honors God as truthful and trustworthy; consequently, it creates God's deity "in us," not in himself. He writes, "To attribute glory to God is to believe in Him, to regard Him as truthful, wise, righteous, merciful, and almighty, in short, to acknowledge Him as the Author and Donor of every good. Reason does not do this, but faith does."[63] Where faith is absent, God loses the essence of who he is. God does not "require anything greater" than a "believing heart" that gives him all glory, obedience, and sacrifice. "When He has obtained this, God retained His divinity, sound and unblemished."[64] From this, Luther avers, we know "what

59. *Comm. Rom.* 4:20, in *CNTC* 8:99.

60. *LW* 3:21; *WA* 42:563.

61. *Comm. Gen.* 15:6, in *CTS* 1:405.

62. *LW* 26:241; *WA* 40.1:381.

63. *LW* 26:227; *WA* 40.1:360.

64. *LW* 26:227; *WA* 40.1:361.

great righteousness faith is and, by antithesis, what a great sin unbelief is."[65] Faith, not law and reason, renders to God what is his; it regards God "not as an idol, but as God,"[66] who looks upon us with his mercy. Hence "Abraham increased in his faith as he gave glory to God" (Rom 4:20). When our circumstances are at odds with God's promises, as in Abraham's story, Calvin exhorts us to "close our eyes, disregard ourselves and all things connected with us, so that nothing may hinder or prevent us from believing that God is true."[67] Similarly, Luther avers, "In faith, one must close our eyes to everything but the Word."[68] Faith seizes, in Calvin's phrase, "the power of God alone," exalting it above all else; it abandons all our imperfections and miseries but simply clings to God, who can "accomplish what He has spoken," and receives from him "what is effected by His Word."[69] Calvin, in his reply to the Council of Trent, declares, "Faith brings nothing of our own to God, but receives what God spontaneously offers. Hence it is that faith, however imperfect, nevertheless possesses a perfect righteousness, because it has respect to nothing but the gratuitous goodness of God."[70] What is crucial for Calvin, in Godfrey's words, is "the object of faith, the perfect righteousness of Christ."[71]

Faith has "nothing of its own," says Luther, unless it grasps Christ's benefits.[72] In *The Freedom of the Christian*, Luther likens faith to the "wedding ring" through which union between bride (believer) and groom (Christ) occurs, and from this, believers receive Christ's virtues in exchange for their vices. He writes:

> Faith unites the soul with Christ as a bride is united with her bridegroom. . . . Christ and the soul became one flesh (Eph. 5:31-32). . . . Christ is full of grace, life, and salvation. The soul is full of sins, death, and damnation. Now let faith come between them and sins, death will be Christ's, while grace, life, and salvation will be the soul's; for if Christ is a bridegroom, he must take upon himself

---

65. *LW* 26:227; WA 40.1:361.
66. *LW* 26:227; WA 40.1:361.
67. *Comm. Rom.* 4:20, in *CNTC* 8:99.
68. WA 10.3:423, 17–18, as cited in Kolb, *Luther's Treatise*, 46.
69. *Comm. Rom.* 4:21, in *CNTC* 8:100.
70. Calvin, "Acts of the Council," 125.
71. Godfrey, "Calvin and the Council," 124.
72. *LW* 35:120.

the things which are his bride's and bestow upon her the things that are his.[73]

The marital imagery here portrays a joyous exchange, that what is Christ's is transferred to us, and what is ours is imparted to him. The believer by faith is free in Christ, who swallows up all sins, death, and hell, and bestows on her his righteousness, life, and salvation. The significance of faith lies in its function as a vehicle by which the believer "takes hold of Christ and has Him present, enclosing Him as the ring encloses a gem."[74] The marital imagery highlights the intrinsic linkage between faith and love but with an emphasis on faith as the unitive principle of the believer and Christ. "This Bridegroom, Christ, must be alone with His bride in His private chamber, and all the family and household must be shunted away. But later on, when the Bridegroom opens the door and comes out, then let the servants return to take care of them and serve them food and drink. Then let works and love begin."[75] Faith that consummates the marriage precedes the activity of love. Luther speaks of love as integral to faith: "Because you have taken hold of Christ by faith, you should now go and love God and your neighbor."[76] Good works that stem from faith are "truly good works"; otherwise they are sin (Rom 14:23).

Luther and Calvin maintain the unity and distinction of justification and sanctification. For Luther, justification is prior to and grounds sanctification. For Calvin, both flow from union with Christ as the twin benefits accrued to those who were baptized (Gal 3:27). What is Christ's is communicated to those who "put on Christ" (Gal 3:27) in baptism, as one would put on a garment. Calvin uses this garment metaphor to describe that "believers are united to Christ in such a way that, in the sight of God, they bear the name and person of Christ and are viewed in Him rather in themselves."[77] Calvin locates his treatment of justification, Johnson claims, within what he calls "the soteriological priority of union with Christ."[78] To grasp Christ, Calvin asserts, is to "principally receive a double grace," the twin benefits—"namely, that being reconciled to God through Christ's blamelessness, we may have in heaven instead of a Judge a gracious Father;

73. *LW* 31:351.
74. *LW* 26:132; WA 40.1:233.
75. *LW* 26:137; WA 40.1:241.
76. *LW* 26:133; WA 40.1:234.
77. *Comm. Gal.* 3:27, in *CNTC* 11:68.
78. Johnson, "Luther and Calvin," 71.

and secondly, that sanctified by Christ's Spirit we may cultivate blamelessness and purity of life."[79] In subsuming justification under the rubric of
union with Christ, Calvin does not undermine its importance. Justification, Calvin claims, is "the main thing on which religion turns."[80] Calvin
elaborates on the primacy of union with Christ in which believers receive
Christ's righteousness:

> I confess that we are deprived of this utterly incomparable good
> [righteousness] until Christ is made ours. Therefore, that joining
> together of Head and members, that indwelling of Christ in our
> hearts—in short, that mystical union—are accorded by us the
> highest degree of importance, so that Christ, having been made
> ours, makes us sharers with him in the gifts with which he has
> been endowed. . . . For this reason, we glory that we have fellow-
> ship of righteousness with him.[81]

For both Reformers, justification occurs outside us, in Christ. Based
on Gal 3:6, "Abraham believed God and it was reckoned to him as righteousness," Luther teaches that God reckons "imperfect faith as perfect
righteousness for the sake of Christ."[82] He explains how this occurs:

> Christ protects me under the shadow of His wings and spreads
> over me the wide heaven of the forgiveness of sins, under which
> I live in safety. This prevents God from seeing the sins that still
> cling to my flesh. My flesh distrusts God, is angry with Him, does
> not rejoice in Him etc. But God overlooks these sins, and in His
> sight they are as though they were not sins. This is accomplished
> by imputation on account of the faith by which I begin to take hold
> of Christ; and on His account God reckons imperfect righteous-
> ness as perfect righteousness and sin as not sin, even though it
> really is sin.[83]

Faith simply receives God's justifying action apart from works of love.
Calvin asserts, "For, as regards justification, faith is something merely passive, bringing nothing of ours to the recovering of God's favor but receiving
from Christ that which we lack."[84] Apart from any virtues or actions, faith

79. *Inst.* 3.11.1.
80. *Inst.* 3.11.1.
81. *Inst.* 3.2.10.
82. *LW* 26:231; *WA* 40.1:366.
83. *LW* 26:231–32; *WA* 40.1:367.
84. *Inst.* 3.13.5.

"adorns us with the righteousness of another, which it begs from God."[85] God justifies those who are in themselves ungodly; his mercy favors sinners whom he might justly punish. Contrary to the Roman Catholic view of justification as an infusion of grace, Calvin furnishes a forensic interpretation in which God's affective word of declaration is that which justifies us. For the Reformers, grace consists in God's favor, with a righteousness freely imputed to us. Righteousness is acquired by faith; as Pannenberg noted, it is not acquired by cultivating "a habit of acting in accordance to the law."[86] Calvin writes, "To declare that by [Christ] alone we are accounted righteous, what else is this but to lodge our righteousness in Christ's obedience, because the obedience of Christ is reckoned to us as if it were our own?"[87] Through union with Christ, we grasp both his righteousness and his holiness; the two are inseparably one because, Calvin reasons, "Christ must not be torn into parts."[88] Just as justification is linked to Christology, so too is sanctification; Calvin declares, "Therefore Christ justifies no one whom he does not at the same time sanctify."[89] The inclusion of sanctification in the understanding of faith allows both Calvin and Luther to affirm that true faith is never inactive; it operates, or else it is not faith at all. In *The Freedom of the Christian*, Luther sees the righteousness of faith as both justifying and sanctifying. There, he operates with the conception that the faith that trusts the gospel of forgiveness and sees the self as righteous in God's sight will want to, and strive to, act righteously. Faith, in Calvin, as in Luther, does not undercut but impels human actions; as Calvin says, "Faith can in no wise be separated from devout disposition." He expands:

> Since faith embraces Christ, as offered to us by the Father . . .—that is, since he is offered not only for righteousness, forgiveness of sins, and peace, but also for sanctification . . . and a fountain of water of life . . .—without a doubt, no one can duly know him without at the same time apprehending the sanctification of the Spirit.[90]

Christ is our justifier as well as the sanctifier; for Calvin, the two are distinguished but are "constantly conjoined and cohere." He illustrates, "The light of the sun, though never unaccompanied with heat, is not to

85. *Comm. Rom.* 4:5, in *CNTC* 8:85.

86. Pannenberg, "Theology of the Cross," 162–63.

87. *Inst.* 3.11.23.

88. *Inst.* 3.16.1.

89. *Inst.* 3.16.1.

90. *Inst.* 3.2.8.

be considered heat. . . . We acknowledge, then, that as soon as any one is justified, renewal also necessarily follows."[91]

Faith's Location: The Social Relation

Justification by faith does not concede ethical passivity as the acceptable disposition of the total Christian life. Though Luther excludes love as the basis of justification, he includes it in his doctrine of sanctification, showing how faith becomes a tangible reality. The veracity of faith must be accompanied by works of love; otherwise, its reality is called into question. The focus of Paul here is not the acquisition of faith through the instrumentality of love but the practical outworking of faith through it. "Where the Spirit reigns," says Calvin, "the law no longer has any dominion."[92] In the *Small Catechism*, Luther explains commandments two through ten by beginning with a recurring phrase, "we should fear and love God so that . . ."[93] All obedience flows out of trust or fear and love of the first commandment. Luther articulates this, by way of Gal 5:23, "against which there is no law," that faith naturally expresses outwardly in love. "The unrighteous man . . . has to live a good life, because he does not live the good life which the Law requires."[94] However, the righteous person performs good works spontaneously, though he does not have to, "because he owes the Law nothing, since he has the love which performs and fulfills the Law."[95] Luther illustrates, "Just as the three plus seven (the example is Augustine's) do not have to be ten but are ten, and there is no law or rule that one must seek in order that they may become ten . . . so a righteous man does not have to live a good life, but he lives a good life and needs no law to teach him to live a good life."[96]

Luther grounds his explanation of the effective nature of faith in terms of dual-nature Christology: "And yet Scripture sometimes speaks of Christ as God, and sometimes it speaks of Him as 'composite and incarnate.'"[97] Likewise, Scripture presents faith in two ways: sometimes it is conceived of

91. Calvin, "Acts of the Council," 116.
92. *Comm. Gal.* 5:23, in *CNTC* 11:106.
93. See "The Small Catechism," in *BC*, 351–54.
94. *LW* 27:378; WA 2:596.
95. *LW* 27:378; WA 2:596.
96. *LW* 27:378; WA 2:596.
97. *LW* 26:264; WA 40.1:414.

"apart from work," which Luther labels "abstract" or "absolute" faith, and sometimes "with the work," which he calls "a concrete, composite, incarnate" faith.[98] Luther could accept the distinction between abstract faith and incarnate faith, Mikkonen points out, as long as the distinction is employed to differentiate a false faith from a true kind.[99] The scholastic doctrine of faith assigns the justifying function to love, which for Luther is an erroneous faith; abstract faith—faith apart from works—justifies, and thus is a true faith. Yet true faith is never alone; it must become incarnate by its outward works of love. Luther writes, "Therefore in theology, let faith always be the divinity of works diffused throughout the works in the same way that the divinity is diffused throughout the humanity of Christ. . . . Therefore faith is the 'do-all' in works."[100] To explain that true faith is never idle or lazy but diffused throughout works, Luther resorts to the christological doctrine of the "communication of properties": "Thus justification belongs to faith alone, just as creation belongs to the divinity; nevertheless, just as it is true to say about Christ the man that He created all things, so justification is attributed to incarnate faith or to faithful 'doing.'"[101] Participation in the communion of the church is the incarnate expression of the new creature seized by grace. Hays rightly captures the two mutually related implications of the Reformers' doctrine of the incarnate faith.

> For one thing, a participatory soteriology ensures that salvation always has an *ecclesial* character: we are not saved as solitary individuals, but we become incorporate in Christ, so that our fate is bound together not only with him but also with our brothers and sisters in him. Second, participation in Christ entails a conformity to the pattern of self-sacrificial love that he embodied and enacted on our behalf (as Gal 2:19b–20 elegantly suggests).[102]

About the christological phrase "in Christ," Barclay writes, "Paul has ruled out numerous qualifying criteria for divine selection: birth (natural rights of descent), status (comparative 'greatness'), and practice ('works'), all forms of symbolic capital humanity ascribed or achieved."[103] Everything changes because of our relation to Christ. For one, the commandment of

---

98. *LW* 26:264; WA 40.1:414.

99. Mikkonen, *Luther and Calvin*, 124.

100. *LW* 26:266; WA 40.1:417.

101. *LW* 26:266; WA 40.1:416.

102. Hays, "Christ Died for Ungodly," 62.

103. Barclay, *Paul and the Gift*, 531.

circumcision God gave Abraham was operative until the advent of Christ. Paul contrasts circumcision, a thing of the old creation, with the new creation inaugurated in Christ. Our identity or worth is no longer bound up with circumcision but with Christ's advent. Of this discontinuity, Paul declared, "For in Christ neither is circumcision anything or uncircumcision, but a new creature" (Gal 6:15). Circumcision, which is of no significance, is set opposite the new creation, which is what counts. The antithesis, Calvin writes imaginatively, seems to reflect God's intention: "Therefore it is as if Paul had said, 'God does not keep us nowadays under ceremonies; it is enough if we exercise ourselves in love.'"[104] The same sentiment occurs in Luther, who writes, "Paul did not say: 'That which makes a Christian is a cowl or a fasting or a vestment or a ceremony.' . . . Not one of these . . . makes a man a Christian; only faith and love do so."[105] Christ is the center through which we view our relationship to God by faith and people by love. Christ has made us a new creature of faith, but not in separation from the works of love, or else faith would be reduced, as Barclay writes, merely to "an interior, individual phenomenon."[106]

Love does not justify but is a location in which faith becomes a social reality. Just as for our sake God has become incarnate in the human Jesus, so too for the sake of people true faith becomes incarnate in the works of love. For the Reformers, Paul's public reproof of Peter in Antioch in Gal 2:11–14 was an instance of faith becoming incarnate in a communal context, testifying to the reality of true faith. Paul's harsh rebuke was motivated theologically, for the concretization of a true faith in the context of ecclesial life was at stake. By the grace of God, Jewish and Gentile people are incorporated into the body of Christ. They share the common experience of being grasped by the power of God (Gal 4:1–7), which delivers them from the "present evil age" (Gal 1:4). Ethnic identity and ancestry, Jewish or otherwise, and any outward accomplishments are no legitimate measures of our worth before God. As Barclay notes, "It is the incongruous grace that Paul traces in the Christ-event and experiences in the Gentile mission that is the explosive force that demolishes old criteria of worth and clears space for innovative communities that inaugurate new patterns of social existence."[107] However, Jewish converts in the early church insisted

104. *Comm. Gal.* 5:6, in *CNTC* 11:96.
105. *LW* 27:31; *WA* 40.2:38.
106. Barclay, "Text of Galatians," 64.
107. Barclay, *Paul and the Gift*, 572.

it was necessary to "Judaize" the Gentiles for them to be fully integrated into the church. Some Jewish people dissociated from other Gentiles and refused to dine with them. Peter, the pillar of the church, refrained from eating with the Gentiles himself, and others joined him. Consequently, the church in Antioch was divided. By separating themselves from the Gentiles, who were of the same church, Paul charged that Peter and Jewish believers were "deviating from the truth of the gospel" (Gal 2:14). The following sentence—"If you, though a Jew, live like a Gentile but not a Jew, how can you compel the Gentiles to live like Jews?"—reveals the change of the mode of existence. As Seifrid writes appropriately, "Cephas's life as a Jew in this fallen age (see Gal 1:4) has been transcended by another life, that of the new creation (see Gal 6:15), even if for the time being these two 'times' are simultaneously and paradoxically present."[108] Believers are introduced into "the sphere of Christ," De Boer writes, "the territory where Christ is Lord. . . . That territory is the community of people, both Jew and Gentile, who have 'come to believe in Jesus Christ.'"[109] All external factors such as race, culture, ethnicity, and economic status are relativized; they do not define an authentic church except by Christ alone. Believers in Christ are introduced into "new relational realities . . . established by the Holy Spirit," Rabens says, "not by [their] ethical actions or feelings of being emotionally close to God."[110] Any attempt to segregate the people of God by religious customs, practices, or conditions not only acts contrary to the truth of the gospel but also falsifies it. In matters of faith and practice, Luther binds himself to the word of God; he does not allow reason to reign above faith. In plain language, Luther propounds, "As soon as reason and the law are joined, faith immediately loses its virginity."[111] He continues, "This is the issue at stake: Either Peter must be severely rebuked, or Christ must be removed entirely. Rather let Peter perish and go to hell, if need be, than that Christ be lost."[112] The purity of gospel, which the Holy Spirit taught through Paul, Calvin argues, was in danger of being adulterated by human reason or traditions.[113] He shows no tolerance to those who try to separate themselves from the body of Christ in which all—Jewish people

108. Seifrid, "Paul, Luther, and Justification," 216.

109. De Boer, *Galatians*, 157.

110. Rabens, "Indicative and Imperative," 303.

111. *LW* 26:113; WA 40.1:204.

112. *LW* 26:119; WA 40.1:212.

113. *Comm. Gal.* 2:14, in *CNTC* 11:36.

or otherwise—are incorporated. Calvin chastises the separatists harshly: "Thus, having separated themselves in their pride from the company of believers, they can only really become monks of the devil. . . . He simply seeks to persuade them to live separately from others so that he might eventually turn them away from God altogether."[114] Peter's action of withdrawal from the Gentiles was an instance of a public sin that would fall under church discipline; in Calvin's words, "This example teaches us that those who have sinned publicly must be chastised publicly, so far as it concerns the Church. The aim is that their sin may not, by remaining unpunished, do harm by its example."[115]

Christ as Sacrament and as Example: Gift as Prior to Model

Luther's Christology is primarily conceived in terms of Christ's expiatory death on the cross, yet he does not exclude imitating Christ's example. In his 1519 lecture on Gal 2:20, he regards the expiatory and exemplary functions of Christ as coinherent realities. There Luther incorporates into Christ's sacrificial death Christ as both a gift and a model. He endorses Augustine's Christology: "Saint Augustine teaches that the suffering Christ is both a sacrament and an example—a sacrament because it signifies the death of sin in us and grants it to those who believe, an example because it also behooves us to imitate Him in bodily suffering and dying."[116] The redemptive action of Christ is set alongside our action of following Christ, but the logical order begins with Christ as Savior, followed by Christ as example. As Luther declares, "Whoever, therefore, would imitate Christ as He is the *exemplum* must believe first with a firm faith that Christ suffered for him as *sacramentum*."[117] Commenting on the phrase "putting on Christ" (Gal 3:27), Luther furnishes two ways in which it is to be understood. The first way is "according to law," when we put on the "garment of imitation" and follow him; the second is "according to the gospel," when we put on Christ as "the garment of our righteousness" and trust him.[118] These two

---

114. *SG,* 661.

115. *Comm. Gal.* 2:14, in *CNTC* 11:36.

116. *LW* 27:238; *WA* 2:501.

117. *WA* 57.3:114, as cited in Lage, *Martin Luther's Christology,* 101.

118. *LW* 26:352–53; *WA* 40.1:542.

garments correspond to the distinction between Christ as sacrament and Christ as example.

The unity and distinction between Christ as sacrament and Christ as example, Luther argues, is in line with Scripture, which presents Christ in two ways: first, as a "gift," which "nourishes your faith and makes you a Christian"; and second, as an "example," which "exercises your works. These do not make a Christian."[119] Faith is naked; it "possesses nothing of its own" except Christ's benefits; "works have something of your own in them," which benefit the neighbors.[120] What benefits one's neighbors does not effect our justified status before God; as Luther states, "It is not the imitation that makes sons; it is sonship that makes imitations."[121] The pair of the gift and example, Lohse writes, corresponds to the pair of "faith and discipleship."[122] Iserloh offers an ethical implication of the cross of Christ as a sacrament: "It is an event that does not have its termination in itself but is a sign, that is, it points toward an event in the person affected by it."[123] "Cruciform"[124] discipleship is a consequent aspect of Christ the sacrament. The one who stands beneath the cross cannot remain neutral or passive. He would be so moved by it that he willingly "offers his own body . . . to death or to the cross";[125] as Lohse argues, not for the purpose of "supplementing" the efficacy of the cross through works of love, but simply in accordance with Augustine's idea of Christ as our example.[126]

With Luther, Calvin uses the same garment metaphor to speak of our identity in Christ. Those who are "baptized into Christ" (Gal 3:27) have put off the old garment of Adam's sin but "put on" (Gal 5:27) a new garment

---

119. *LW* 35:120.

120. *LW* 35:120.

121. *LW* 27:263; WA 2:518.

122. Lohse, *Martin Luther's Theology*, 48. Lohse argues that the Augustinian pair permeates Luther's writings throughout his life. However, Lage observes that Norman Nagel argues for the contrary view that Luther abandons Augustine's sacrament-example Christology in his "mature" theology (Lage, *Martin Luther's Christology*, 104n29). See Nagel, "*Sacramentum et Exemplum*," 175, 183, 188.

123. Erwin Iserloh, *Gnade and Eucharistie in der philosophischen Theologie des Wilhelm von Ockham: Ihre Bedeutung für die Ursachen der Reformation*, VIEG 8 (Wiesbaden: Steiner, 1956), 110, as cited in Lohse, *Martin Luther's Theology*, 48n10.

124. The word "cruciform" comes from Gorman, *Inhabiting the Cruciform God*.

125. WA 9.18:19–22, as cited in Lohse, *Martin Luther's Theology*, 48.

126. Lohse, *Martin Luther's Theology*, 48.

of Christ's righteousness.[127] The theme of Christ as an example emerges in Calvin's sermon on Gal 6:18, where Paul speaks of "the rule" by which the Christian lives—namely, conformity to the image of Christ and his teaching following Christ's expiatory work.[128] Having been incorporated into the body of the church, we must discard personal preferences and heed the command to be united to one another. He elaborates, "When Christ speaks, may we submit to his teaching, so that each of us keeps his commands. Also, let us help one another. . . . [Otherwise,] it is certain that we are still serving Satan and are like slaves serving under the tyrannical rule."[129] The form in which a new creation relates to neighbors is the cross of Christ. The cruciform life, which was laid upon Christ, is now laid upon us, as we bear the "marks" of Christ in "our body" (Gal 6:17). These marks differ from the others, Calvin writes, as they bear "the nature of the cross."[130] The possession of the cross—not in books or painting or theory, but in living reality (Paul says "in my body")—is a distinguishing mark of a true disciple of Christ. Luther writes, "Every Christian carries this cross [which Luther calls 'the living image'] in the body—and in my own body, not in someone's else."[131] The world regards the suffering Christians endure as disgraceful, but in God's sight it is glorious.[132] For both Reformers, it is not either Christ as sacrament or Christ as example; it is both-and, and the redemption achieved by the suffering and humiliated Christ is to be grasped by faith first before the example of Christ is to be imitated.

In his 1535 commentary on Gal 5:8, Luther applauds the Anabaptists for the emphasis they place on Christ as example and on cross-bearing as distinctive of their entire teaching, but he offers a warning on the "proper time" in which the proclamation of Christ as gift and example occurs.[133] He then specifies the proper time, lest "the proclamation of salvation becomes a curse":

> But I will not let this Christ be preached to me as exemplar except at a time of rejoicing, when I am out of reach of temptations (when I can hardly attain a thousandth part of His example), so

127. *Comm. Gal.* 3:27, in *CNTC* 11:68.
128. *SG*, 661.
129. *SG*, 661.
130. *Comm. Gal.* 6:17, in *CNTC* 8:119.
131. *LW* 27:407; *WA* 40.2:616.
132. *Comm. Gal.* 6:17, in *CNTC* 8:119.
133. *LW* 27:34–35; *WA* 40.2:43–44.

that I may have a mirror in which to contemplate how much I am still lacking, lest I become smug. But in a time of tribulation I will not listen to or accept Christ except as a gift, as Him who died for my sins, who has bestowed His righteousness on me, and who accomplished and fulfilled what is lacking in my life. For He "is the end of the Law, that everyone who has faith may be justified" (Rom. 10:4).[134]

Commenting on Gal 5:13, "Do not use your freedom as an opportunity for the flesh, but through love be servants of one another," Luther teaches that if Christ as gift is not preached, the wounded conscience under the law would not be healed. However, "if faith is preached as it must be preached, the majority of men understand the teaching about faith in a fleshly way and transform the freedom of the spirit into the freedom of the flesh."[135] In such an instance, Christ as example must be proclaimed as a form of mortification of the old flesh. When there is abuse of liberty, Calvin writes, Christ as example must be announced, so that God, not self, must "reign," and his law, not human inventions, be the "rule" of conformity.[136] Liberty must be put to its "lawful use," he continues, so that "it shall not be turned into a pretext or occasion for license."[137] In order to curb licentious abuse of grace-spirited freedom, we must discipline ourselves so that through love we serve our neighbors as examples of Christ. The freedom we have vertically before God ought to be put to its proper use horizontally before people, serving them freely and willingly. Luther avers, "Now Paul shows beautifully on the basis of the Decalog what it means to be a servant through love."[138]

Two Kinds of Love:
God's Love and Human Love

There are two kinds of love: one has flesh as its origin, and the other, faith. God's love is not causally dependent on the quality of the object of love; nor does it seek to secure some good from its object. Thesis 28 of Luther's *Heidelberg Disputation* identifies two mutually exclusive kinds of love: "The

134. *LW* 27:34; WA 40.2:43.
135. *LW* 27:48: WA 40.2:60.
136. *SG*, 656.
137. *Comm. Gal.* 5:13, in *CNTC* 11:100.
138. *LW* 27:51; WA 40.2:64.

love of God does not find, but creates, that which is pleasing to it. The love of man comes into being through that which is pleasing to it."[139] Mannermaa labels them "the descending God's Love and the ascending Human Love";[140] in his words:

> The movement of God's Love and Human Love are polar op-posites. The direction of Human Love is upwards, that is, turns toward what is grand, wise, alive, beautiful, and good. God's Love, in turn, turns itself or is oriented downward, that is, toward what is lowly, disgraceful, weak, foolish, wicked, and dead. Therefore God's Love irresistibly involves emptying oneself, suffering, and loving the cross.[141]

God's love is hidden in its opposite; it, Luther writes, "turns in the direction where it does not find good which it may enjoy, but where it may confer good upon the bad and needy person."[142] Such understanding of-fers a proper way of how we ought to treat people. Luther says, "Therefore, sinners are attractive because they are loved; they are not loved because they are attractive."[143] The works faith does through love take the form of kenosis, that is, after the manner of Christ, who empties himself purely for our sake, not for any good he could gain from doing so. These works are characterized not by pomposity but by poverty, not by power but by weakness, and not by glory but by lowliness. This kenotic love is directed toward the low and despised. Just as God is most glorious in his opposites, in the humility and weakness of the cross, so too are we most glorious when we share in Christ's suffering and become, to use Luther's phrase, a "little Christ" to our neighbors.[144] What counts is not the pomp of external cer-emonies but the love we as new creatures in Christ manifest to others, re-flecting our justified status. The responsive life of faith assumes freedom to love as its instantiation; Luther writes, "Behold, from faith thus flow forth love and joy in the Lord, and from love a joyful, willing, and free mind that serves one's neighbor willingly and takes no account of gratitude or ingrati-tude, of praise or blame, of gain or loss. . . . He most freely and willingly spends himself and all that he has, whether he wastes all on the thankless

139. *LW* 31:57.

140. Mannermaa, *Two Kinds of Love*, 5.

141. Mannermaa, *Two Kinds of Love*, 3.

142. *LW* 31:57.

143. *LW* 31:57.

144. *LW* 31:57.

or whether he gains reward."[145] Luther establishes what Jüngel calls "a rule of superabundance,"[146] by which the good things we receive from God must be commonly shared with others.[147] What flows from Christ to us by faith now flows from us by love to those who need them. We bear, Luther writes, "the form of God," that we by faith receive from God's abundance in Christ, which we now through love give to others, proving that we are "gods, children of the Most High" (Ps 82:2).[148] Just as Christ assumes as his own, to borrow Barclay's phrase, "the kenotic and non-circular"[149] vocation, giving himself completely for our sake without reciprocal demand from us, so is the truly Christian life marked by self-emptying love for others without any reciprocal benefits. This cruciform understanding of love finds expression in Calvin's *Sermons on Galatians*:

> Our Lord Jesus shows us that if we return a favour to someone who has helped and served us, or if we love people who are pleasing to us or from whom we expect to gain, we cannot call that love. Even the pagans do the same, but not because they are obeying either God or the law (Matt. 6:46). When we seek self-advancement, it is not love for others but love for self which is displayed. True love has as its goal God and the sense of community that ought to exist amongst us. . . . Therefore, by seeking to do good even to those who are unworthy of it, we are truly providing that we desire to show love for God.[150]

Christ has reoriented our lives, from self to Christ, from inwardness to outwardness, from self-absorption to self-emptying love. The "cruciform" expression of faith in communal or social locations proceeds from the new identity in Christ. This new creation is God's action, a "gift" freely bestowed, not conditioned by any prior quality we may have. This "gift" lifts us out of ourselves and leads us to live not in ourselves but in our neighbors by love, without any thought of reward or return. Barclay clarifies:

> As a community founded on and shaped by the incongruous gift of Christ, this "new creation" is evident precisely in (and not independently of) reordered patterns of social and personal behavior.

145. *LW* 31:365.
146. Jüngel, *Freedom of a Christian*, 86.
147. *LW* 31:371.
148. See WA 10.1.1:100, as cited in Mannermaa, *Two Kinds of Love*, 66.
149. Barclay, *Paul and the Gift*, 113.
150. *SG*, 521.

> Without such difference, it is hard to see how the gift of Christ
> differs from a reward for socially conformist behavior: but for
> Paul the gospel stands or falls on its announcement of an uncon-
> ditioned gift.[151]

Speaking of the object of love, Paul uses "the neighbor" (Gal 5:14)
without differentiation. By this, Luther argues, Paul collapses all distinctions of persons, as we by faith share equal status before God as one humanity. However, by love we bear different relationships to our neighbors
before the world, as we all possess different vocations and are placed in different life stations in which our calling is performed.[152] Calvin avers that all
humanity is united by "a common nature."[153] The image of God is universal,
in all without distinction. We love our neighbors, just as we love our own
flesh, for all are one flesh (Isa 58:7).[154] "The image of God," says Calvin, is "a
specially sacred bond of union. Thus no distinction occurs between friend
and foe, for the wickedness of men cannot annul the right of nature."[155]

Paul adds "as thyself," Calvin intimates, not to suggest that we love
ourselves first before we love others. "No, the Lord is exposing the disease
that prevents us from loving one another," that is, "excessive love" of self.[156]
He continues, "This excessive love blinds us and robs us of all reason, good
judgment and fairness."[157] The love of ourselves [amor] is opposed to the
love of our neighbors [charitas]. The love of self springs from the agency of
the flesh, the systemic problem which Calvin describes as "the depravity of
corrupt nature."[158] No one can love their neighbors in truth and sincerity.
Calvin writes, "The Lord therefore commanded that [the love of self] be
changed to love (charitatem)," that is, love for others without self-preoccupation.[159] The old nature still abides and is the root of all vices; it must be
buried with Christ so that the new nature might be raised up. Unless the old
nature is corrected by grace and renewed by the Holy Spirit, there cannot
be true virtues. Of "the fruit of the Spirit" (Gal 5:22), Calvin writes, "All

151. Barclay, "Text of Galatians," 64.

152. *LW* 27:351; *WA* 2:577.

153. *Comm. Gal.* 5:14, in *CNTC* 11:101.

154. *Comm. Gal.* 5:14, in *CNTC* 11:101.

155. *Comm. Gal.* 5:14, in *CNTC* 11:101.

156. *SG*, 521.

157. *SG*, 521.

158. *Comm. Gal.* 5:24, in *CNTC* 11:106.

159. *Comm. Gal.* 5:14, in *CNTC* 11:101.

virtues, all good and well-regulated affections, proceed from the Spirit, that is, from the grace of God and the renewed nature which we have in Christ. Nothing but evil comes from man; nothing good comes but from the Holy Spirit."[160] The inward power of the Holy Spirit in creating a changed heart appears in Luther's interpretation of Gal 5:14, where he explains, "When this emotion [i.e., love] of the heart has been set on the right course, the other parts no longer need any commandments; for everything flows out of this disposition of the heart. As this is, so is everything; and without it all other things are foolish exertions."[161] Unless the Spirit governs us and manifests his power there, no one could perform works out of a willing and cheerful heart. The Holy Spirit remakes us and instills in us aspiration for righteousness. Luther expands this in his *Preface to Romans*:

> But [a right] heart is given only by God's Spirit, who fashions a man after the law, so that he acquires a desire for the law in his heart, doing nothing henceforth out of fear and compulsion but out of a willing heart. . . . How shall a work please God if it proceeds from a reluctant and resisting heart? To fulfill the law, however, is to do its works with pleasure and love, to live a godly and good life of one's own accord, without the compulsion of the law. This pleasure and love for the law is put into the heart by the Holy Spirit, as St. Paul says in [Rom] chapter 5[:5].[162]

Concluding Reflections

The Reformers do not concede any dichotomy between faith and love, theology and ethics; both are integrated into a seamless garment. Any doctrine of salvation that does not incorporate sanctification is not to be predicated of them. "And while my works of love are never good enough to save me," Cary states, "they can be good enough to be a real help to my neighbor. In that way the Gospel frees me to live in love, concerned for the good of my neighbor rather than wrapped up in my spiritual anxieties about myself. It is precisely because I am justified by faith alone that I am free to love."[163] Justifying faith is fertile and never futile. Faith in which Christ is present is that which arouses us to do works of love. As Kolb and Arand aptly write,

160. *Comm. Gal.* 6:22, in *CNTC* 11:105.
161. *LW* 27:350; *WA* 2:576.
162. *LW* 35:367–68.
163. Cary, *Meaning of Protestant Theology*, 204.

"The passive righteousness of faith provides the core identity of a person; the active righteousness of love flows from that core identity into the world."[164] Faith defines our righteous status before God and grants us equal access to the heavenly riches in Christ. Love describes our righteous deeds before the world, with its various obligations depending on one's vocation. Works benefit our neighbors but do not merit justification. Wengert sums up aptly, "Thus faith suffices before God, while works and examples are for this world and the neighbor."[165] The life that is pleasing to God is marked by faith in Christ, and love for others flows out of a life of faith as a consequence. Love is not the basis of justification but the means whereby faith finds its social concretization. Those whom the Spirit places "in Christ" trust and show that faith in love. Just as the soul inhabits the body, Calvin avers, animating every member to act effectively, so too the Spirit indwells us, effecting in us the power to do what we by ourselves could not.[166]

What is so good about good works? In what sense could the Reformers call good works "good"? Westerholm offers a helpful summary of the Reformers' position: "No deed of one who does not delight in the good can be truly good, and love of the good is not found where God is not loved. The seeming virtues of untransformed human beings are thus, in reality, splendid vices."[167] Virtue is not a predicate of nature but solely of grace. Such an understanding has its root in Augustine, who, in *The City of God* argues that moral deeds performed by the unregenerate are "hostile . . . to pious faith."[168] Virtue, for Augustine, is obtained "not by law and teaching uttering their lessons from without, but by a secret, wonderful and ineffable power [of God] operating within" a human heart.[169] Such an axiom resonates with Luther and Calvin, according to whom an impasse between vice and virtue cannot be breached except by faith. Commenting on Rom 14:23, "Whatsoever is not done of faith or in faith is sin," Calvin writes, "God does not regard outward show, but the inward obedience of the heart. On this alone depends the value of our works. . . . To condemn all that is not of faith is to reject all that is not supported and approved by the

164. Kolb and Arand, *Genius of Luther's Theology*, 26.

165. Wengert, "Martin Luther," 106.

166. *Comm. Gal.* 5:25, in *CNTC* 11:106.

167. Westerholm, *Justification Reconsidered*, 45.

168. Augustine, *The City of God*, translated by Marcus Dods (New York: Random House, 1950), 5.14, as cited in Westerholm, *Justification Reconsidered*, 43.

169. Augustine, "Grace of Christ," ch. 25, 601.

Word of God."[170] Faith is not borne out of human works but drawn from no other source than God's word, which specifies what good works are. Luther regards faith as "the chief work and from no other work that we are called believers in Christ. A sinner may also do all other works; but to trust firmly that he pleases God is possible only for a Christian who is enlightened and strengthened by grace."[171] From faith stems all good works; human goodness is not inherent but a derivative of faith. The goodness we have is, in Luther's phrase, "a borrowed goodness."[172] Bertram writes creatively, "Love is not love, good work is not good unless it is the function of faith—that very faith which justifies."[173] Yet this faith is not something we create but that which God creates in us through the love of the cross. Knowing that "God is so kindly disposed toward you that he even gives his Son for you," Luther writes, "your heart in turn must grow sweet and disposed toward God. And in this way your confidence must grow out of pure good will and love—God toward you, and yours toward God."[174] With Luther, Calvin teaches the fallen will is spiritually dead and cannot choose God. The ability to turn to God is credited to God's grace alone, without human cooperation with God. In his *Acts of the Council of Trent with the Antidote*, Calvin faults Trent for "sharing the work between God and ourselves, so as to transfer to ourselves the obedience of a pious will in assenting to divine grace, whereas this is the proper work of God himself."[175]

The critical question, in the end when we appear before God's judgment throne, is this: In what does justifying righteousness consist? Luther would say, nothing but "the love and favor of God." But Aquinas would reply "the works that grace produces." This "theological parable"[176] constructed by Kolb clarifies that God's unconditional love in Christ, expressed in his promise and grasped by faith, and not in "grace-assisted"[177] deeds, grants us free access into heaven. Luther admittedly "declare[s] that even if I did have and perform [active righteousness], I cannot trust in it or stand up before the judgment of God on the basis of it. Thus I put myself beyond all

---

170. *Comm. Rom.* 14:23, in *CNTC* 8:302.

171. *LW* 44:25.

172. *LW* 44:24.

173. Bertram, "Radical Dialectic," 222.

174. *LW* 44:38.

175. Calvin, "Acts of the Council," 112.

176. Kolb, "Luther on Two Kinds," 454–55.

177. Kolb, "Luther on Two Kinds," 454–55.

active righteousness, all righteousness of my own or of the divine law, and I embrace only the passive righteousness which is the righteousness of grace, mercy, and the forgiveness of sins."[178] We approach the judgment seat of God not through the infused grace of the scholastics, but through Christ's perfect obedience in which we participate. Calvin writes, "Thus, we, being joined and united to his person and to his body, are accounted righteous, because his obedience [to the Father who sent him] was so perfect that it was sufficient to cleanse and remove our sins."[179] In this regard, Luther offers an all-inclusive claim of Christ's perfect obedience: "No, it is entirely outside and above us; it is Christ's going to the Father, that is, his suffering, resurrection, and ascension,"[180] that forms the foundation of the transference of his righteousness to sinners. Our trust is not on the proof of our good works, not even in, to use Luther's own phrase, "borrowed goodness,"[181] a goodness produced by grace, but solely on the infallible promises offered in the gospel. We "ascend into heaven" not by a righteousness of our own creation but by that righteousness that "descends to us" from heaven.[182] The solid rock of the Reformers is the righteousness of grace, which effects a return to our righteous identity in the garden of Eden.

178. *LW* 26:6; WA 40.1:42.
179. *SG*, 180.
180. *LW* 24:347; WA 46:44.
181. *LW* 44:24.
182. *LW* 27:225; WA 2:493.

4

THE ATTRIBUTION OF CONTRARIES

Christ, the Blessed Curse

LUTHER AND CALVIN SHARE the Chalcedonian Christology that Christ has two distinct natures in one person. Both Reformers perceive the soteriological focus of their Christology in Gal 4:4–5, "When the fullness of time came, God sent forth His Son, born of woman, born under the Law, to redeem those who were under the Law, that we might receive adoption."[1] From what God does in Christ, we see who God is as God for us (*pro nobis*). The person and the work are inseparably one. Because the identity of the incarnate Son and the office he was enjoined to perform correspond to each other, the full significance of this identity is to be derived from the mission he was "sent" to achieve in time—namely, atonement for sins. Christ being human is not identical to his accursedness; his accursedness is the goal of his mission in history. Assuming flesh and assuming sin must be viewed as one act, with Christ's divine-human sinlessness as an underlying presupposition of the Son's mission encapsulated in this: "he who knew no sin" (2 Cor 5:21) became "a sinner" and a "curse" under the law to give us his righteousness and blessing. As Paul proclaimed, he "loved me and gave himself for me" (Gal 2:20). Both Reformers turn to Gal 3:13, "Christ redeemed us from the curse of the law,

---

1. See George, *Galatians*, 330, where he states "verses 4–5 contain one of the most compressed and highly charged passages in the entire letter because they present the objective basis, the Christological and soteriological foundations, for the doctrine of justification. . . . The early incorporation of these verses into the traditional liturgy of Christmas also points to their appeal as a basic kerygmatic text."

having become a curse for us," as the key text for their atonement theology. Christ engages in a duel with the contraries of justification—law, sin, death, wrath, and hell—and triumphs over them in exchange for grace, righteousness, life, mercy, and heaven. The gospel lies in an effective attribution of all contraries to Christ, who in his body willingly endured them in order that he might end them. Hidden in his accursedness is victory over all curses; all opposites of justification are banished for those who believe. His accursedness under the law thus is a blessed curse, which offers us bountiful comfort and indescribable joy.

Dual-Nature Christology: Fully God and Fully Man

First, the divinity of Christ was already proclaimed and taught in the Gospel of John (cf. John 8:23; 1:14; 14:6). If God were to "send forth his Son" (Gal 4:4), Luther writes, the Son must preexist before his bodily appearance.[2] That "God sent forth his Son" also established the distinction of persons within the one Godhead, that the Son is a different person, equally God as are the other two persons (Gal 4:6).[3] "The Spirit of the Son" for Luther means the Spirit "has the divine essence from the Son, as He has it from the Father."[4] No creature can say that the Spirit is his, as the Spirit is "God's own Spirit," that is, exclusively his.[5] The Son is God, Luther reasons, because God's Spirit is the Son's Spirit.[6] Only God can be the one, "the highest good," on whom the soul relies for satisfaction and salvation.[7]

Calvin teaches that the Lord Jesus Christ existed eternally before he was "sent" (Gal 4:4).[8] Not only is Christ God's Son by nature, but he is also a true, natural man, the Son of man by physical birth. Regarding his physical origin, Christ "was made out of a woman."[9] Calvin acknowledges both words "made" and "born," though he prefers the former.[10] Christ differs

2. *LW* 75:382; WA 10.1.1:355.

3. *LW* 75:391–92; WA 10.1.1:370.

4. *LW* 75:392; WA 10.1.1:370.

5. *LW* 75:392; WA 10.1.1:370.

6. *LW* 75:392; WA 10.1.1:370.

7. *LW* 75:382; WA 10.1.1:354.

8. *Comm. Gal.* 4: 6, in *CNTC* 11:73.

9. *Comm. Gal.* 4:4, in *CNTC* 11:73; *LW* 75:383; WA 10.1.1:355.

10. *Comm. Gal.* 4:4, in *CNTC* 11:73.

from other creatures as having been "created of the seed of his mother," not through physical copulation between men and women.[11] This was a fulfillment of the testament God made to Abraham (Gen 22:18). As Abraham's Seed, Christ is one of us; as Calvin writes, "He put on our nature."[12]

Paul said "born out of woman" instead of "born of a virgin." Both Reformers put the emphasis on "woman."[13] "Virgin" is not "a name and status of a nature," Luther argues, but a woman is.[14] Mary was "a true, natural woman" who bears Christ "out of herself alone, not out of man."[15] "This man alone" of all was from her and is the "blessed fruit" of her womb.[16] Apostles lay stress on Jesus's birth rather than on Mary's virginity. While her virginity is her virtue, "only beneficial for herself," her womanhood was beneficial to both her and the child she bears. Luther expands, "For, to Christ, not so much depends on the virginity as on the womanhood. She was also chosen as a virgin not for her own sake, but for Christ's sake, so that He would have as His mother a woman from whom He could be born without sin. He could not [be born that way] unless she were a virginal woman who conceived and gave birth without a man's assistance."[17] The "blessed seed" God promised in his testament must be innocent, "full of blessing," if it were to free those who are accursed in Adam.[18] The "bodily birth"[19] is accursed, as it originates through Adam and his sin; the virginal birth is blessed, as it is through Mary, without physical help, that the child emerges out of her body as the blessed Seed. Adam's birth in sin, which is completely cursed, is contrasted with Mary's virginal birth, which is completely blessed. Christ's "fleshly birth"[20] is not born in sin as in Adam but from Mary's body from which his humanity comes. The blessed fruit of Mary's body, Luther contends, is the remedy for the curse of the Adamic race: "No man but only a woman was involved, and thus He became a true, natural child of a woman, the true Seed of Abraham, and yet not born in sin, but full of blessing, so

11. *Comm. Gal.* 4:4, in *CNTC* 11:73.

12. *Comm. Gal.* 4:4, in *CNTC* 11:73.

13. *Comm. Gal.* 4:4, in *CNTC* 11:74; *Inst.* 2.13.3; *LW* 75:384; WA 10.1.1:356.

14. *LW* 75:384; WA 10.1.1:356.

15. *LW* 75:384; WA 10.1.1:356.

16. *LW* 75:384; WA 10.1.1:357.

17. *LW* 75:384; WA 10.1.1:357.

18. *LW* 75:384; WA 10.1.1:357.

19. *LW* 75:384; WA 10.1.1:357.

20. *LW* 75:384; WA 10.1.1:358.

that through Him all who were cursed at their own birth are blessed."[21] By the phrase "made of a woman," Calvin lays stress on the purpose of Christ's virginal birth, claiming that "Christ clothed himself in human flesh, for this was the only way he could render obedience to God on our behalf and set us free."[22]

The Right Picture of Christ: God's Love "For Me"

Galatians 1:1, "though Jesus Christ and God the Father" and "from God the Father and the Lord Jesus Christ," evinces for Luther and Calvin a proper way of knowing God. Paul's prayers were presented to both Christ and his Father in unity, not in separation. The linkage between Christ and God is essential to the Reformers' doctrine of God. Luther said, "It is the rule and principle" of biblical interpretation, which refrains us from speculation about the supreme majesty but leads us to the incarnate Son.[23] "For as in his own nature God is immense, incomprehensible, and infinite, so to man's nature He is intolerable."[24] To be safe and saved, Luther advises that we are to follow Scripture, which teaches us to gaze upon the incarnate Son, "this incarnate and human God."[25] Justification is to be found in "no other God than this Man Jesus Christ. Take hold of Him, cling to Him with all your heart, and spurn all speculation about Divine Majesty; for whoever investigates the majesty of God will be consumed by His glory."[26] We must begin with "this man,"[27] Luther teaches, who offers himself as the mediator between God and sinners, and be persuaded of "the love, the goodness, and the sweetness of God."[28] Christ is the "lovely picture" of "His majesty sweetened and mitigated to our ability to stand it."[29]

Similarly, Calvin lays stress on the true humanity of Christ as God's way of reaching us. He writes, "Because the Holy Spirit speaking through

21. *LW* 75:384; WA 10.1.1:358.

22. *SG*, 371.

23. *LW* 26:28; WA 40.1:75.

24. *LW* 26:29; WA 40.1:77.

25. *LW* 26:29; WA 40.1:78.

26. *LW* 26:29; WA 40.1:78.

27. *LW* 26:29; WA 40.1:78.

28. *LW* 26:30; WA 40.1:78.

29. *LW* 26:30; WA 40.1:78.

Paul knew our weakness, at the right moment he used a most appropriate remedy to meet it: he set the Son of God familiarly among us as one of ourselves."[30] Human creatures, full of sin, cannot "see God in all his glory" without being terrified by it.[31] Christ's humanity is where we should begin if we are to reach God. Calvin avers, "It is for this reason that Jesus Christ was revealed. For it is only through him that we may taste the love of God and enjoy his blessings."[32] "The awesome majesty of God"[33] that terrifies the totally depraved, Calvin argues, can be conquered only by the "all-sufficient sacrifice" of our Lord Jesus Christ through which God accepts us as "his children."[34] The phrase "from God the Father" points to the origin of God's gifts, that is, from the Father; the phrase "and the Lord Jesus" points to where God's gifts are located. Because all goods are in the Son of God, "the heir" (Heb 1:2), we are to seek him to benefit from them. "He who knows Christ aright," Calvin asserts, "holds Him fast, embraces Him with both arms, is completely taken up with Him and desires nothing beyond Him."[35] Paul begins his letter with the grace of Christ as the foundation of the Galatians' faith in God. By "commending the grace of Christ," Calvin avers, Paul intended to recall the Galatians to how Christ was to them and what he has achieved for them as to keep them safe in Christ.[36] "Grace" means "the favour of God";[37] "peace" encompasses for Calvin "all worldly prosperity."[38] Grace precedes peace. Earthly blessings may offer us comfort, but a peaceful conscience is a result of the knowledge that God loves us. It is through grace that we are accepted by God. In creation, God has made us, and loves us as his creatures. Due to the fall, he hates us and judges us justly. Calvin expands, "Because we were his creatures, and although we were wretched in his sight, lost and condemned because of sin, he took pity on humanity, not willing that any should perish. Thus, God loved us despite the fact that we had fallen in Adam and become totally depraved. Yet, at the same time, he hated us, because he is the source of all righteousness and had to hate

30. *Inst.* 2.12.1.
31. *SG*, 20.
32. *SG*, 20.
33. *SG*, 21.
34. *SG*, 21.
35. *Comm. Gal.* 1:3, in *CNTC* 11:11.
36. *Comm. Gal.* 1:3, in *CNTC* 11:11.
37. *Comm. Gal.* 1:3, in *CNTC* 11:11.
38. *SG*, 18.

the evil within us."[39] This "mortal conflict" between God and the sinner remains until we enter God's favor through Jesus Christ.[40] "Before we were reconciled to God," Calvin writes, "God both hated and loved us."[41] The separation between God who loves us as his creation and God who hates us as sinners is resolved by the sacrifice of Christ through which our sins are canceled and his righteousness bestowed. This is, Calvin writes, the meaning of Paul's words "he gave himself for our sins":

> Although at one time God hated us, he now designs to accept us into his love. Why? Because our Lord Jesus Christ has atoned for all our sins and transgressions by the obedience he rendered throughout sufferings and death. The sacrifice he offered has made satisfaction for our sins. His blood has brought us cleansing and has washed all our sinful stains.42

Christ's death has removed sin, that barrier between God and sinners; it has appeased God's wrath, reconciling God to us. Hence, God is no longer a judge, but "our merciful Father, because of reconciliation effected through Christ . . . , and Christ has been given to us as righteousness, sanctification, and life."[43]

"Grace" and "peace" for Luther constitute "the whole of Christianity."[44] They cure the "two monsters" that assault the Christian life: "sin and conscience, the power of the Law and the sting of sin" (1 Cor 15:56).[45] Grace deals with sin and its forgiveness, and as a result, a peaceful conscience is possible. Without grace, the conscience suffers under the accusatory function of the law because of sin. Thus, Luther exalts grace above peace. He exhorts us to recall "the true picture" of Christ from whom the blessings of redemption come. A proper definition of Christ is a source of comfort and joy. Luther stresses, "The highest art among Christians is to be able to define Christ. . . . But if this true picture of Christ is removed or even obscured, there follows a sure confusion of everything; for the unspiritual man cannot judge about the Law of God."[46] We must not confuse Christ

39. *SG*, 23–24.

40. *SG*, 21.

41. *SG*, 21.

42. *SG*, 21.

43. *Inst.* 3.2.2.

44. *LW* 26:26; WA 40.1:73.

45. *LW* 26:26; WA 40.1:73.

46. *LW* 26:178; WA 40.1:298–99; *LW* 26:373; WA 40.1:568–69.

with Moses. Neither is Christ a taskmaster or a lawyer, and such titles terrify us. Luther writes, "He is the Dispenser of grace, the Saviour, and the Pitier. . . . He is nothing but sheer, infinite mercy, which gives and is given."[47] With the "sweetest of titles," Luther writes, Paul describes Christ as the one "who loved me and gave Himself for me" (Gal 2:20). God's boundless love is revealed in the fact that God wills to be "for us" in the suffering of the Son on the cross. God in Christ chooses to meet we "who are in anguish, sin and death" as the committed "lover," says Luther, "the kind of lover who gives Himself for us."[48] God's love is the cause of the death of his Son for sinners. "This love," Calvin writes, "with which Christ embraced us, led Him to unite Himself to us."[49] God's love moves God to bestow grace upon sinners, and he has "completed" that love by suffering God's judgment "in our person."[50] Calvin thus perceives "no other reason" for Christ's self-sacrifice than the fullness of love, expressed in "the order" proceeding from God to us: "He loved us and gave himself for us." This assertion excludes any merits or actions of ours as a cause of justification. Paul, says Calvin, "ascribes the whole [redemption] to love," something freely given to us despite our hostility to God (Rom 5:10).[51] All the "fruit" of Christ's death, including atonement, forgiveness, and satisfaction, are gathered up in the phrase "gave himself up."[52] The love with which God redeems us extends to all. Grace is universal, as Christ died for all as "a price for our redemption"; the appropriation of its "effect" is individual.[53] Each one must personally possess for himself the benefits Christ's cross accomplished for us.

The Reformers' focus is the purpose of Christ's bodily coming—namely, the redemption he came to achieve as a fulfillment of his Father's will. As Calvin explains, "And it is proper to both; for, on the one hand, the Father by His eternal purpose decreed this atonement and in it gave this proof of His love for us that He spared not His only-begotten Son but delivered Him up for us all. And Christ, on the other hand, offered Himself as a sacrifice to reconcile us to God."[54] The Father's sending of his Son to the

47. *LW* 26:173; WA 40.1:298.
48. *LW* 26:178; WA 40.1:299.
49. *Comm. Gal.* 2:20, in *CNTC* 11:43.
50. *Comm. Gal.* 2:20, in *CNTC* 11:43.
51. *Comm. Gal.* 2:20, in *CNTC* 11:44.
52. *Comm. Gal.* 2:20, in *CNTC* 11:44.
53. *Comm. Gal.* 2:20, in *CNTC* 11:44.
54. *Comm. Gal.* 1:4, in *CNTC* 11:11.

cross and the obedient death of the Son on the cross are one. As one deity, both the Son and the Father work together in achieving atoning efficacy for us. Calvin exclaims, "So glorious is this redemption that it should ravish us with wonder."[55] In the incarnate Son, God comes in lowliness or humility, giving his life to save us. This is reflected in the apostolic language of the self-giving of God in the Son, "who loved me and gave himself for me" (Gal 2:20). The Son's suffering of "a shameful death, yes, even a cursed death," Calvin avers, is not "in vain" but effective "to free and acquit us, to the end that we might find grace at the judgment seat of God."[56] George captures this point well, explaining that "the curse Christ bore upon the cross was not a curse that wrongly rested upon him; it was a curse that rightly rested upon him as the sinless substitutionary sacrifice 'sent' by the Father for this purpose."[57] The sacrificial act of self-giving in the Son, Linebaugh writes, is "the gift that grounds justification."[58] It is not our love for Christ that wins God's favor but God's love "for us" manifested in the cross of Christ. "The foundation upon which faith rests," Calvin teaches, lies in the opposite of human action, that is, in God's action for us in the cross of Christ where "the effect of faith ought to be judged." Therefore, Calvin writes, "we live by the faith of Christ,"[59] the subjective genitive, which underscores the gift of God. God's salvific action of self-giving is the cause of our faith in Christ, the objective genitive, which underscores the human appropriation of God's gift.[60]

God's coming to us in Christ is his redemptive action in history. As Siggins puts it, "God will not be known in any other way: the knowledge of the one sent is the only possibility of knowledge of the Sender. But what we know of the one sent is that He comes to take away sin, wrath, condemnation, and death, and instead to bring us grace, mercy, and forgiveness—in short, to show us that we have a gracious God, Who will not be known by any other name."[61] The knowledge of God's being is determined by the knowledge of God's atoning work in Christ. Because God is known in his atoning act, the knowledge of what God has done "for us" in Christ

---

55. *Comm. Gal.* 1:4, in *CNTC* 11:11.

56. *SG*, 212.

57. George, *Galatians*, 268.

58. Linebaugh, "Christo-Centrism of Faith," 543.

59. *Comm. Gal.* 2:20, in *CNTC* 11:43.

60. See chs. 1, 2, and 5 for more discussion of "the faith of Christ" and "faith in Christ."

61. Siggins, *Martin Luther's Doctrine*, 60.

discloses truly who God is in himself. The event of Christ's self-sacrificial love is revelatory of God's true nature, Luther writes, which "is nothing but burning love and a glowing oven of love."[62] God not only gives us his beloved Son—as Althaus puts it, "the greatest gift of God's love"—but also "himself."[63] God's way of being love "for us" miserable sinners is known in Christ. "If all this is true," Luther exults, then "Christ is the joy and sweetness of a trembling and troubled heart";[64] otherwise "the whole Gospel is false."[65] The Son's suffering on the cross for Luther was a predicate of God's will to be "the Lover," who offers himself as "our High Priest," interposing himself as the Mediator between God and sinners to placate God.[66] Sinners, full of vices and corruption, could not have access to God unless through the Son's mediatorial activity. Similarly, for Calvin, Christ's mediatorship includes two things: "reconciliation," through which we are accepted as righteous, and "intercession," by which we are welcomed as a child to her father's bosom.[67] Calvin elaborates this in his *Sermons on Galatians*:

> It was sufficient for the High Priest to enter in the name of all the people, having blood in his hands in order to appease the wrath of God. He had these symbols upon his chest, on which the names of the twelve tribes, God's people, were engraved. . . . He also had them upon his shoulders, to show that he was representing the whole congregation. . . . For through him we are welcomed into the kingdom of heaven; the door is now open and we have personal access.[68]

62. WA 36:425, as cited in Althaus, *Theology of Martin Luther*, 116.
63. Althaus, *Theology of Martin Luther*, 116.
64. *LW* 26:178; WA 40.1:299.
65. *LW* 26:179; WA 40.1:299.
66. *LW* 26:178–79; WA 40.1:299.
67. *Comm. Gal.* 3:19, in *CNTC* 11:62.
68. *SG*, 375.

Justification in Christ: Revelation in Its Opposites

Christ, says Luther, is "greater and more excellent than all creation."[69] Even the law of God, the "necessary"[70] blessing "greater than the entire world,"[71] cannot equal the Son of God.[72] In justification, law and gospel are in conflict: "But if my salvation was worth so much to Christ that He had to die for my sins, then my works and the righteousness of the Law are vile—in fact, nonexistent—in comparison with such an inestimable price."[73] If the law had the power to save, then the cross on which the Son of God was crucified was superfluous (Gal 2:21). Concerning justification, law and Christ are opposed to each other. Luther "pointed out carefully that Paul declares the desire to be justified through the Law is to be nothing else than being separated from Christ and being made completely useless by Him."[74] To advocate works-righteousness is to renounce Christ altogether. Commenting on Gal 5:4, "You are severed from Christ, you who would be justified by the law, you have fallen from grace," Luther opts for either-or: "If you keep Christ, you are righteous in the sight of God. If you keep the Law, Christ is of no avail to you; then you are obligated to keep the whole Law, and you have your sentence."[75]

Any admixture of Christ and the law, says Calvin, renders Christ "useless."[76] To attribute righteousness, even "its smallest part," to the law is tantamount to "renouncing Christ and His grace."[77] "Righteousness," Calvin writes, "lies in faith and is obtained in the Spirit, without ceremonies."[78] There is no preexistent or residual goodness in us that might cause God to justify us. Calvin is at odds with the Papists' view that Christ came to meet our weakness because we, by ourselves, could not fulfill the law. Such understanding contradicts, he writes, "the infallible principle" established by

69. *LW* 26:175; WA 40.1:295.

70. *LW* 26:175; WA 40.1:295.

71. *LW* 26:141; WA 40.1:246.

72. *LW* 26:141; WA 40.1:246.

73. *LW* 26:183; WA 40.1:304.

74. *LW* 27:17; WA 40.2:19.

75. *LW* 27:17–18; WA 40.2:19.

76. *Comm. Gal.* 5:4, in *CNTC* 11:95.

77. *Comm. Gal.* 5:4, in *CNTC* 11:95.

78. *Comm. Gal.* 5:5, in *CNTC* 11:95.

Paul: "If we think there is anything good in us, we are accursed, until God accepts us through his pure grace alone."[79] With Calvin, Luther declares with joy, "Everything is forgiven by grace."[80]

Just as the knowledge of God is revealed, so too is the knowledge of sin. Luther asserts, "[Our knowledge of sin] flowed from Christ."[81] True knowledge of sin, the human condition, and the proper use of the law are not naturally known; rather, they flow from divine revelation, specifically from the kind of Savior we are given. Luther writes:

> Therefore those who fall away from grace do not know their own sin, or the Law they follow, or themselves, or anything else at all . . . For without the knowledge of grace, that is, of the Gospel of Christ, it is impossible for a man to think that the Law is a weak and beggarly element, useless for righteousness. In fact, he supposes the very opposite about the Law, namely, not only that it is necessary for salvation, but that it strengthens the weak and enriches the beggarly, that is, that those who keep it merit righteousness and eternal salvation. If this opinion stands, the promise of God is denied and Christ is removed, while lies, wickedness, and idolatry are established.[82]

The redemptive action of Christ on the cross underscores its opposites: the inefficacy of the law and its works, the horror of the sinful nature, and the terror of divine wrath against sin. Luther writes:

> These words, "the Son of God," "he loved me," and "he gave himself for me," are sheer thunder and heavenly fire against the righteousness of the Law and the doctrine of works. There was such great evil, such great error, and such darkness and ignorance in my will and intellect that I could be liberated only by such an inestimable price . . . For I hear in this passage that there is so much evil in my nature that the world and all creation would not suffice to placate God, but that the Son of God himself had to be given up for it.[83]

Justification occurs outside us, in Christ. The extrinsic nature of justification is reinforced in Gal 2:17, "But if, in our endeavor to be justified in Christ, we ourselves were found to be sinners, is Christ then an agent of

79. *Comm. Gal.* 2:20, in *CNTC* 11:216.
80. *LW* 32:227.
81. *LW* 42:12.
82. *LW* 26:408–9; WA 40.1:619–20.
83. *LW* 26:175; WA 40.1:295.

sin?" The justifying event includes God's judgment on who we are—namely, sinners before him—and in us, there is no righteousness of our own. Jewish people who sought justification in Christ are "found" to be sinners, just as the Gentiles; in Seifrid's words, "This judgment, moreover, is passively received: the Gospel does something more than call for a decision; it *effects* self-judgment, the knowledge of oneself as a sinner."[84] The justifying action of Christ is hidden in its opposite, that sinners, though unworthy in themselves, are deemed the objects of God's justifying grace. Paul's language in Gal 2:17, "in Christ," shows that there is only one way to justification, irrespective of the person. Calvin captures "the force of the participle, *also*" (as in "we ourselves *also* were found sinners"), meaning both Jewish and Gentile people inherit the same disease and share a common remedy—the knowledge of both flows from "the grace of Christ."[85]

Both Luther and Calvin accentuate the revelatory nature of the cross in which sin is revealed for what it really is, a systemic disease, and Christ is revealed for who he is, the remedy. Jewish people ascribe holiness to themselves "outside Christ,"[86] but Christ unveils the contrary that they are equally sunk in sin as are the Gentiles (Gal 2:17). Calvin paraphrases Gal 2:17: "'If the consequence of the righteousness of faith is that even we Jews, who were sanctified from the womb, are reckoned guilty and polluted, shall we say that Christ is the author of sin, in that he makes the power of sin vigorous in his people?'"[87] Christ performed the task of revelation through which he stripped Jewish people of their false claim to holiness. Christ functions as a revealer, not the author, of sin. Calvin writes, "Sin is already within us; he simply exposes and declares it."[88] No mortal flesh could perceive sin unless by Christ, just as no patient can perceive poison in his blood unless by a physician. Christ exposes our spiritual diseases, and the infection in the blood, not so they remain in us but that he might dispose them.[89] He reveals sin, not to leave us in a painful condition of sin, but to lead us out of it. This befits the character of Christ, who was "sent" to annihilate sin and bestow righteousness. Calvin avers, "For what does gospel doctrine teach us, but that we are full of iniquity and that we need to be

84. Seifrid, "Paul, Luther, and Justification," 219.

85. *Comm. Gal.* 2:17, in *CNTC* 11:41.

86. *Comm. Gal.* 2:17, in *CNTC* 11:41.

87. *Comm. Gal.* 2:17, in *CNTC* 11:40.

88. *SG*, 191.

89. *SG*, 192–93; *LW* 26:152; *WA* 40.1:263.

cleansed by the One who was appointed to be a Lamb without blemish, and who has also brought us the Spirit of holiness?"[90] Human creatures in their pride cannot "perceive" that they are sinful, estranged from God and fall under the curse, unless they are made "apparent" by the redemptive action of the cross.[91] Jesus Christ, "by the light of his gospel," Calvin avers, presents himself as the "only One" who could diagnose the systemic condition of fallenness and provide the cure for it.[92] The negative function of Christ in revealing sin is for the purpose of removing it. Christ is not the agent of sin but of righteousness. "For Christ, by uncovering the sin that lay concealed," Calvin avers, "is not the minister of sin, as if, by depriving us of righteousness, He opened the gate to sin or even established its dominion."[93]

Sinners may boast about their rectitude and purity, but the truth lies in the opposite. Through the illumination of the gospel, Calvin states, they are found to be full of sins that provoke God's wrath and are lost forever unless they apply to themselves Christ's blood.[94] Calvin goes further to include the sanctifying agency of the Spirit in regeneration. Christ is the bestowal of the Spirit through whom we are renewed and restored in God's image so that we may live a godly life.[95] This is what Christ came to do—to deliver us from the curse and cleanse us of all sins. Should we resist him? "God forbid" (Gal 2:17), Paul exclaims, that we should blame him for being the remedy of the sins he has disclosed!

Voluntary Submission: "Under the Law"

"An exposition of Luther's Christology," Lienhard contends, "is incomplete if it did not show that Christ saves us by liberating us from the law."[96] Christ alone has fulfilled the law voluntarily. Believers are free from the law through Christ, who was "born under the Law, to redeem those who are under the Law" (Gal 4:4). To be "born under" the law is to be "made

90. *SG*, 192.

91. *SG*, 193.

92. *SG*, 193.

93. *Comm. Gal.* 2:17, in *CNTC* 11:41.

94. *SG*, 192–93.

95. *SG*, 192.

96. Lienhard, *Luther*, 274.

under" it.[97] By nature, Christ was not under the law, but for our sake, both the Father and the Son, united in one will, voluntarily place the Son under it.[98] By contrast, Luther avers that we "were not willingly placed" under the law but "were naturally and essentially under it, against our will."[99] The distinction between "being placed" under the law and "being under" the law is one of "will" and "nature."[100] What we do at will differs with what we do by nature. What we willingly do lies in our power; what we naturally do is an outflow of nature. Luther illustrates, "You can go to the Rhine [dance] or not, but you must eat, drink, sleep, grow, digest, and become old, whether you want to or not."[101] By nature, we are under the law, and have no power to escape its domain. By nature, Christ was not under the law; he willingly subjected himself to it. Luther identifies two amazing aspects of Christ's innocence: first, "He did not need to suffer, even if He had obeyed no law"; and second, "He was also not obliged to suffer because He had kept [the law] willingly."[102] For our sake, he willingly and innocently suffered the severe punishment of the law.

The apostle Peter's story of deliverance from Herod gives Luther and Calvin the occasion to illustrate how Christ redeems us from the law. Peter was imprisoned under Herod, bound with two chains between two soldiers, with the sentries at the door. The angel appeared in a bright light, awoke him, and broke him loose from the chains (Acts 12:6–7). Peter was in prison not willingly but naturally. The angel entered the prison at will for Peter's sake, though he could have chosen otherwise. The two chains are the fear of punishment or the hope of a reward; they hold us under the custody of the law. The sentries represent "the teachers" of the law, who highlight our bound condition from which we cannot break free. Christ, the angel, willingly enters the prison to free us from its bondage. Luther writes, "He willingly does just those works which we did reluctantly, for He does them for our good, so that He may attach us to Himself and lead us out."[103] He knows the way out, because he was, in Luther's phrase, "willingly and freely

---

97. *Comm. Gal.* 4:4, in *CNTC* 11:74.

98. *LW* 75:387; *WA* 10.1.1:363.

99. *LW* 75:387; *WA* 10.1.1:363.

100. *LW* 75:387–88; *WA* 10.1.1:363.

101. *LW* 75:388; *WA* 10.1.1:363.

102. *LW* 75:389–90; *WA* 10.1.1:367.

103. *LW* 75:388; *WA* 10.1.1:364.

outside."[104] Peter was liberated from the prison as he followed him, trusting in what he said; as Luther frequently says, "As he believes, so is it with him" (cf. Matt 8:3).[105] Whoever believes that Christ came to liberate him from the law is indeed saved, just as the word declares. Having been freed from the prison of the law, we now can do everything voluntarily and joyfully, without constraint.

Similarly, Calvin acknowledges that all the details in Luke's report attest more fully to the liberating power of God from the tyranny of law.[106] "A light shone" unexpectedly upon Peter, who was sleeping, arousing him to God's presence. "Sleep," Calvin notes, "is a kind of image of death, which keeps our senses stifled and subdued."[107] In such condition when we are weak and incapacitated to seek God, God remains solicitous toward his own, as "their sleep also calls on God."[108] Peter's liberation was solely of divine origin, as the guards were also asleep, as Peter was, seemingly unaware of the unexpected deliverance. Peter was content with the mere words of God brought by the angel, God's appointed instrument. His incredible deliverance from Herod is sure proof of God's wonderful power that triumphs over the power of the enemy. The two chains fall off; we no longer fear nor seek for reward. We then can do everything with a free, willing, and joyful spirit. The law's jurisdiction over us is null, so that we might "receive adoption as sons" (Gal 4:5). We now live, Calvin stresses, on God's "verdict"[109] that the curse of the law has been abolished. By faith, we follow him, liberated from the custody of the law.

With Luther, Calvin puts an emphasis on what the person of Christ came to do for the sinful race. Christ clothed himself in human flesh to render obedience to God on our behalf and free us. Christ places himself under the verdict of the law, and suffers death, curse, and damnation as a transgressor, though he was completely innocent. His subjection to the law is not imposed from without but is willed by himself. His free and willing submission to the law, says Calvin, "involved him in a sort of servitude," but not in the way that might diminish his deity, which is one being with the Father. He expands, "There is no contradiction here; as it is written

104. *LW* 75:388; *WA* 10.1.1:365.

105. *LW* 75:388; *WA* 10.1.1:365.

106. *Comm. Acts* 12:6–7, in *CNTC* 6:340.

107. *Comm. Acts* 12:6–7, in *CNTC* 6:340.

108. *Comm. Acts* 12:7, in *CNTC* 6:340.

109. *SG*, 372.

in the second chapter of Philippians, verse six, he 'thought it not robbery to be equal with God.' He emptied himself voluntarily. Thus because he humbled himself out of his own pure and free bounty, he retained his position of honor, though he appears before men in the form of a servant."[110] He, the sovereign Lord of all, assumed our human nature and freely became a humble servant to obtain for us freedom from the curse of the law. Calvin summarizes succinctly:

> Christ, the Son of God, who was by right exempt from all subjection, became subject to the law: Why? In our name, that He might obtain freedom for us. A free-man redeemed a slave by constituting himself a surety; by putting the chains on himself, he takes them off the other. In the same way Christ chose to become liable to keep the law that He might obtain exemption for us. Otherwise He would have submitted to the yoke of the law in vain, for it was certainly not on His own account that he did so.[111]

Real Communication: He Became a "Sinner"

Christ has truly redeemed and freed us from the law and its verdict—namely, sin and death. As Paul said, "Christ redeemed us from the curse of the law by becoming a curse for us" (Gal 3:13). Scriptural language about Christ's death for Luther is not given in vain; it accomplishes its own mission. Commenting on Ps 63:33, "He will make His voice a mighty voice," Luther extols the peculiar power of God's speech to achieve its own purpose, just as "wine has the power to delight the heart."[112] He believes God truly accomplishes what he says through the spoken or written gospel on earth and does not with these words simply point to a heavenly reality. The fourth word of the cross—"My God, my God, why hast thou forsaken me?"—for Luther accentuates that guilt and just condemnation are "in fact"[113] transferred to Christ. The attribution is not figurative but actual, that Christ truly was cursed by his Father. This is borne out in Luther's christological

---

110. *SG*, 371.

111. *Comm. Gal.* 4:4, in *CNTC* 11:74.

112. *LW* 13:35.

113. *LW* 26:292; *WA* 40.1:454.

interpretation of Isa 53:6, "God has laid the iniquity of us all on Him."[114] Here lies, Luther claims, the "wonderful exchange": "His chastisement is the remedy that brings peace to our conscience."[115]

Unlike Jerome, Luther takes with earnestness the word "cursed" used by Paul in Gal 3:13, claiming it is an effective word that does what is says.[116] When Christ was "made a curse for us," he truly "endured the anxiety and the terror of a frightened conscience which feels eternal wrath."[117] He does all this not so that he might be destroyed by them but that he might destroy them for us, which Luther stresses as "fact."[118] Our salvation depends on Christ appearing in our place before God as "the person of all men, the one who has committed the sins of all men," to make satisfaction for them with his own blood.[119] Christ's identification with sinners for Luther is "of His own free will and by the will of the Father."[120] Christ is guilty, not "in his own person" but in us, bearing "the person of a sinner."[121] That Christ became "a sinner" is the meaning and force of Paul's teaching on 2 Corinthians 5:21, "For our sake God made Him to be sin who knew no sin."[122] Christ not only bore the sins of the world but also became "the greatest" sinner and "a curse," says Luther; not only "adjectivally," but also "substantively."[123] Bertram captures Luther's point: "This drastic conclusion is suggested by Paul's strong use of 'curse' in its substantive rather than its adjectival sense."[124] The death Christ dies under God's wrath, Althaus writes, is that of "a sinner" he became.[125] Unlike our death, Christ's death was, Luther writes, "an innocent and pure death."[126] The innocent Son became guilty, says Luther, "in order to do the Father's will, by which we would be sanctified eternally."[127] The

114. *LW* 26:292; WA 40.1:454.
115. *LW* 17:224; WA 31.2:435.
116. *LW* 26:278; WA 40.1:434.
117. WA 5:602ff, as cited in Althaus, *Theology of Martin Luther*, 205.
118. *LW* 26:292; WA 40.1:454.
119. *LW* 26:280; WA 40.1:437.
120. *LW* 26:278; WA 40.1:434.
121. *LW* 26:277; WA 40.1:434.
122. *LW* 26:277; WA 40.1:434; *LW* 26:288; WA 40.1:448.
123. *LW* 26:288; WA 40.1:448; *LW* 26:277; WA 40.1:434.
124. Bertram, "Luther on Unique Mediatorship," 256.
125. Althaus, *Theology of Martin Luther*, 203.
126. WA 37:59, as cited in Althaus, *Theology of Martin Luther*, 203.
127. *LW* 26:292; WA 40.1:454.

gospel lies hidden in the actuality of Christ's vicarious act for us (*pro nobis*), that very act of obedience he renders to the Father. For us, Christ offers up himself, says Luther, as "the price of redemption."[128] Through Christ's obedient sacrifice, God has expiated sin and wrath and granted us righteousness and mercy. Luther declares, "God does not want to see anything else in the world . . . except sheer cleansing and righteousness. And if any remnants of sin were to remain, still for the sake of Christ, the shining Sun, would not notice them."[129] Had Christ not truly assumed sin, guilt, wrath, condemnation, and death as "his own," says Luther, these mighty "monsters" would have ever remained "in us," in which case salvation would be lost.[130] That Christ truly "became sin" in us offers "the most delightful comfort," that we have truly become "the righteousness of God" in him (2 Cor 5:21).[131] Scriptural language about "this fortunate exchange"[132] in which Christ assumed our sinful person and gave us his righteous person, Siggins writes, does not "mislead us."[133] It is, as Luther puts it, "a very sweet and truly apostolic doctrine."[134]

Two extreme contraries—"curse, sin, and death," and "blessing, righteousness, and life"—coinhere in Christ, "the one and only Person."[135] "In himself," they are at war with each other: "the highest, the greatest, and the only sin; and the highest, the greatest, and the only righteousness."[136] Sin has entered "a mighty duel" with righteousness, and one of them must surrender.[137] It sought to conquer Christ but failed, because Christ is "a Person of invincible and eternal righteousness" before whom sin must yield. "In Christ, all sin is conquered, killed, and buried; and righteousness remains the victor and the ruler eternally."[138] Similarly, Christ enters the battle where

---

128. *LW* 26:295; WA 40.1:458.

129. *LW* 26:280; WA 40.1:437.

130. *LW* 26:282; WA 40.1:434; *LW* 26:292; WA 40.1:454.

131. *LW* 26:278; WA 40.1:434.

132. *LW* 26:284; WA 40.1:443.

133. Siggins, *Martin Luther's Doctrine*, 113.

134. *LW* 26:279; WA 40.1:436; *LW* 26.292–93; WA 40.1:455.

135. *LW* 26:281–82; WA 40.1:440.

136. *LW* 26:281; WA 40.1:440.

137. *LW* 31:352.

138. *LW* 26:281; WA 40.1:440.

"blessing" clashes with "curse" but conquers it for faith.[139] Luther expands on the victory motif:

> For the blessing is divine and eternal, and therefore the curse must yield to it. For if the blessing in Christ could be conquered, then God Himself would be conquered. But this is impossible. Therefore Christ, who is the divine power, Righteousness, Blessings, Grace, and Life, conquers and destroys these monsters—sin, death, and the curse—in His own body and in Himself, as Paul enjoys saying (Col. 2:15): "He disarmed the principalities and powers, triumphing over them in Him."[140]

Christ's humanity alone cannot conquer sin and death, but his divinity, united to the humanity, says Luther, "did all this, and death and hell could not swallow him up, these were necessarily swallowed up by him in a mighty duel; for his righteousness is greater than the sins of all men, his life is stronger than death, his salvation is more invincible than hell."[141] All these conquering acts lie not in our power but in God's, exclusively his; or else God would be robbed of his glory. In this, Christ's divinity is affirmed. "Therefore when we teach that men are justified through Christ and that Christ is the Victor over sin, death, and the eternal curse," Luther avers, "we are testifying at the same time that he is God by nature."[142]

Luther retains the gravity of sin and wrath. The attribution of sin and judgment to Christ is real and "effective." He writes, "Christ felt the attribution. . . . It was an effective attribution, wholly genuine, except that he did not deserve [punishment], and was delivered up for us without having done anything to merit it."[143] Foregoing speculation on the mystery of the cross, Luther writes, "However, this is a thing rather to be experienced than to be discussed and grasped in words."[144] George captures Luther's point: "The suffering of the Son of God on the cross—his being made a curse for us (see Gal 3:13)—makes no sense by the canons of human logic. But, from the standpoint of biblical faith, it is a window into the heart of God and the only means by which we see God's eternal purpose fulfilled in history."[145]

---

139. *LW* 26:282; WA 40.1:440.

140. *LW* 26:281–82; WA 40.1:440.

141. *LW* 31:352; also quoted in Zachhuber, *Luther's Christological Legacy*, 69.

142. *LW* 26:283; WA 40.1:441.

143. *LW* 32:201.

144. *LW* 32:201.

145. George, "Afterword," 207.

Like Luther, Calvin does not weaken sin or curse, both of which God laid on Christ. Our sins were transferred to Christ, and his suffering thus entails a penal quality. Robert Paul states, "Calvin argues, in language reminiscent of Luther, that Christ was numbered with transgressors so that he might 'bear the character of a sinner.'"[146] Christ, "the unspotted Lamb of God, full of blessing and grace," Calvin says, "took our place and thus became a sinner and subjected Himself to a curse, not in Himself indeed, but in us."[147] In becoming human, Calvin avers, the Son of God assumes "what was ours as to impart what was his to us, and to make what was his by nature ours by grace."[148] A real exchange occurs in Christ: sins, death, and the curse are transferred to Christ; righteousness, life, and blessing are transferred to us. Christ died a sinner's death, for he died in our place. Calvin writes, "For he suffered death not because of innocence but because of sin."[149] With Luther, Calvin renders Gal 3:13 as follows:

> Now [Paul] does not say that Christ was cursed, but something more, that He was a curse, signifying that the curse of all was placed on him. If this seems harsh to anyone, let him be ashamed also of the cross of Christ, in the confession of which we glory. God was not ignorant of what death His Son would die when He pronounced, "Cursed is everyone who hangs on a tree." . . . He took our place and thus became a sinner, and subject to the curse, not in Himself indeed, but in us; yet in such a way that it was necessary for him to act in our name.[150]

The death the Lord Jesus Christ suffered on the cross, says Calvin, was no "accident"; it was "ordained" by God.[151] Christ became our substitute and made himself, he says, "the chief of sinners" on our behalf.[152] Christ makes satisfaction for our sins, Calvin continues, "not by display of divine and heavenly power that he paid our debt of eternal death . . . [but in] weakness; indeed, not only so, but he was accursed. If this had not been the case, our burdens would have crushed us and all would have perished in

---

146. Paul, "Atonement," 147.

147. *Comm. Gal.* 3:13, in *CNTC* 11:55.

148. *Inst.* 2.7.2.

149. *Inst.* 2.16.5.

150. *Comm. Gal.* 3:13, in *CNTC* 11:55.

151. *SG*, 284.

152. *SG*, 284.

the abyss."[153] That the Son became a curse for us should cause us to become aware of the miserable and hopeless condition about which we cannot do anything until God comes to our rescue. The knowledge of redemption at such cost condemns all self-confidence and merits of works. It humbles us before God so that we might "magnify the grace bought for us by the Son of God, and be careful not to detract from his worth in any way whatsoever, even though he became a curse."[154] By his accursedness, Christ has proved that our salvation is of immense worth to him that he would spare nothing but give himself totally to set us free from the curse. "Therefore," Calvin writes,

> we must trust that whenever we come in his name to ask for mercy, it will be bestowed upon us. But if we come believing that we have a scrap of merit, what good is it? We know that the Father loves the Son, and how precious his death was in his sight. For this reason, we can have full confidence that God will forgive us and be favorable and kind to us if we cleave to what Paul shows us here: namely, that our Lord Jesus Christ spared nothing for us, even to the point of bearing our curse.[155]

Both Reformers consider propitiation as a provision of God's love. In his sermon on Gal 2:20, Calvin affirms "the Son of God suffering" death in our person, not as a vain but "a shameful death, yes, even a cursed death; he endured the pains of hell for a time in order to free and acquit us, to the end that we might find grace at the judgment seat of God."[156] A "mere bodily death," for Calvin, is "ineffectual" in the appeasement of God's wrath.[157] The Son of God must become one of us and "in our name," says Calvin, "fight" against all enemies of life—"the devil's power," "the dread of death," and "the pains of hell," and finally triumph over them via his death and resurrection.[158] With Luther, Calvin interprets the cry of dereliction on the cross by means of Isa 53:5, holding that Christ truly must undergo what sinners do; in his words, Christ "experienced all the signs of a wrathful and avenging God."[159] However, he must also be embraced as God's "beloved Son," he

153. *SG*, 286.
154. *SG*, 287.
155. *SG*, 286.
156. *SG*, 212.
157. *Inst.* 2.16.10.
158. *Inst.* 2.16.11.
159. *Inst.* 2.16.11.

continues, "in whom his heart reposed" (cf. Matt 3:17), or else his death is of no avail.[160] "Therefore, just as human sinners are both loved and hated by God," Zachman writes, "so also to free sinners from the impasse of God's love and hatred, Christ himself must not only experience God's vengeance, but must also be loved by God."[161] To quote Calvin's exposition of Gal 3:13:

> He could not be outside God's grace, yet He endured His wrath.
> For how could He reconcile Him to us if He regarded His Father as
> an enemy and was hated by Him? Therefore the will of the Father
> always reposed in Him. Again, how could he have freed us from
> the wrath of God if He had not transferred it from us to Himself?
> Therefore He was smitten for our sins and knew God as an angry
> judge.[162]

The "Communication of Attributes": Luther and Calvin

What sets Luther and Calvin apart is their usage of the doctrine of the "communication of attributes" in their Christology.[163] In his Galatians lectures, Luther comments on it more than Calvin, in a few places, especially when dealing with soteriology. Calvin hardly discusses the communication of attributes in his commentary and sermons on Galatians. His explicit comment on it occurs in his commentary on Gal 2:20, where he upholds union with Christ as the context in which a "true and genuine communication" (*veram cum ipse et substantialem communicationem*) of his life and benefits to believers who are one with him occurs.[164] As part of his explanation of Gal 3:10, Luther also acknowledges that Scripture speaks of Christ in different ways. Sometimes Christ is spoken of as the whole person; sometimes as two natures separately, either divine or human. To speak about the natures

160. *Inst.* 2.16.11.

161. Zachman, "Did Death of Christ," 79–80.

162. *Comm. Gal.* 3:13, in *CNTC* 11:55.

163. For discussion of the doctrine of *communicatio idiomatum*, see Lienhard, *Luther*, 335–46; Kolb, *Martin Luther*, 111–17; Siggins, *Martin Luther's Doctrine*, 227–38; Bayer, *Martin Luther's Theology*, 234–38; Wendel, *Calvin*, 219–24; Zachhuber, *Luther's Christological Legacy*, 46–63; Cross, *Communicatio Idiomatum*, 59–70 (Luther), 122–40 (Calvin).

164. *Comm. Gal.* 2:19, in *CNTC* 11:43.

THE ATTRIBUTION OF CONTRARIES

"separately" is to speak of him "absolutely."[165] To speak about the divine nature united to the human nature in one person is to speak of Christ as "composite and incarnate."[166] Luther uses the communication of attributes to make sense of the various depictions of Christ in Scripture. The sentence "The infant lying in the lap of His mother created heaven, and is the Lord of the angels" refers to the man. But the word "man" acquires a new meaning, as it "stands for the divinity."[167] It means "this God who became man created all things."[168] Creation is a predicate of Christ's divinity, not of his humanity. "Nevertheless," Luther explains, "it is said correctly that 'the man created,' because the divinity, which alone creates, is incarnate with the humanity, and therefore the humanity participates in the attributes of both predicates."[169] Such understanding rests on the Ockhamist influence, Kolb writes, that enabled Luther to operate with the presupposition that God works in, with, and under selected elements of the created order, including human flesh.[170] In stressing the personal unity of Christ, Luther does not overlook his humanity. It is God's plan to reconcile sinners to himself through Jesus's assumed humanity. So, it is appropriate to attribute redemption to the man Jesus, understood not in abstract separation but in concrete unity with the Creator in one person. The divine attributes can be ascribed to the human nature, achieving divine work through it. The personal union of Christ means "the Man, Mary's Son, is and is called almighty, eternal God, who has eternal dominion, who has created all things and preserves them 'through the communication of attributes' because he is one person with the Godhead and is also very God."[171] Luther elaborates:

> The kingly authority of the divinity is given to Christ the man, not because of His humanity but of His divinity. For the divinity alone created all things, without the cooperation of the humanity. Nor did the humanity conquer sin and death; but the hook that was concealed under the worm, at which the devil struck, conquered and devoured the devil, who was attempting to devour the worm. Therefore the humanity would not have accomplished everything

165. *LW* 26:265; WA 40.1:416.
166. *LW* 26:265; WA 40.1:416.
167. *LW* 26:265; WA 40.1:416.
168. *LW* 26:265; WA 40.1:416.
169. *LW* 26:265; WA 40.1:416.
170. See Kolb, *Martin Luther*, 114–16.
171. *LW* 15:293; WA 54:49.

by itself; but the divinity, joined with the humanity, did it alone, and the humanity did it on account of the divinity.[172]

The indivisibility of the person of Christ allows a genuine christological predication of each nature's properties. Luther writes, "Those things that are attributed to the human being may rightly be asserted with respect to God; and on the other hand, those things that are attributed to God may rightly be asserted with respect to the human being. So it is true to say: this human being created the world and this God has suffered, died, was buried, etc."[173] This leads Bayer to affirm the christological predication between the two natures, that "in Christ, the human being, God suffered, died, and was victorious over death; in Christ, who is God, the human nature has become omnipresent, omniscient, omnipotent."[174]

Reason may claim that God cannot suffer and die. Against such, Luther says:

> That is true, but since the divinity and humanity are one person in Christ, Scripture ascribes to the divinity, because of this personal union, all that happens to humanity, and vice versa. And in reality it is so. Indeed, you must say that the person (point to Christ) suffers and dies. But this person is truly God, and therefore it is correct to say: the Son of God suffers. Although, so to speak, the one part (namely, the divinity) does not suffer, nevertheless, the person who is God, suffers in the other part (namely, in the humanity).[175]

This person, who is God—namely, the Son of God—truly is crucified for us. Against Zwingli, who regarded the expressions "God suffered" or "God died" as "rhetorical, not real" predications, Luther considers them as real predications.[176] Calvin could not conceive of the idea that God could really suffer and die. In his *Institutes*, he acknowledges the New Testament language of passion, such as "God purchased the church with his blood" (Acts 20:28) and "the Lord of glory was crucified" (1 Cor 2:8).[177] But such

172. *LW* 26:267; *WA* 40.1:417.

173. *WA* 39.2: 93.1–94.8, 100.25–102.27, as cited in Kolb, *Martin Luther*, 117n44.

174. Bayer, *Martin Luther's Theology*, 236.

175. *LW* 37:210.

176. See "Formula of Concord, Solid Declaration, Article 8, Person of Christ," in *BC* (Tappert), 595n6. Kolb's and Wengert's translation is "not *realiter*, that is, real, in fact and in truth" (see *BC*, 620). See also *LW* 41:103–4.

177. *Comm. Acts* 20:28, in *CNTC* 7:184. Partee, *Theology of John Calvin*, 151,

language is figurative. Calvin elaborates, "Paul attributes blood to God, because the man Jesus Christ, who shed His blood for us, was also God. This figure of speech was called the *communicatio idiomatum* by the Fathers, because the property of one nature is applied to the other."[178] So Calvin rejects the attribution of suffering to Christ's divinity. He claims, "Surely God does not have blood, does not suffer, cannot be touched with hands. But since Christ, who was true God and also true man, was crucified and shed his blood for us, the things that he carried out in his human nature are transferred *improperly*, although not without reason, to his divinity."[179] When Scripture says "God laid down his life for us" (1 John 3:16), the property of human suffering for Calvin is predicated "improperly" of Christ's divinity because Christ is indivisibly one person with two natures. In his sermon on Gal 2:20, Calvin does not affirm that God suffers in Christ but that the person does, that is, "the Son of God suffer[s]" a most despicable death in order that he might free us.[180]

For Luther, the personal union of the two natures is so complete that they share their attributes. All the attributes of Christ's dual nature must be ascribed to Christ, the one indivisible person. He writes, "Consequently Christ is God and human being in one person because whatever is said of him as human must also be said of him as God, namely, Christ had died, and Christ is God; therefore God died, not the separated God, but God united with humanity."[181] The assertion that God dies is crucial, for our salvation depends upon it. Salvation for both Reformers resides in the person of Christ, who has suffered God's wrath against human sin, effecting for us reconciliation with God. Against Nestorius, Luther says:

> If it cannot be said that God died for us, but only a man, we are lost; but if God's death and a dead God lie in the balance, his side goes down and ours goes up like a light and empty scale. Yet he can also readily go up again or leap out of the scale! But he could not sit on the scale unless he had become a man like us, so that it could be called God's dying, God's martyrdom, God's blood, and God's

comments that both Luther and Calvin are Chalcedonian but not Nestorian or Eutychian. The Reformed school argued that Lutheranism tended toward Eutychianism, resulting in a denial of Christ's real humanity; the Lutheran school argued that Reformed theology tended toward Nestorianism, resulting in the denial of real personal union.

178. *Comm. Acts* 20:28, in *CNTC* 7:184.

179. *Inst.* 2.14.1.

180. *SG*, 212.

181. *LW* 41:103.

death. For God in his own nature cannot die; but now that God and man are united in one person, it is called God's death when the man dies who is one substance or one person with God.[182]

The way in which Luther and Calvin deploy the communication of attributes leads to different eucharistic theologies. For Luther, the divine attribute of omnipresence is communicated to Jesus's humanity so that he could say Christ's humanity is in the Eucharist.[183] Calvin concedes that Jesus's glorified humanity is "circumscribed" in heaven, while his divinity is omnipresent.[184] Lutherans operate with the conceptual framework, Braaten notes, that "the finite is capable of the infinite (*finitum est capax infiniti*),"[185] and thus ubiquity is to be predicated of Jesus's humanity. The Reformed operate with an axiom different from Luther, Braaten writes; "the finite is not capable of the infinite (*finitum non capax infiniti*),"[186] and thus Jesus's humanity, even when joined to his divinity, cannot receive any divine attributes such as omnipresence. Lutherans coined the phrase *extra-Calvinisticum* as a description of the Calvinists,[187] who held that because the Logos is infinite, it must therefore exist "*extra Carnem* (outside the flesh)" and not be bound to the flesh the Logos assumes.[188] Lutherans countered the *extra-Calvinisticum* by coining the phrase "*totus intra carnem* and *numquam extra carnem* (wholly in the flesh and never outside the flesh)."[189] The Logos is united to the flesh in such a way that it never exists outside the flesh but always within it.

Concluding Reflections

Luther and Calvin warn against speculating on the essence of God, for such an attempt would only lead us into the terror of the divine majesty. Faith must not be fixed on knowing that God is or on what God is, but on knowing how he is for us so that we may cling to him for all good. Christ for

182. *LW* 41:103–04.

183. *LW* 31:212–23.

184. *Inst.* 4.17.30.

185. Braaten, "Person of Jesus Christ," 508.

186. Braaten, "Person of Jesus Christ," 509.

187. For a major study of the *extra-Calvinisticum*, see Willis, *Calvin's Catholic Christology.*

188. Braaten, "Person of Jesus Christ," 509.

189. Braaten, "Person of Jesus Christ," 509.

Luther is "the divine majesty sweetened and mitigated to your ability to stand it."[190] Likewise, Calvin teaches that we cannot approach the divine majesty without a propitiator. Christ's death appeases God's wrath and reconciles God to us. Calvin avers, "Until we realize that there is no other cleansing from the stains of sin but the shed blood of the Lord Jesus Christ, applied by the Holy Spirit, and until we learn to trust in his grace and love alone, we will never be able to have free access to God."[191]

Despite their different understanding of the communication of attributes, Luther and Calvin affirm that the motif of God's suffering is required by the doctrine of salvation. For them, the reality of Christ's human suffering is bound up with two other aspects of their Christology: the man Christ and Christ as God incarnate are one; thus they could assert God suffers in the man Jesus of Nazareth, the incarnate Son. The death of Jesus is real, and not to be conceived, Ebeling writes, "docetically as mere appearance. Quite the contrary: this death was suffered in its full horror, and was sealed by Christ's burial, as the tradition in 1 Cor. 15:4 expressly emphasizes."[192] Christ bore our sin and mortality, doing away with them through his death and resurrection to give us his righteousness and life. Resurrection renders the cross effectual in that Christ's righteousness conquers our sin, proving his victory is nothing else than the victory of the crucified. "Just as Christ by his death takes our unrighteousness upon himself," Zachman writes, "so by his rising he bestows his righteousness upon us."[193] The two events—cross and resurrection—comprise a single meaning: a celebration of victory over all contraries—sin, death, and the devil. Commenting on Rom 4:25, "He died for our sins and rose for our justification," Luther writes, "[Christ's] victory is a victory over law, sin, our flesh, the world, the devil, death, hell, and all evils; and this victory of his he has given to us."[194] All contraries— "sin, death, and our mask"—truly are swallowed up by his resurrection so that "sheer righteousness, life, and eternal blessing"[195] become ours by faith. Commenting on "to glory on the cross of Christ" in Gal 6:14, Calvin teaches that "the whole of redemption and all its parts" are encapsulated in

---

190. *LW* 26:30; WA 40.1:78–79.

191. *SG*, 22.

192. Ebeling, *Truth of the Gospel*, 145.

193. Zachman, *Assurance of Faith*, 172.

194. *LW* 26:21–22; WA 40.1:65.

195. *LW* 26:84; WA 40.1:443. The word "mask" refers to our sinful person.

the cross in which Paul glories.[196] The cross and resurrection of Christ, says Calvin, are so closely linked that the latter does not "lead us away" from the former.[197] Instead, resurrection leads us to the cross, rendering it efficacious. Let nothing distract us from glorying in the cross; as Paul exclaims in Gal 6:14, "God forbid!"

The Reformers hold that the sole reason for the incarnation was to appease the wrath of God by suffering chastisement for our peace.[198] Jesus, the one human being in whom dwells the fullness of God's deity, endures our alienation from God in order to bestow on us his reconciliation to us. The mediatorship of Christ presupposes Luther's prefatory statements about this "human God," "no other God than this man Jesus Christ."[199] The "human God" is indeed a vehicle of God's self-revelation but is more than that; his significance is found in the act of atonement he came to achieve as a fulfillment of God's will. In the doctrine of justification, we are to look at Christ, the righteous one who has acted and suffered in his self-humiliation according to the joyous exchange between the sinner and himself, that our sins are Christ's and his righteousness ours. The principle of communication of attributes means that God as God does not suffer immanently, for there is nothing in God's being that would cause God to suffer; rather, he suffers economically in the Son's assumption of our sinful person so that he might bestow on us his righteous person. The predication of contraries is "real," Forde writes, "not an abstract metaphysical transaction."[200] Suffering is not an attribute of God, just as sin is not; rather, it is a predicate of the mission of the Son, who was "sent" by the Father to be the blessed curse so that he might redeem the fallen creation from the curse of the law. Suffering belongs to his accursedness and not essentially to God. Luther draws great comfort from a real attribution, that "our sin must be Christ's own sin, or we shall perish eternally."[201] The greatest marvel of the gospel consists in that God in Christ enters a "mighty duel"[202] with the enemies of life (sin, death, and the curse), triumphs over them, and bestows on us

196. *Comm. Gal.* 6:14, in CTNC 11:117.

197. *Comm. Gal.* 6:14, in CTNC 11:117.

198. *LW* 26:292; WA 40.1:454; *Inst.* 2.12.5.

199. *LW* 26:29; WA 40.1:78.

200. Forde, "Luther's Theology of Cross," 52.

201. *LW* 26:278; WA 40.1:435.

202. *LW* 31:352.

his eternal goods (righteousness, life, and blessing).[203] In so doing, God assumes that which is alien to himself but proper to humanity—namely, the opposition between God and humankind—and eventually conquers it. Hence the curse of God's repulsion from us is overcome by the blessing of his attraction to us in Christ. God's love moves God to draw nigh to us; it abolishes his distance from us in exchange for his reconciliation to us.

Calvin also reaps from this christological attribution full enjoyment of all heavenly riches. He writes, "We enjoy Christ only as we embrace Christ clad in his own promises. . . . We possess in Christ all that pertains to the perfection of heavenly life."[204] The sonship, which is essentially Christ's by nature, is imparted to us by grace, and as a result, we share the same inheritances as Christ does, even as God's adopted sons. God's love begins from eternity and has conquered his hate of sinners through the blood of his Son in history to constitute a people under God's blessing rather than under God's curse. Calvin quotes Augustine, saying:

> The fact that we were reconciled through Christ's death must not be understood as if his son reconciled us to him that he might now begin to love those whom he had hated. Rather we have already been reconciled to him who loves us, with whom we were enemies on account of sin . . . Therefore, he loved us even when we practised enmity toward him and committed wickedness. Thus in a marvelous and divine way he loved us even when he hated us. For he hated us for what we were that he had not made; yet because our wickedness had not entirely consumed his handiwork, he knew how, at the same time, to hate in each one of us what we had made, and to love what he had made.[205]

The "mortal conflict" of God's loving us and hating us is resolved in Christ's act of offering himself as a sacrifice. God in Christ suffers the contraries of wrath and mercy, sin and righteousness, curse and blessing, but conquers them for faith. That Christ became "for us" a blessed curse through which he emerged victorious over sin, death, and wrath, Calvin advises, should not be converted into a discursive and dispassionate exercise that often does not move our hearts.[206] Christ did this "for us," before

---

203. *LW* 26:282; *WA* 40.1:441.

204. *Inst.* 2.9.3.

205. See Augustine, *John's Gospel* cx. 6 (PL 35:1923f.; tr. NPNF[1] 7:411), as cited in *Inst.* 2.16.4n7.

206. *SG*, 213.

which we can do nothing except be enraptured in wonderment and trust, a response that is proper to God. The cross is God's suffering love by which we live, and this picture of Christ ought to captivate troubled hearts, who find joy and relief not in the works of law but in the work of Christ, the Justifier of sinners. Luther exults, "I am revived by this 'giving' of the Son of God into death, and I apply it to myself. This applying is the true power of faith."[207] Calvin, too, feels the power of Paul's language of divine self-giving through which we are drawn into the "one act [Christ's] which accomplished the redemption of the world [so that] we can all personally say, 'The Son of God loved me so much, that he gave himself to die for me.'"[208]

207. *LW* 26:177; WA 40.1:298.
208. *SG*, 213.

5

Justification and Assurance

The Holy Spirit, Faith, and the Person

THE DISCUSSION OF THE RELATIONSHIP between the Holy Spirit and justification is scattered throughout the book of Galatians. There Luther and Calvin present an adequate picture of the doctrine of the Holy Spirit as the effective agent of justification, though not in a systematic fashion. By "the Spirit of God's Son," we apprehend God as our gracious Father, not a tyrant, and we come to know our status as God's adopted children, not as slaves. The Trinitarian shape and substance of the gospel, Swain argues, is "implied" in Gal 4:6, "And because you are sons, God has sent the Spirit of His Son into your hearts, crying Abba! Father!"[1] The Reformers assume the Trinitarian nature of Paul's gospel, but with an emphasis on how the Triune God relates to us rather than on how he relates to himself. The Reformers' reading of Galatians is governed by what Swain calls "the Pauline grammar of divine agency."[2] Just as Christ is conceived in terms of the redemptive action upon sinners, so also the Holy Spirit is understood in terms of the salvific action upon them. Our identity as God's elect is forged in Christ, accepted by the Father as well as the Son, and made certain in our hearts by the Holy Spirit. All three persons work together as one God in constituting a people of God, translated from God's wrath to God's mercy. The whole of the Christian life and actions is attributed to the efficacy of the Spirit. Not only does the Holy Spirit come in visible

---

1. Swain, "Heirs through God," 260–61, where he discusses the Trinity in Gal 4:4–7.
2. Swain, "Heirs through God," 262.

forms, ushering in God's kingdom, but he also continues his work, causing his gifts to increase in our lives (Gal 3:5).

Both Reformers discuss two opposite ways to God: law or faith, merit or grace. Justification occurs not by anything we bring, but solely by faith in Christ; not by personal merits, but purely by free grace. The subjective genitive "the faith of Christ" refers to the saving action of God in Christ, the causative factor of justification; the objective genitive "faith in Christ" refers to its human reception, the responsive factor. Luther and Calvin do not consider them as opposed to each other; both are required theologically for a proper understanding of the gospel of justification. The movement of God's justifying action is from person, whom God first justifies, to works, which flow from the justified status. We by our depraved nature cannot draw near to God; nor could God draw nigh to us unless we have been first clothed with his Son's righteousness. Justification consists in a negation of all self-righteousness and works of law, and a confession of Christ's righteousness as all-sufficient. By "the Spirit of His Son," we are given, to use Luther's phrase, a "filial confidence in the Father"[3] who loves us dearly, as he does his dear Son, despite the abhorrent sins God finds in us. Justification and assurance come when we see ourselves only in Christ, whose Spirit is sent into our hearts, assuring us that we are truly God's sons and "brothers and co-heirs" with Christ.[4] The terrifying cry of fear under the law is liberated by the consoling cry of the Holy Spirit under the gospel.

A Triadic Interaction: The Holy Spirit, Faith, and Word

For Luther, justification comprises four interrelated points: preaching, hearing, believing, and calling upon God. It begins with the word addressing us outside ourselves through the instrument of proclamation, followed by the word heard and believed, and we thereby are saved by calling upon God. This is taught in Luther's commentary on Rom 10:14.

> For these four points are so interrelated that the one follows upon
> the other, and the last is the cause and antecedent of all the others,
> that is, it is impossible for them to preach unless they are sent;
> from this it follows that it is impossible for them to hear unless
> they are preached to; and from this, that it is impossible for them

3. *LW* 26:152; WA 40.1:262.

4. *LW* 75:391; WA 10.1.1:370.

to believe if they do not hear; and then it is impossible for them to call upon God if they do not believe; and finally it is impossible for them to be saved if they do not call upon God.[5]

The four points presuppose the mission of the Holy Spirit, who works through the preached word to create faith in the hearer's heart. It is here that Femiano speaks of a triadic "interaction of faith, the word, and the Holy Spirit."[6] Galatians 3:2, "Did you receive the Spirit by the works of the Law, or by hearing with faith?," presents Luther an occasion to weave together his teaching on the triadic relationship between preaching, hearing with faith, and the reception of the Spirit in his doctrine of justification. The Enthusiasts of Luther's time revert the order, holding that the Spirit works independently of the word. In Galatians, as in Romans, Luther gives priority to "the external word," followed by the "inward revelation." Luther expands:

> This sort of doctrine, which reveals the Son of God, is not taught, learned, or judged by any human wisdom or by the Law itself; it is revealed by God himself, first by the external word and then inwardly through the Spirit. Therefore the Gospel is a divine word that came down from heaven and is revealed by the Holy Ghost, who was sent for the same purpose. Yet this happens in such a way that the external word must come first. For Paul himself did not have an inward revelation, until he had heard the outward word from heaven, namely, "Saul, Saul, why do you persecute me?" (Acts 9:4). Thus he heard the outward word first; only then did there follow revelations, the knowledge of the Word, faith, and the gifts of the Spirit.[7]

In the opening verse of Gal 2:1, "Then after fourteen years I went up again to Jerusalem," Luther indicates his conviction that the Spirit's descent upon the Gentiles came through hearing with faith, not through circumcision or keeping the law.[8] The Spirit seals the gospel in the hearts of these Gentiles that have been visited with the word. As proof, Luther cites Cornelius, a pagan, who was without the law, but upon whom the Spirit descended through Peter's preaching (Acts 10:44).[9] The entire book

5. *LW* 25:413; WA 46:422.

6. Femiano, "Holy Spirit," 44. See also Carlson, "Luther and the Doctrine," 139.

7. *LW* 26:73; WA 40.1:141.

8. *LW* 26:79; WA 40.1:150.

9. *LW* 26:204; WA 41.1:331.

of Acts, says Luther, has substantiated the truth, that the gospel, not the law, bestows the Holy Spirit.[10] The Spirit fell upon the three thousand who heard the word proclaimed, causing them to yield to it (Acts 2:10). Luther expands, "The Law never brings the Holy Spirit; therefore it does not justify, because it only teaches what we ought to do. But the Gospel does bring the Holy Spirit, because it teaches what we ought to believe. And to put righteousness into the Law is simply to conflict with the Gospel."[11] Justification occurs only through faith in Christ, the fruit of the gospel, and apart from the law.[12]

With Luther, Calvin writes in his *Institutes*, "God breathes [the Spirit] faith into us only by the instrument of his gospel, as Paul points out that 'faith comes from hearing.'"[13] Proclamation, Calvin asserts, is "dead and useless, unless the Lord gives effective power to it by His Spirit."[14] Commenting on Rom 10:17, he teaches that when the Spirit is present, preaching "is the instrument of his power."[15] When Christ's power accompanies preaching, Leith avers, "the words, their sound and their meaning [become] the occasion of the voice of God."[16] Calvin cites the conversion of Lydia in Acts 16:14 as an instance of the Spirit's work in making effectual the ministry of the word. Calvin writes:

> If the mind of Lydia had not been opened, the preaching of St. Paul would have been mere words (*literalis*); yet God inspires her not only with mere revelations but with reverence for His Word, so that the voice of a man, which otherwise would have vanished into thin air, penetrates a mind that has received the gift of heavenly light.[17]

The unity of the word and the Spirit guards against "a false imagination, or the semblance of secret illumination" and deviation from "the Word," faith's very foundation.[18] "The efficacy of preaching," Calvin avers,

---

10. *LW* 26:204; WA 41.1:331.

11. *LW* 26:208; WA 41.1:337.

12. *LW* 26:205; WA 41.1:333.

13. *Inst.* 4.1.5.

14. *Comm. 1 Cor.* 3:7, in *CNTC* 9:70.

15. *Comm. Rom.* 10:17, in *CNTC* 8:233.

16. Leith, "Calvin's Doctrine of Proclamation," 31.

17. *Comm. Acts* 16:14, in *CNTC* 7:73.

18. *Comm. Acts* 16:14, in *CNTC* 7:63.

lies in God and is not to be transferred to the preacher, his instrument.[19] Faith is "too exalted" to be generated by a human voice; it is God who acts not in separation from but in unity with the preacher to create faith in us.[20]

External Forms and Inward Change: Discernment of the Spirit's Presence

Luther and Calvin read Gal 4:6, "And because you are sons, God has sent the Spirit of His Son into your hearts," together with the book of Acts to speak of two ways in which the Spirit comes: externally and internally. In the "primitive church," the Spirit appeared externally "in a manifest and visible form," such as in signs and miracles.[21] The Spirit came upon Christ in the form of a dove (Matt 3:16), and upon the apostles in the form of fire (Acts 2:3); as Paul says, "Tongues are a sign, not for believers but unbelievers" (1 Cor 14:22). The external manifestations of the Spirit were necessary for the establishment of the "primitive church," primarily for the sake of the unbelievers. Once confirmed, Luther opines, such visible forms of the Spirit's presence ended.[22]

Similarly, Calvin avers that the material signs of miracles and tongues attest to the effects of the Holy Spirit via the preached word. By them, the hearers of faith were assured they possessed the Spirit, Calvin writes, "because it is the power of God, breathed forth as it were by Him into all His creatures."[23] Prophecies and external manifestations in New Testament times were "meant to beautify the first beginnings of the gospel."[24] The outpouring of the Spirit's gifts at Peter's preaching to non-Jewish people demonstrates what "an effectual instrument of God's power" preaching is.[25] External manifestations were meant by Christ "to set forth the beginning of his kingdom"; once the kingdom was inaugurated, the material signs cease their function.[26] The cessation of these phenomena, says Calvin, testifies

19. *Comm. Rom.* 10:17, in *CNTC* 8:233.

20. *Comm. 1 Cor.* 3:7, in *CNTC* 9:70.

21. *LW* 26:374; WA 40.1:570.

22. *LW* 26:374–75; WA 40.1:572.

23. *Comm. Acts* 2:2, in *CNTC* 6:50.

24. *Comm. Acts* 21:9, in CTS 19:270.

25. *Comm. Acts* 10:44, in CTS 18:451–52.

26. *Comm. Acts* 2:38, in CTS 18:121.

"that the end and perfection was present in Christ."[27] The causative power of the Spirit manifested to the disciples in visible forms assures us that "the church," says Calvin, "will never lack His invisible and hidden grace."[28] The gifts of the Spirit are not to be confused with "the grace of regeneration."[29] These various gifts, Calvin avers, had served their proper purpose and thus have now ceased; "but the Spirit of understanding and regeneration" remains operative and fruitful "that he may keep us in reverence of the word."[30]

Second, the sign now in which the Spirit is sent is not a visible form but is that which occurs in the hearts, as borne out in Gal 4:6, "God has sent the Spirit of His Son into your hearts." This sign of inward change assures the heart that it possesses the Spirit by whom we are justified. By the work of the Holy Spirit, we have become a new creature, who is now adorned with the garment of Christ's righteousness.[31] This change happens by rebirth via baptism, as Paul taught: "As many of you as were baptized have put on Christ" (Gal 3:27). The baptized, a new creature, is given "a new judgment, new sensations, and new drives."[32] The "glow and yearning for the Word," which Luther calls "this feeling," is not self-generated; it "has been infused into our hearts by the Holy Spirit."[33] "This feeling" cannot be acquired by human reason but by the Spirit's working through the spoken word (Ps 77:1).[34] The Spirit generates a transposition from the condition of the fall into the condition of grace. Luther further enumerates some of the external signs by which we are "confirmed *a posteriori*" to have been regenerated by the Holy Spirit: delighting to hear of Christ, preaching and teaching Christ, praising him, confessing him, hate sin, loving others, and fulfilling our calling.[35] The Spirit continues his efficacious work, communicating to us, in Calvin's phrase, "the fruit of the gospel, of that gospel that

---

27. *Comm. Acts* 21:9, in CTS 19:271.
28. *Comm. Acts* 2:2, in CNTC 6:51.
29. *Comm. Gal.* 3:5, in CNTC 11:49.
30. *Comm. Acts* 10:44, in CNTC 6:317.
31. *LW* 26:353; WA 40.1:540.
32. *LW* 26:353; WA 40.1:540.
33. *LW* 26:377; WA 40.1:574.
34. *LW* 26:377; WA 40.1:574.
35. *LW* 26:379; WA 40.1:577.

had been preached amongst them by his own mouth,"[36] and enabling us to cry, "Abba! Father!"[37]

Cain and Abel:
The Person as Prior to Work

An important indication of the Spirit's presence is the performance of law in faith. Only when we are justified as doers [the person] could we ever begin to do [action] the law. A "true doer of the law" (Rom 2:13) thus is predicated upon faith, the cause of good works. Luther avers, "Faith takes the doer himself and makes him into a tree, and his deeds become fruit . . . So faith makes the person, who afterwards performs works."[38] As such, "the doer of the Law is justified" (Rom 2:13); that is, the person (the doer) is declared righteous in God's eyes. Paul reinforced the declarative aspect of justification, Parsons notes, by a "negative" comment in Rom 3:20, "Therefore, no one will be declared righteous in God's sight by observing the law."[39] So "to do," Luther continues, "is first to believe, and so, through faith, to keep the law. For we must receive the Holy Spirit, illumined, and renewed by Him, we begin to keep the Law."[40] Likewise, for Calvin, "the hearing or the knowledge of the law" (Rom 2:13) cannot justify; as per Gal 3:10, "For all who rely on the works of the Law are under the curse." The law cannot bestow righteousness; thus, it requires another righteousness outside us, one that flows from faith. Commenting on Gal 3:12, "And the law is not of faith," Calvin writes, "The contradiction between the law and faith lies in the cause of justification. You will more easily unite fire and water than reconcile the two statements that men are justified by faith and by the law. The law is not faith, that is, it has a method of justifying a man which is completely foreign to faith."[41] Righteousness obtained by faith and righteousness by works are irreconcilables.

In his 1522 Christmas sermon on Gal 4:1–7, Luther distinguishes between the person and the work to demonstrate Paul's central thesis that

36. *Comm. Gal.* 3:4–5, in *CNTC* 11:49.

37. The Spirit's role in assurance will be expanded later in the section "Assurance and the Spirit's Cry" below.

38. *LW* 26:255; *WA* 40.1:402.

39. Parsons, *Since We Are Justified*, 3.

40. *LW* 26:255; *WA* 40.1:400.

41. *Comm. Gal.* 3:12, in *CNTC* 11:54.

"no work justifies the person but [the person] must first without any works be justified."[42] The order of God's justifying action is from person to work, from being to act. In this, both Luther and Calvin compare Abel to Cain to describe the relationship between faith and works. Commenting on Gen 4:4, "God had regard for Abel and his offering," Luther argues that Abel, the person, was "first godly" and approved of God, followed by his offering. His work does not merit justification but rather flows from it.[43] God does not justify Abel on account of his performance; rather, God justifies his work because he was already reckoned as just. By contrast, "for Cain and his offering He had no regard" (Gen. 4:5). This is because of his person, which had not been made godly. Related to this are the two kinds of good works performed before and after justification. Those preceding justification have an appearance of good but are of no avail because unjustified people "in their nature and first birth" are sinful;[44] only those good works performed following justification are perfectly good, for they flow from a justified person. As support, he quotes Ps 116:11, "All men are liars," saying that "our name is sin, falsehood, vanity, and folly."[45] Thus, all born in Adam can only perform evil works, the kind that Cain does, unless they are changed. This runs contrary to Aristotle, who taught, "Whoever does much good will become good in that way."[46] The "Cain-saints"[47] follow Aristotle, seeking to justify themselves by means of their works without first being justified in their person. While God looks at the person, bestowing on her the righteousness by which she is justified, Cain looks at the works by which he seeks to gain God's approval. The order from person to work produces "Abel-saints" whose lives are transformed by the hearing of the word with faith, from which good works follow. But the Cain-saints remain in their first birth and condemned both in their person and their works; as Christ said, "Whoever does not believe will be damned" (Mark 16:16). Both groups seek to enter heaven by "the narrow gate" of which Christ spoke in Luke 13:24; but whereas the Abel-saints' narrow gate is "faith," reducing them to naught and causing them to despair of their works so their trust is

---

42. *LW* 75.364; WA 10.1.1:325.

43. *LW* 75.364; WA 10.1.1:325.

44. *LW* 75:365; WA 10.1.1:326.

45. *LW* 26:220; WA 2:490.

46. See *Nicomachean Ethics* 2.1 (Loeb 71 [1926]), 72–73, as cited in *LW* 75:365; *LW* 27:219; WA 2:489.

47. *LW* 75:365; WA 10.1.1:327.

not in themselves but only in God,[48] the Cain-saints' narrow gate is "good works," by which they magnify themselves; they glory in their good deeds, "hang[ing] them around [their necks]"—and these eventually hinder them from entering through the door to heaven.[49] While Cain-saints seek to please God by good works but to no avail, Abel-saints believe Christ's word and are liberated for good works. Luther avers, "Therefore, nothing belongs to justification except hearing and believing Jesus Christ, our Savior. However, both are not the work of nature. . . . On the other hand, nothing belongs to good works except justification."[50] Luther thus insists we heed the "order of man's salvation" prescribed by God: "first, above all things, to hear the Word of God, and then to work, and thus be saved."[51]

With Luther, Calvin teaches us to observe "the order" prescribed by Moses, who "does not simply state that the worship which Abel had paid was pleasing to God, but he begins with the person of the offeror; by which he signifies, that God will regard no works with favour except those the doer of which is already previously accepted and approved by God."[52] Related to the story of Abel and Cain, Calvin mentions two equally important points. First, works performed outside faith may appear holy but are sins, Calvin writes, "being defiled from their root."[53] Thus God's acceptance of the person precedes his acceptance of the works. Second, all sinners are "hateful to God" and cannot approach God's throne other than through "faith," which is, in Calvin's words, "a gratuitous gift of God, and a special illumination of the Spirit."[54] Consequently, Calvin infers that "we are *prevented* by his mere grace, just as if he had raised us from the dead."[55] Unless we first are made alive by grace, our works remain impure, as they are done in unbelief. All good works are attributed to grace—namely, the "prevenient grace, which anticipates and goes before everything that is good in man."[56] Cain attempted to appease God by external sacrifices and without "the mediator's

---

48. *LW* 75:367; WA 10.1.1:330.

49. *LW* 75:367; WA 10.1.1:330.

50. *LW* 75:366; WA 10.1.1:327.

51. *LW* 75:366; WA 10.1.1:327.

52. *Comm. Gen.* 4:4, in CTS 1:194.

53. *Comm. Gen.* 4:4, in CTS 1:195.

54. *Comm. Gen.* 4:4, in CTS 1:195.

55. *Comm. Gen.* 4:4, in CTS 1:195.

56. *Comm. Gen.* 4:4, in CTS 1:195n. This is the editor's explanation of what "*prevented* by his mere grace" means.

grace."[57] In his attempt to constitute himself by performance, he incurs divine displeasure, and thus God treats his offering with disdain (Gen 4:5).[58] Calvin writes, "In the person of Cain is portrayed to us the likeness of a wicked man, who yet desires to be esteemed just, and even arrogates to himself the first place amongst the saints. Such persons truly, by external works, strenuously labour to deserve well at the hands of God; but, retaining a heart inwrapped in deceit, they present to him nothing but a mask; so that, their laborious and anxious religious worship, there is nothing sincere, nothing but mere pretense."[59] No one can break free from the curse that falls on sinful humanity unless God intervenes and reconciles us to himself; and apart from expiation of God's wrath, no one can find acceptance with God.[60] No human works can effect purity, Calvin asserts, except by faith, as taught by the Spirit through the words of Peter that "hearts are purified by faith" (Acts 15:9).[61] Purity is to be sought not in the work of merits but in grace through the mediation of God's Son. Calvin repeatedly stresses, "The chief point of well-doing is, for pious persons, relying on Christ the Mediator, and on the gratuitous reconciliation procured by Christ, to endeavour to worship God sincerely and without dissimulation. Therefore two things are joined together by a mutual connection: that, the faithful, as often as they enter the presence of God, are commended by the grace of Christ, their sins being blotted out; and yet that they bring thither true purity of heart."[62] Iwand's description of Luther's view fits Calvin's: "Thus, our works are born out of our condition, and we are not born out of our works."[63] The person of faith produces good works, and not vice versa. Both Luther and Calvin concur in affirming the person as prior to the work: righteous deeds flow from, and do not make, a righteous person.

---

57. *Comm. Gen.* 4:4, in CTS 1:195.

58. *Comm. Gen.* 4:5, in CTS 1:196.

59. *Comm. Gen.* 4:5, in CTS 1:197.

60. *Comm. Gen.* 4:5, in CTS 1:196.

61. *Comm. Gen.* 4:5, in CTS 1:196.

62. *Comm. Gen.* 4:5, in CTS 1:201.

63. Iwand, *Righteousness of Faith*, 61–62.

The Efficacy of Christ's Death: Faith of and in Christ[64]

The very purpose of Christ's coming was to destroy "the kingdom of sin" (1 John 3:8) so that he might give us his righteousness.[65] It is in this context where "the faith of Christ" occurs, referring either to the gospel itself or to the narrative of Christ's life and death, which, Calvin stresses, is to be preached as a remedy to the plight of sin and its destructive force.[66] The efficacy of Christ's death, not faith itself, is the cure of the sinful predicament. Though the phrase "the faith of Christ" rarely surfaces in Luther, the same accent is placed on the gospel of Christ, which he sets in opposition to the law of Moses. Luther writes:

> Thus by the preaching of the Gospel I have destroyed the Law, lest it continue to rule in the conscience. For Moses, the old settler, has to yield and emigrate somewhere else when Christ, the new guest, comes into the new house to live there alone. And where He is, there the Law, sin, wrath, and death have no place. In their stead there is present now nothing but grace, righteousness, joy, life, and a filial confidence in the Father, who is now placated, gracious, and reconciled.[67]

Luther's exegesis of Gal 2:16, 19–20 does not consider human faith as contributing to justification and hence is Christocentric.[68] The phrase "faith in Christ" receives its meaning in the context of Pauline antithesis—"not by works of the law, but through faith in Jesus Christ"; as Luther avers, Paul is "contrasting the righteousness of faith with the righteousness of the entire law, with everything that can be done on the basis of the Law, whether by divine power or by human."[69] Luther's main point is that if Christ's righteousness is ineffectual in justifying us, we remain in sin and without hope; no active righteousness of works could justify us. Linebaugh writes, "The negation of justification by works of the law provides a negative definition of the phrase 'faith in Jesus Christ.' In other words, for Luther, 'by works of the

64. See also my comments on "faith in Christ" and "the faith of Christ" in chs. 1, 2, and 4.

65. *Comm. Gal.* 2:18, in *CNTC* 11:41. Calvin uses the phrase "the kingdom of sin."

66. *Comm. Gal.* 2:18, in *CNTC* 11:41.

67. *LW* 26:152; *WA* 40.1:262.

68. See Linebaugh, "Christo-Centrism of Faith," 540–45, for his discussion of faith in Christ.

69. *LW* 26:122; *WA* 40.1:218.

law' is a soteriological antonym to 'faith in Christ' and thus, as its excluded opposite, entails and partially defines the debated phrase: not by works of the law indicates that the human is not a salvific subject; faith in Christ identifies Jesus as the savior."[70] Luther often contrasts works with faith, as he contrasts the law with the gospel, to repudiate works-righteousness. Justification by faith means, for Luther, that "we work nothing, render nothing to God; we only receive and permit someone else to work in us."[71] Faith is not self-created but created by God; it merely receives the righteousness procured by Christ through hearing his word. Luther expands, "Faith is a divine work in us. It changes us and makes us to be born anew of God. It kills the old Adam and makes altogether different people."[72] The objective genitive "faith in Christ" denies the human subject the justifying function. Christ, whom faith grasps, is the sole basis of one's saving relationship with God.

Paul applies, Luther writes, the "Hebraic figure of speech" to shed light on the genitive case;[73] it could be interpreted, as he notes, either in an "active" or "passive" sense.[74] For instance, actively, the genitive "the glory of God" means the glory that is rightly God's; passively, it means that "by which we glory in God."[75] Likewise, the genitive "the faith of Christ," Luther notes, usually takes on a passive sense, referring to "that by which Christ is believed."[76] As Hamm writes, "faith is the way of pure receiving" the gift of Christ's righteousness that is pressed upon us from outside us.[77] In his commentary on Gal 3:25, "But now faith comes," Calvin gives a Christocentric account of faith, referring it to "the brighter revelation of grace after the veil of the temple had been rent. And this, we know, was effected by the manifestation of Christ."[78] Calvin's emphasis is on the objective content of Christ's saving action over against the terrors of the law. Likewise, Luther

---

70. Linebaugh, "Christo-Centrism of Faith," 539. See also p. 535, where he identifies that the Pauline antithesis consists in "an anthropological negation and a Christological confession: it excludes the human as the subject of salvation and confesses Christ, who is present in faith, as the one by, in, and on the basis of whom God justifies the ungodly."

71. *LW* 26:5; WA 40.1:41.

72. *LW* 35:370; WA DB 7:11.

73. *LW* 26:101; WA 40.1:185.

74. *LW* 26:102; WA 40.1:185.

75. *LW* 26:102; WA 40.1:185.

76. *LW* 26:102; WA 40.1:185.

77. Hamm, *Early Luther*, 217.

78. *Comm. Gal.* 3:25, in *CNTC* 11:67.

interprets the phrase "faith comes" as the coming of Christ in human flesh in order that he might deliver us from sin and death.[79] The conscience in which Christ reigns through grace suffers neither condemnation nor despair (cf. Rom 8:1). However, on the same text, Luther admits faith as a human action of grasping the grace of Christ through which we mitigate the terrors of the law. Luther writes personally, "To the extent that I take hold of Christ by faith, therefore, to that extent the Law has been abrogated for me."[80] With respect to the question "Where does faith derive such power as to convey the life of Christ?," Calvin declares "the foundation on which faith rests is the love and death of Christ; for it is from this that the effect of faith must be judged."[81] Luther, too, contends that "faith . . . does not originate in works; neither do works create faith, but faith must spring up and flow from the blood and the wound and death of Christ."[82] Faith that grasps has as its foundation the self-giving love of God "for me." The believer lives by faith in the efficacious activities of the cross. Seifrid comments, "Christ's work is not an isolated event of the past: in that it took place 'for me,' it embraces me, and thus creates my faith here and now. For this reason, . . . [Paul] is able to say that he (and all believers) lives by that faith which has its source in and flows forth from the Son of God."[83] God's love goes ahead of us and moves him to suffer for us; he redeems us *ex nihilo*, not through human merits, but through the suffering love of the cross, the basis of our faith. Christ is the "rock" from which faith draws for our benefits, our "oil and honey" (cf. Deut 32:13).[84] Calvin raises a further question, implicating the subjective genitive: "How comes it that we live by the faith of Christ?"[85] His reply:

> Because He loved us and gave Himself for us. The love . . . with which Christ embraced us, led Him to unite Himself to us. And this He completed by His death. By giving Himself for us, He suffered in our person (*in nostra persona passus est*). Moreover, faith

79. *LW* 26:349; *WA* 40.1:534.

80. *LW* 26:350–51; *WA* 40.1:538.

81. *Comm. Gal.* 2:20, in *CNTC* 11:43.

82. *LW* 44:38.

83. Seifrid, "Paul, Luther, and Justification," 219.

84. *LW* 44:38.

85. For a major proponent of the subjective genitive position, see Hays, *Faith of Jesus Christ*. For further discussions, see Just, "Faith of Christ"; Chester, "When Old Was New." See also Chester, *Reading Paul with Reformers*, 377–86.

makes us partakers of everything that it finds in Christ. This mention of love means the same that John said, 'Not that first we loved him, but he anticipated us by his love' (1 John 4:9). For if any merit of ours had moved him to redeem us, such a cause would have been stated. But now Paul ascribes the whole to love; it is therefore free. Let us observe the order, 'He loved us and gave Himself for us.' It is as if he said, 'He had no other reason for dying than because He loved us,' and that when we were enemies, as he says in Rom. 5:10.[86]

Where the phrase "the faith of Christ" appears in Calvin's commentary on Gal 2:20, the phrase "faith in the Son of God" occurs in Luther's commentary. This does not mean Luther and Calvin are at odds with each other. By the subjective genitive, "the faith *of* Christ," Calvin's emphasis is on the salvific action of God in Christ, not ours; the sacrificial love of Christ for us, not ours for him. "The faith of Christ" is contrasted with "the works of the law," the two contrary ways to justification. Calvin paraphrases Gal 2:15: "What is the purpose of our believing? That we might be justified by the faith of Christ. For what reason? Because we were convinced that a man cannot achieve righteousness by the works of the law."[87] And yet, in the same paragraph, Calvin complements "the faith of Christ," that which reckons us righteous, with our "faith in Christ," that by which we are made righteous. In speaking of the receptive nature of faith, Calvin writes, "Moreover faith makes us partakers of everything that it finds in Christ." In his *Sermons on Galatians*, Calvin coins another phrase, "live by faith in the gospel," as an equivalent to "faith in the Son of God."[88] It is clear "the faith *of* Christ" does not exclude "faith *in* Christ"; indeed, as Horrell notes, "[our] faith is often mentioned alongside the crucial phrase 'the faith of Christ' (e.g., Rom 3.3; Gal 2.16)."[89]

86. *Comm. Gal.* 2:20, in *CNTC* 11:43–44.

87. *Comm. Gal.* 2:15, in *CNTC* 11:38.

88. *SG*, 212.

89. Horrell, *Introduction to the Study*, 108. I am indebted to Stephen Chester, who recognizes "an added layer of complexity: Luther and Calvin are commenting in Latin on the Greek text of Galatians and their comments are then being translated into English. However, the main issue remains the same despite the intervening use of Latin: when Calvin's comments are read in English the contemporary English reader will most naturally hear the phrase 'the faith of Christ' as a subjective genitive. However, it is grammatically possible for it to be an objective genitive and it is clear that Calvin (and for that matter the KJV translators) in fact hears Paul as using an objective genitive. The potential for confusion arises from the evolution of English and the diminishing use in English today

By the objective genitive "faith in Christ," Luther's emphasis is not so much on faith per se, but on the object of faith—namely, "[Christ] who is present in the faith itself."[90] The justified person lives not by faith that is vacuous of its object, but by faith in the one who gave himself "for me." Faith's "decisive content," Lohse writes, is nothing other than "in faith Christ is present";[91] in Luther's words: "Faith takes hold of Christ and has Him present, enclosing Him as the ring encloses the gem. And whoever is found having this faith in the Christ who is grasped in the heart, him God accounts as righteous. This is the means and merit by which we obtain the forgiveness of sins and righteousness."[92] Luther does not see Christ and faith as opposites; they presuppose each other. Althaus captures Luther well: "Christ is what he is for *me* in God's judgment only in that faith in which I 'grasp' him; and that faith is meaningful in God's judgment only because Christ is present with a man."[93] Those tormented by sin and terrified by God's accusing law find relief in Christ, in whom God has become, to borrow Mattes's phrase, "a graspable God."[94] What justifies us for Luther is not faith itself but "faith in Christ"[95]—namely, faith's very object. Luther interprets "believed in Jesus Christ" or "faith in Christ" as saying it is through Christ's presence in faith that we have been imputed with his righteousness. Here three items, Chester discerns, interlock in Luther's doctrine of justification: "faith, Christ, and acceptance or imputation."[96] As Chester writes aptly, "The presence of Christ in faith secures an intimate relationship between imputation and the participation of believers in Christ. God imputes because the Christian believes but the faith of the Christian itself is a divine gift in which Christ is present."[97] Faith alone, Hamm writes, places us in "a cognitive and affective relationship to Christ's righteousness" and "thus became the Christocentric relational basis for participation in Christ."[98]

---

of objective genitive phrases" (from personal communication with Stephen Chester).

90. *LW* 26:129; WA 40.1:229.

91. Lohse, *Martin Luther's Theology*, 261.

92. *LW* 26:132; WA 40.1:233.

93. Althaus, *Theology of Martin Luther*, 231.

94. Mattes, *Martin Luther's Theology*, 102.

95. *LW* 26:130, 133; WA 40.1:229, 234.

96. *LW* 26:132; WA 40.1:233; also quoted in Chester, "No Longer I," 321.

97. Chester, "No Longer I," 321–22.

98. Hamm, *Early Luther*, 79.

Both Reformers stress the effectual function of faith, that by which we grasp Christ who first grasps us. Calvin anticipates that some may dispute that since faith possesses no causal power to produce a perfect person, one cannot say that faith justifies.[99] With Luther, Calvin's focus is on Jesus Christ, faith's treasure, rather than on faith itself; he writes, "Our attention is drawn to the Lord Jesus Christ [his suffering and death], when we consider 'faith.'"[100] Faith, says Calvin, has "no merit in itself; it is not a question of weighing in the balances to assess its value or virtue."[101] Its worth lies in the object it grasps—namely, Christ, who "is set before as the one in whom we rest all our faith."[102] Allen writes, "The steadiness of faith is not in itself but in its object";[103] only the object of faith is causative of its reality. The accent on faith's object causes Calvin to stress "it is [Christ] who is called God's beloved Son (Matt. 3:17), so that we might be beloved in him; he is called the Righteous One (Isa. 53:11), so that we may partake of his righteousness; and he is called the Holy One (Lk. 1:35), so that we may be sanctified in him."[104] All that Christ has done remains useless unless grasped by faith, the responsive factor. Calvin says, "This kind of faith brings grace: when we recognize that we are wretched creatures, and abominable in God's sight, seeking the remedy in the Lord Jesus Christ."[105] "To believe" in Gal 2:16 for Calvin means more than giving assent to historical knowledge about Christ; it means "truly receiving him" as one given to us by his Father.[106] Contrasting faith with works, Calvin writes, "Faith looks at nothing but the mercy of God and Christ dead and risen. All merit of works is therefore excluded from being the cause of justification when the whole is ascribed to faith."[107] Commenting on Rom 3:22, Calvin uses the language of causality to underscore the connection between the faith of Christ and faith in Christ. God's mercy is "the efficient cause" of justification, Christ is its "substance," and faith is its "instrumental cause."[108] Calvin raises a pertinent question:

99. *SG*, 179.

100. *SG*, 181.

101. *SG*, 342.

102. *SG*, 180.

103. Allen, *Justification and the Gospel*, 113.

104. *SG*, 181.

105. *SG*, 181.

106. *SG*, 342.

107. *Comm. Gal.* 3:6, in *CNTC* 11:50.

108. *Comm. Gal.* 3:6, in *CNTC* 11:50; *Comm. Rom.* 3:22, in *CNTC* 8:73.

"Is salvation through faith?" His reply is "Yes," providing that "the Lord Jesus is the object of faith and belief."[109] Then he further qualifies faith instrumentally: "Faith is therefore said to justify, because it is the instrument by which we receive Christ, in whom righteousness is communicated."[110] Allen observes rightly that in his *Institutes*, Calvin speaks of the receptive character of faith, in a way akin to Luther,[111] as that by which the person and benefits of Christ become ours when we are joined to him.[112] Since "faith alone obtains" God's blessings, Calvin advises us to discard all other means to God except by "the straight and narrow path of faith."[113]

Hays considers "faith in Christ" as "anthropological," with the emphasis on the soteriological efficacy of the human decision for Christ; he views the "faithfulness of Christ" as "christological," but with an emphasis on the soteriological efficacy of God's action in Jesus for us.[114] The antinomy of "anthropological" (faith in Christ) versus "christological" (the faith of Christ) in Hays's formulation is not part of the Reformers' theological framework. The contrast between "anthropological" and "christological," Linebaugh argues, does not correspond to the contrast between works of the law and the faithfulness of Christ.[115] Hays's rendering, Watson writes, is "disingenuous," for both are christological.[116] When speaking of "faith in Christ," Barclay asserts, "Paul has no interest here in faith as a religious disposition, only as

---

109. *SG*, 180.

110. *Comm. Rom.* 3:22, in *CNTC* 8:73; *SG*, 342.

111. See Canlis, *Calvin's Ladder*, 130, where she argues that "in Luther's *Praefatio* to his Latin works (1545) he describes his exegetical breakthrough as realizing that God's righteousness is to be grasped by faith. Calvin contradicts this, noting that Luther's emphasis on the responsive faith of the believer *to* Christ should instead be construed as the "'active' faithfulness *of* God as the stable foundation of salvation.'" Her analysis is based on Calvin's exegesis of Pss 7:17 and 22:31. Allen differs from Canlis, arguing that her position ignores the passive nature of faith framed "within the context of a broader discussion" about how one receives Christ and his benefits via union with him. He also suspects that Canlis's account does not do justice to Luther, "who does frequently use the shorthand term 'faith' to speak of what saves, but who often clarifies by saying that faith saves instrumentally by uniting one to Jesus, who is salvation in his person and work." See Allen, *Justification and the Gospel*, 113.

112. *Inst.* 3.2.10.

113. *SG*, 343.

114. Hays, *Faith of Jesus Christ*, 277. See Chester, *Reading Paul with Reformers*, 379, and Barclay, *Paul and the Gift*, 378–84, for further discussion.

115. Linebaugh, "Christo-Centrism of Faith," 535.

116. F. Watson, "By Faith (of Christ)," 159; also cited in Barclay, *Paul and the Gift*, 382.

belief (or better, trust) in the generative event of the death and resurrection of Christ. What matters is not the subjectivity of belief, but the focus and basis of that faith: the unconditional gift of God in Christ."[117] The faith of Christ and faith in Christ are mutually constitutive; they are not opposites. Barclay offers a helpful summary of the significance of "faith in Christ" in the Reformers, without converting the gospel into the currency of a form of works-righteousness:

> So, what is the new currency? Hardly some other human capacity or some inherent token of worth, but "faith in Christ"—the acknowledgment that the only thing of value is Christ himself. Faith is not an alternative human achievement nor a refined human spirituality, but a declaration of bankruptcy, a radical and shattering recognition that the only capital in God's economy is the gift of Christ crucified and risen. Faith directed to, and centered on, Christ recognizes, under the impact of the good news, that there is no element of value locatable in the human being. It invests everything in the only capital that counts: Christ.[118]

Assurance and the Spirit's Cry: "Abba! Father!"

Paul said the people of God were under "the elements of the world" (Gal 4.3) before the time was fulfilled. They were first slaves under the law before being made children subsequently under the gospel. For that reason, the Spirit was sent to make that transition, from slaves to children. They were given the Spirit, who enables them to call out "Abba! Dear Father!" The Spirit given is specifically "the Spirit of God's Son," not just "His Spirit" generically. God constitutes us his children. How? By "the Spirit of the Son." The Son is God's "child" by nature; he possesses the Spirit, which is exclusively his.[119] Together with him, we by adoption share his sonship and call out "Abba! Father!" The Spirit was sent to our hearts, bearing witness that we are God's children who are as precious as God's child, his Son. Luther paraphrases, "God sends you His Spirit, who dwells in the Son, so that you may be His brothers and co-heirs, and call out just as He does: 'Dear

---

117. Barclay, *Paul and the Gift*, 382.

118. Barclay, *Paul and the Gift*, 383–84.

119. *LW* 75:391; *WA* 10.1.1:370.

Father!'"[120] "The Spirit of his Son" makes us co-heirs with Christ and creates in us a filial confidence in the Father who loves us equally, as does the Son, causing our hearts to cry "Abba! Father!" The right to sonship occurs through possessing the Son's Spirit when we are united to Christ. As Calvin writes, "We belong to him, and he, in turn, is not willing to separate himself from us . . . Similarly, we must have the Spirit of the Lord Jesus Christ, otherwise we cannot boldly approach our God or call upon him as our Father."[121] As "brothers and co-heirs" with Christ, we partake together with him of the same blessings of God.

Similarly, Calvin lays out his argument in three propositions, showing the role the Spirit plays in God's adoption of us:

> Adoption by God precedes the testimony of adoption given by the Holy Spirit. But the effect is the sign of the cause. And you dare to call God your Father only by the instigation and incitement of the Spirit of God. Therefore it is certain that you are the sons of God.[122]

The Holy Spirit for Calvin is "the earnest and pledge of our adoption,"[123] through which our hearts are assured of God's fatherly love for us revealed in his Son. The testimony of adoption is given to believers, but not to unbelievers; these cannot receive "the Spirit of truth" because they do not know God (John 14:17).[124] "The Spirit of the Son" for Calvin assures us we are the sons of God as truly as is Christ, because we possess the gift of his Spirit. Calvin affirms, "We are the sons of God because we are endowed with the same Spirit as His Son."[125] By the Spirit, we know for sure that the Father loves us as he does his Son; he, too, accepts us as he accepts his own. Calvin avers, "Thus, we pray by the Spirit of our Lord Jesus to God the Father, with full confidence that he owns and accepts us as members of the body of his Son."[126] Where such certainty that we are God's own is wanting, Calvin avers, certainly there is "no faith."[127]

120. *LW* 75:391; WA 10.1.1:370.
121. *SG*, 374.
122. *Comm. Gal.* 4:6, in *CNTC* 11:75.
123. *Comm. Gal.* 4:6, in *CNTC* 11:75.
124. *Comm. Gal.* 4:6, in *CNTC* 11:75.
125. *Comm. Gal.* 4:6, in *CNTC* 11:75.
126. *SG*, 375.
127. *Comm. Gal.* 4:6, in *CNTC* 11:75.

Both Luther and Calvin combine Gal 4:6, "And because you are sons, God sent forth the Spirit of his Son into our hearts, crying, 'Abba! Father!,'" with Rom 8:15–16, "You have received the Spirit of God's gracious adoption, by whom we cry: 'Abba! Father!' The Spirit of God bears witness to our spirit that we are children of God."[128] As Paul says, "So through God you are no longer a slave but a son" (Gal 4:7). As sons of God, we are joint "heirs" with God's beloved Son and share the same inheritance with him. The inheritances—forgiveness of sins, righteousness, resurrection, and eternal life—are freely offered to us "merely by being born" of the word, not by human efforts.[129] We receive these goods passively, that is, without any works we do except by faith we "permit God to do His Work in us."[130] Faith grasps "the Word," which is, in Luther's words, "the divine womb" in which we are made a new creation.[131] We receive our identity passively, that we are "known by God" rather than by actively "coming to know God" (Gal 4:8–9). How does this happen? Luther answers, "He gives the Word, and when we take hold of this by the faith that God gives, we are born as sons of God."[132] Therefore we become God's children, for Luther, "in a purely passive, not in an active way"; that is, we simply "let ourselves be made and formed as a new creation through faith in the Word."[133] No human works can produce son, heir, and inheritance unless through hearing the word by faith. None could perceive the gospel or believe it unless the Holy Spirit reveals it to our hearts so that, as Luther puts it, "the truth of the Gospel is shining."[134]

A true knowledge of God is a predicate of the illumination of the Holy Spirit; as Paul teaches in 1 Corinthians 12:3, "No one can say 'Jesus is Lord' except by the Holy Spirit." Carlson aptly summarizes the meaning of this verse: "In short, by the activity of the Holy Spirit, faith is first conceived in man, who thus becomes a believer."[135] Not by human efforts but by God's efficacious call, they "come to know God." Calvin affirms, "The beginning of our calling is the free election of God, by which we are foreordained to life

128. *LW* 75:392; WA 10.1.1:371; *Comm. Rom.* 8:15, in CTS 19:295–96.
129. *LW* 26:392; WA 40.1:597.
130. *LW* 26:401; WA 40.1:610.
131. *LW* 26:392; WA 40.1:597.
132. *LW* 26:401; WA 40.1:610.
133. *LW* 26:392; WA 40.1:597.
134. *LW* 26:213; WA 40.1:342.
135. Carlson, "Luther and the Doctrine," 138.

before we are born. On this depends our calling, our faith, the fulfillment of salvation."[136] The phrase "known by God" highlights the corruption of the fallen nature that we, by ourselves, cannot manufacture true knowledge of God. Calvin writes, "All that men worship can be nothing more than vain fancy until God leads them onto the right path, for their own nature will entice them to devote themselves to all that is erroneous and illusory."[137] Therefore the Holy Spirit comes to our aid, apart from which we can neither know God nor believe in him. The passivity of faith means the Galatians have come to be known by God, Calvin writes, "not by the merit of the law, but from the grace of faith."[138] For Luther, the phrase "known by God" reinforces the passive righteousness of faith, not the active righteousness of the law, as the basis of one's saving relationship to God.[139] To return from grace to law, as the Galatians did, is to invert the order God has ordained. They defected from the gospel they formerly received, and in so doing, they relapsed into the former condition of ignorance of God (Gal 4:8).

The godly are more aware of the contraries of justification, that is, of sin, wrath, judgment, and death. These negative forces could work in us the cry of despair until the Spirit begins to cry in our hearts "Abba! Father!" Rather than using "whispers or speaks or sings," Luther writes, Paul selectively uses the word "crying," which the Spirit does "in full force, that is, with a full heart, so that everything would live and move in this confidence."[140] The Spirit releases a tiny "sob and sigh of the heart," which become in God's sight "a loud cry."[141] This cry, though small, will not go unnoticed; it will be heard by God. Luther imagines the Father saying, "'I do not hear anything in the whole world except this single sigh, which is such a loud cry in My ears that it fills heaven and death and drowns out all the cries of everything else.'"[142] The faint cry of the Spirit is made not to a tyrant or an angry judge, but to a Father whose heart is turned toward those who sigh "Abba! Father!" Our status as God's children is made certain in us through the crying of the Spirit in our hearts.

---

136. *Comm. Gal.* 4:9, in *CNTC* 11:77.

137. *SG*, 389.

138. *Comm. Gal.* 4:9, in *CNTC* 11:76.

139. *LW* 26:401; *WA* 40.1:610.

140. *LW* 75:393; *WA* 10.1.1:373.

141. *LW* 26:384; *WA* 40.1:584.

142. *LW* 26:384; *WA* 40.1:586.

Trials, for Luther, are God's "alien work" through which the Spirit calls out and awakens us to that call as God's "proper work." Those who spurn the cross place themselves outside the orbit of the Spirit's calling out and thus fail to perceive the benefit of the Spirit's outcry. We should not only desire the outcry of the Spirit in us but also a "fearful outcry" of trials, which is causally helpful, as it stimulates us to call out for God's aid, his proper work.[143] Gritsch writes, "The more there is *Anfechtung* [trials] and suffering, the more one must cry as a child of God, 'Abba, dear Father.'"[144] Luther avers, "Your sins will also cry out; that is, they will produce greater despair in your conscience. But Christ's Spirit will and must cry down that outcry, that is, cause your conscience to be stronger than your despair (cf. I Jn. 3:19–22)."[145] Human nature cannot generate filial confidence in God as our dear Father; it can only emit a cry of despair, Luther argues, as Cain did: "'Oh, woe is me! You are a strict and intolerant Judge! . . . From Your face I must hide.'"[146] Any "self-chosen spirituality and humility"[147] prompting us to look to ourselves and our works for assurance of salvation leads us to sheer despair. The afflicted should cling to the Spirit's cry, which draws us away from ourselves to God's Son, through whom the cry of despair disappears.

Similarly, Calvin underscores the participle "crying" as "a sign of certainty and unwavering confidence" with which we approach God.[148] He elaborates, "Uncertainty does not let us express calmly, but keeps our mouth half-shut, so that the half-broken words can hardly escape from a stammering tongue."[149] The believers, Calvin says, "felt the power of the Holy Spirit drawing us to God," enabling us to cry out to him, expressing in full confidence that we are indeed God's children, despite the many flaws God sees in us.[150] Drawing from Rom 8:15, Calvin distinguishes between "the spirit of bondage" to fear, the fruit of the law, and "the spirit of adoption" to freedom, the fruit of the gospel.[151] This distinction corresponds to

143. *LW* 75:393; WA 10.1.1:374.
144. Gritsch, "Martin Luther's Commentary," 109.
145. *LW* 75:393; WA 10.1.1:374.
146. *LW* 75:393; WA 10.1.1:374.
147. *LW* 75:380; WA 10.1.1:351.
148. *Comm. Gal.* 4:6, in *CNTC* 11:75; *Comm. Rom.* 8:15, in *CTS* 19:299.
149. *Comm. Gal.* 4:6, in *CNTC* 11:76.
150. *SG*, 200–1.
151. *Comm. Rom.* 8:15, in *CNTC* 8:168.

the distinction between the law, which incites fear, and the gospel, which comforts the terrorized. Calvin qualifies, "Fear is connected with bondage, as it cannot be otherwise, but that the law will harass and torment the souls with miserable disquietness, as long as it exercises its dominion."[152] The spirit of adoption conquers the spirit of fear, just as the gospel does to the law. It incites confidence in God to whom we can call out "Abba, dear Father!" Calvin writes:

> He now confirms the certainty of that confidence, in which he has already bidden the faithful to rest secure; and he does this by mentioning the special effect produced by the Spirit; he has not been given for the purpose of harassing us with trembling or of tormenting us with anxiety but on the contrary, for this end—that having calmed every perturbation, and restoring our minds to a tranquil state, he may stir us to call on God with confidence and freedom.[153]

The torment that comes from the spirit of bondage remains until the grace of adoption appears. Calvin stresses, "There is no other remedy for quieting them, except God forgives us our sin and deals kindly with us as a father with his children."[154] While fear incapacitates us to cry, faith liberates us to cry. Faith "expands the heart, the emotions, and the voice," says Luther, "but fear tightens up all these things and restricts them."[155] Faith cries "Abba!" with joy, knowing that God is the gracious Father; fear cannot cry "Abba!" with assurance, as it views God as a stern judge.[156] Freedom from fear and a lack of certainty is furnished by the spirit of adoption, just as freedom from the terror of the law comes by the consolation of the gospel.

For Calvin, as for Luther, the doubling of the words "Abba! Father!" is meant to inculcate "assurance and certainty" in the faithful.[157] The repetition of the name given only to God's children, Calvin notes, underscores "the warm, ardent, and intense feeling" that the Father has toward his own.[158] Luther elaborates first that the doubling of the name indicates the fervency of the outcry with which the afflicted person approaches God; and second,

---

152. *Comm. Rom.* 8:15, in CTS 19:298.
153. *Comm. Rom.* 8:15, in CTS 19:295–96.
154. *Comm. Rom.* 8:15, in CTS 19:298.
155. *LW* 25:358; WA 46:368.
156. *LW* 25:358; WA 46:368.
157. *Comm. Rom.* 8:15, in CTS 19:298; *LW* 75:394; WA 10.1.1:375.
158. *Comm. Rom.* 8:15, in CTS 19:298.

that Scripture repeats the same thing to assure and strengthen faith.[159] Luther cites Gen 41:32, where God showed through repeated dreams that the seven years of blessing in Egypt would be followed by seven years of bane.[160] The repetition of the prophetic dream is a surety that God will act, just as the word says. Third, the repetition shows the continual need for the strengthening of our faith. The first word "Abba!" indicates that confidence begins. When confidence wavers, it is strengthened again by the second word "Father." The peculiar word "Abba!" indicates that our faith begins weak. But after having been profoundly tried, Luther writes, the afflicted will become so acquainted with the name that he naturally cries to his "dear Father" for help.[161] The "Father" is called out twice, for the purpose of assuring our hearts that God indeed is our Father, a corresponding reality created by the word. The combined phrase "Abba, Father," Calvin notes, affirms that both Jewish and Gentile people can enjoy the gospel privilege, which was, at one time, restricted to the descendants of Abraham. "Under the gospel," Calvin avers, Jewish and Gentile people "are now equal and in the same condition" and can in one voice call out "Abba, Father!," confident their cries reach God's ears.[162] The promise that we are God's sons through Christ is made effectual by "a tiny faith,"[163] Luther avers, expressed not in the words of "the orators," but in sighs that escape human language.[164] By the cry of the Holy Spirit, the cries that stem from the law, works, our feelings, and our conscience no longer occupy our hearts, but rather, instead, "a very short word, 'Oh, Father!,'" which contains "everything" needful to our identity and well-being.[165] As a result, there is only sonship and no slavery, complete liberty without bondage, adoption with a right to eternal inheritances.[166]

159. *LW* 75:394; *WA* 10.1.1:375.

160. *LW* 75:394; *WA* 10.1.1:375.

161. *LW* 75:395; *WA* 10.1.1:375.

162. *SG*, 381.

163. *LW* 26:389; *WA* 40.1:593.

164. *LW* 26:385; *WA* 40.1:586.

165. *LW* 26:385; *WA* 40.1:586.

166. *LW* 26:385; *WA* 40.1:586.

Concluding Reflections

Reason concedes that it is inconceivable for such inestimable gifts of the Spirit only to be received without any human participation to obtain them. On the contrary, faith declares that there is nothing for us to do except hear and heed his voice through which we are justified. The accent on the grace of salvation safeguards against converting the gifts of the Holy Spirit into a reward for works. Justification occurs when we rest from everything but God's word, the instrument of the Spirit through which God works faith in us. "In faith," Luther avers, "one must close the eyes to everything but God's Word."[167] The gospel shines when the word we proclaim through the Spirit is received in the human heart. The certainty of our salvation rests not on human subjectivity but on the objective word of God in the efficacy of the Spirit. "We, by the grace of God," Luther declares, "are able to declare and judge with certainty, on the basis of the Word, about the will of God toward us, about all laws and doctrines, about our own lives and those of others. On the other hand, the papists and the fanatical spirits are unable to judge with certainty about anything."[168] The work of the Holy Spirit is intrinsically linked to the word so that the one implies the other. The assurance of faith is not drawn subjectively from within but objectively from without— namely, from God's word. The Holy Spirit communicates to our hearts the word of the cross, that we are made the people of God's blessing and are no longer under his curse.[169] The subjective experience of justification is real and is part of God's recreative work. But its reality lies beyond the grasp of human assessment. Justification occurs outside us, apart from the law and in opposition to the law; by implication, the experiential aspect of it has validity outside us, independently of human actions and irrespective of our subjectivity. Chester writes aptly:

> The experiential element in justification for Luther therefore paradoxically relies on the very objectivity of the saving work of God in Christ, setting it against the doubts that arise from the temptations that assail the self. The experiential element in justification is essential, but it is best understood as a kind of "anti-experience" in which learning not to trust in human subjectivity is of fundamental importance.[170]

167. WA 10.3:423, 17–18, as cited in Kolb, *Luther's Treatise*, 46.
168. *LW* 26:375; WA 40.1:572.
169. *LW* 26:388; WA 40.1:591.
170. Chester, "Abba! Father!," 22.

The godly feel a perpetual tension between the hearing of faith and the works of the law. Their conscience murmurs against faith as the basis of the proper reception of God's promises. It considers such teaching extremely insufficient, insisting that it requires additional things such as circumcision and observances of the law to complete it.[171] Reason and flesh remain our enemies, as they continue to work in the godly the opposite of justification. Where there is a lack of joy and freedom, there is the weakness of faith. Luther writes, "The more there is faith, the more there is joy and freedom; the less there is faith, the less there is joy."[172] Because our faith is feeble, and our understanding limited, we suffer "the murmuring of reason and voice of the conscience"[173] against the glad tiding that in Christ, we are God's beloved children. We are constricted by our sinful nature to embrace such "an inestimable gift" (2 Cor 9:15) of salvation. To banish this murmuring and constriction, we should not consider the gravity of our sins or our un-worthiness that lead us into sheer despair. Instead, we should consider the greatness of God's love, which gives up his Son for us, and through which our hearts are filled with joy and gratitude. As faith gradually increases by the word, the murmuring inevitably decreases. Faith, generated by prom-ise, triumphs over the temptation that might cause a believer to forsake God, and in those who boast about God's triumphant grace. The conscious-ness of heinous sins does not conquer but is conquered by the annihilating power of God's promise that we grasp by faith.

Our consciences perpetuate in doubt, Calvin also notes, as they follow the dictates of the "natural sense."[174] For Calvin, where there is no certainty that we are God's sons as surely as is Christ, faith is absent as surely as is the Spirit. "For where the pledge of the divine love towards us is wanting," he affirms, "there is assuredly no faith."[175] We, Calvin avers, feel the justifying action of the Holy Spirit "drawing us to God."[176] However, the certainty of such experience lies not in human subjectivity or feelings, but in Christ's redemptive work, which the Spirit applies to our heart. By the Spirit, we are certain of the Father's acceptance of us in his Son, though we are anxious about our ability to persevere, to remain in Christ till the end. As Bray

171. *LW* 26:215; *WA* 40.1:346.

172. *LW* 75:390; *WA* 10.1.1:368.

173. *LW* 10:99.

174. *Comm. Gal.* 4:6, in *CNTC* 11:75.

175. *Comm. Gal.* 4:6, in *CNTC* 11:75.

176. *SG*, 200–1.

writes, "The proof of [sonship] is the presence of the Holy Spirit in our hearts. The Holy Spirit makes our adoption effective and allows us to claim the promises made to Abraham and fulfilled in Christ."[177] Under the dominion of the Spirit, nothing, not even our residual pollution and demerits, could deter us from appropriating the fruits of justification wrought by Christ. Calvin avers, "As for ourselves, we can serve God freely and boldly, even when the conscience accuses us and we know that we are full of sin."[178] This is possible not on the basis of our merits but purely of God's mercy.

With Augustine, Calvin affirms the Holy Spirit assists believers to act. He quotes Augustine in his *Institutes*, saying:

> "You will say to me, 'Therefore we are acted upon and do not act ourselves.' Yes, you act and are acted upon. And if you are acted upon by one who is good, then you act well. The Spirit of God who acts upon you is the helper of those who act. The name 'helper' indicates that you also do something."[179]

Because the Holy Spirit acts upon us, we are enabled to act in accordance with God's will. Human agency is not removed from agency of the Holy Spirit. From the word "help," Calvin infers that God's action and human action coincide; we "also do something" when God acts.[180] He quotes Augustine favorably: "To will is of nature, but to will aright is of grace."[181] By the Holy Spirit, the will can then be rightly disposed to God.

To be a Spirit-filled Christian for both Reformers is to bid farewell to the lordship of self and come under the lordship of Christ. In light of this, Evans argues that Calvin was a theologian of the Spirit, who "bids reason give way to, submit and subject to, the Holy Spirit so that the man himself may no longer live but hear Christ living and reigning within him (Gal. 2:20)."[182] As evidence, Evans quotes Calvin:

> We are not our own: let not our reason nor our will, therefore, sway our plans and deeds. We are not our own: let us therefore not set it as our goal to seek what is expedient for us according to

177. Bray, *Galatians*, 132.

178. *SG*, 201.

179. Augustine, *Sermons*, clvi. 11:11 (PL 38:855f.; tr. LF 2:769), as cited in *Inst.* 2.5.14n29.

180. *Inst.* 2.5.14.

181. Augustine, *Sermons*, clvi. 9:9; 11:11–12 (PL 38:855f.; tr. LF 2:769), as cited in *Inst.* 2.5.14n29.

182. *Inst.* 3.7.1; also cited in Evans, "John Calvin," 99.

the flesh. We are not our own: in so far as we can, let us therefore forget ourselves and all that is ours.

Conversely, we are God's: let us therefore live for him and die for him. We are God's: let his wisdom and will therefore rule all our actions. We are God's: let all the parts of our life accordingly strive toward him as our only lawful goal.[183]

Similarly, to live a Spirit-filled life, for Luther, is to live a "Christ-life," a life in which Christ lives and reigns in us, not a self-life that stands by itself and lives in itself. In this, Luther could also be labeled a theologian of the Spirit; in his words:

"I am not living as Paul now, for Paul is dead." Who then is living? "The Christian." Paul, living in himself is utterly dead through the law but living in Christ, or rather with Christ living in him, he lives an alien life. Christ is speaking, acting, and performing all actions in him; these belong not to the Paul-life, but to the Christ-life. "You malicious person, do not slander me for saying that I am dead. . . . This death acquires an alien life for me, namely, the life of Christ, which is not inborn in me but is granted to me in faith through Christ."[184]

183. *Inst.* 3.7.1; also cited in Evans, "John Calvin," 99.
184. *LW* 26:170; WA 40.1:287.

6

DISCONTINUITY WITH THE OLD I

"No Longer I . . . but Christ"

GALATIANS 2:20, "It is no longer I who live but Christ lives in me," affords Luther and Calvin the occasion to articulate the believer's existential situation before conversion and after it; in Luther's terms, the former is "Paul-life," the latter "Christ-life."[1] Having been apprehended by the gospel, Augustine once wrote, "For where I am not I, I am more happily I."[2] Not the self that lives by his own life but "the Christ who lives" in him by faith constitutes the core of his identity. The language of dying and rising is encapsulated in the Pauline antithesis of "no longer I but Christ," which sets the stage for the Reformers' discussion of the meaning of being "a new creation" (Gal 6:15). A new form of existence emerges out of our relation to Christ. The fallen I in Paul is set opposite the restored I in Christ. The old I in us no longer lives, for it has died; the new I in Christ lives, for it has been raised up. Sin that results in the loss of salvation is conquered by Christ's righteousness, which confers on us his eternal life. Linebaugh is right to identify two movements: "The movement from the state of creation to the state of fall is the movement from life to death; the movement from sin to salvation, conversely, is a movement from death to life. Within and across these ruptures, salvation is as radical as death and

---

1. *LW* 26:170; WA 40.1:287.

2. Augustine, *On Continence*, Patrologia Latina 44, edited by J. P. Migne (Paris: Garnier, n.d.), 865–66 (29), as cited in Allen, *Justification and the Gospel*, 104n7; and in Linebaugh, "Speech of the Dead," 87.

resurrection."[3] The language of dying and rising in Christ undergirds salvation as a "radical discontinuity"[4] with the old creature to whom we die in exchange for "the recreation"[5] or "reconstitution"[6] of the new creature who now lives to God. The identity of true humanity is not a by-product of human actions but of Christ's redemptive action on the cross, through which we are delivered from the "present evil age" (Gal 1:4) and translated into the kingdom of God's Son. Christ lives in us, imparting his power to us so that the power of nothingness—the world and all its vices—loses its grip on us. It is only through the death of the old self that we begin to live the Christ-life in us. The alien life to which we are appointed is a life lived not in ourselves but in Christ, not from external duties or forms of piety but from Christ. All contraries—sin, death, curse, and hell—die through the Christ who lives in us, communicating to us the fruits of redemption through which we are recreated. The Christ whom faith grasps creates our existence anew; we are no longer enslaved by the sinful flesh but are instead enlivened by the life of God. The gospel is hidden in the paradoxical tension between the two poles: negatively, the passing away of the old self, and positively, the coming to life of the new self. The identity of the justified I is shaped by the cruciform life, where the old Adam undergoes death and is not permitted free rein, and the new person undergoes resurrection and lives again in holiness and righteousness. Self-obsession means we are dead to God; conversely, by dying to it, we are alive to God.

Dead to the Law and Alive to God: The World and I Crucified

Commenting on Gal 2:19, "For I through the law died to the law, that I might live to God," Luther regards the apostle's opposition of "the Law to the Law" as "the most delicious language."[7] Here he observes a distinction between the law of the Decalogue, which holds us in bondage, and the law

---

3. Linebaugh, "Speech of the Dead," 87. Though Linebaugh attributes this double movement to Luther, in my view, it is also in Calvin.

4. Chester, *Reading Paul with Reformers*, 192n52. He quotes Hampson, *Christian Contradictions*, 101, where the word "discontinuity" occurs.

5. Chester, *Reading Paul with Reformers*, 192n52, where the word "recreation" is his.

6. Barclay, *Paul and the Gift*, 568, where he uses the phrase "the reconstitution of an individual self."

7. *LW* 26:155; *WA* 40.1:267.

of "grace and freedom" that liberates us from it.[8] The marvel of the gospel lies in this opposition, that the enlivening law of grace kills the damning law of Moses so that we may be placed outside its condemnation and under Christ's righteousness. Luther presents this as a paradox: "Thus death killed death, but this death which kills death is life itself. But it is called the death of death, by an exuberant indignation of the spirit against death. So also righteousness takes the name 'sin,' because it damns sin; and this damning sin is true righteousness."[9] Just as the law of grace swallows up the annihilating law of Moses, so his righteousness truly conquers our sins. The godly will reap significant comfort from this verse, "I through the law died to the law," knowing that she through the grace of Christ is freed from law's curse and lives to God. Grace bound the law that once bound us and frees us from its bondage.[10] The law of grace that saves is opposed to the law that condemns; the former triumphs over the latter. "Thus death, which bound me, is now bound itself; death, which killed me, is now killed itself through death, that is, through life itself."[11]

Justification consists negatively in dying to the law and positively in living to God. The false teachers taught that unless we live to the law, we are dead in God's sight. However, Paul stated the contrary: unless we are dead to the law, we will not live to God. To live to Christ means to be placed "under another Law, namely the Law of grace, which rules over sin and the Law."[12] To die to the law means to refuse to come under its dominion; to live to God means to come under his lordship. The two are opposites: "To live to the Law is to die to God and that to die to the Law is to live to God."[13] Those who attempt to justify themselves through the law use it improperly; they fall under the curse of the law. Through Christ's victory, the godly are liberated from the law and are placed above it. In this sense, "the godly is dead to the Law as he is dead to sin, the devil, death, and hell, all of which still remain, and all of which the world and the wicked will inherit."[14] The law dies when the godly dies to it and lives to God. Both I and the negative force of the law are nothing: "But because I die to [the Law], it also dies to

8. *LW* 26:156; WA 40.1:267.
9. *LW* 26:156; WA 40.1:267.
10. *LW* 26:161; WA 40.1:276.
11. *LW* 26:163; WA 40.1:278.
12. *LW* 26:158; WA 40.1:271.
13. *LW* 26:159; WA 40.1:271.
14. *LW* 26:157; WA 40.1:268.

me."[15] This is because the I has undergone crucifixion with Christ and is buried in him.

The law is good, yet there is nothing in it that would give rise to new life. Calvin writes, "Quite the opposite: it rejects me, it turns me away, it banishes me from the kingdom of heaven."[16] The law "through which we die to the law" is life-annihilating and casts us into hell; the gospel through which we die with Christ is life-animating and raises us to heaven. Calvin writes:

> In the law, there will always the kind of death that leaves us in the depths of hell, but the death spoken of in the gospel imparts life. How is this so? Well, we are crucified with Jesus Christ so that we may live to God. This means that our old man . . . or what we are by nature, is expelled little by little. . . . Yet, though the progress may be slow, we can be sure that the Lord Jesus Christ is putting to death all that is worldly and fleshly in us, because we are no longer given over to this world. . . . [Crucifixion] does involve dying, but this death will bring us life—unlike the death we experience under the sentence of the law.[17]

Christ's death and resurrection are integral to the reconstitution of the human person. Christ buries the law and its negative function and conquers them through his resurrection. Both the law and the grave are emptied of their destructive power over the I who is liberated through Christ's death and resurrection. In Luther's words:

> Just as the grave in which Christ lay dead opened and was seen to be empty after He had risen, and Christ disappeared, so when I believe in Christ, I rise with Him and die to my grave, that is, to the Law that held me captive. Hence the Law is now empty; and I have escaped from my prison and grave, that is, from the law. Therefore the Law has no further right to accuse or to hold me, for I have risen again.[18]

Justification occurs when the "accusing and damning Law" of Moses dies so that we may rise with Christ through the "Law of grace."[19] "Flesh," that which lives by itself, is ineffectual in dealing with the sin that damns

15. *LW* 26:159; WA 40.1:271.
16. *SG*, 195.
17. *SG*, 199.
18. *LW* 26:158; WA 40.1:270.
19. *LW* 26:158; WA 40.1:271.

us; Christ's flesh is "omnipotent,"[20] capable of removing sin, which otherwise would have devoured us. Sin is laid upon Christ's flesh; it is slain by Christ the crucified—as Paul wrote, Christ "for our sake was made to be sin, so that in Him we might become the righteousness of God" (2 Cor 5:21). Luther writes, "Thus in my flesh I find a death that afflicts and kills me; but I also have a contrary death, which is the death of my death and which crucified and devours my death."[21] Christians undergo two deaths: the death we die "in my flesh" slaughters us, and the "contrary death"—in Luther's words, "the death of my death"—enlivens us.[22] This contrary death becomes the basis of self-constitution: I am no longer I, not through death in my own flesh, which is of no avail, but rather through the death of "the flesh of Christ,"[23] which has the power to annihilate the law and sin and other vices. Christ assumed our sin and entered our death in order that his righteousness and life might be ours by faith. Luther avers:

> All these things happen, not through the Law or works but through Christ the crucified, on whose shoulders lie all the evils of the human race—the Law, sin, death, the devil, and hell—all of which die in Him, because by His death He kills them. But we must accept this blessing of Christ with a firm faith. For just as what is offered to us is neither the Law nor any of its works but Christ alone, so that what is required of us is nothing but faith, which takes hold of Christ and believes that my sin and death are damned and abolished in the sin and death of Christ.[24]

Luther continues, "For by the very fact that He permitted the Law to accuse Him, sin to damn Him, and death to devour Him He abrogated the Law, damned sin, destroyed death and justified and saved."[25] By faith in Christ, these contraries—law, sin, death, and all evils—are extinguished and no longer harm us. The autonomous self and all its vices are crucified through Christ's death so that we now live to God. Thus, Paul could exult "Nevertheless, I live" (Gal 2:20). Luther writes:

> Therefore the crucifixion and death by which I am crucified and die to the Law, sin, death, and all evils is resurrection and life to

20. *LW* 26:159; WA 40.1:272.
21. *LW* 26:160; WA 40.1:273.
22. *LW* 26:160; WA 40.1:273.
23. *LW* 26:159; WA 40.1:273.
24. *LW* 26:160; WA 40.1:273.
25. *LW* 26:164; WA 40.1:280.

me. For Christ crucifies the devil, kills death, damns sin, and binds the Law. As one who believes this, I am liberated from the Law, etc. Therefore the Law is deaf, bound, dead, and crucified to it. Thus I live by this very death and crucifixion, that is, by this grace and liberty.[26]

The law remains still in force and performs its negative function in the world. Only believers in Christ inherit the blessing of being crucified and dead to these monsters of life and have the glory of living to God. To live to the law is to live in bondage to it, from which we cannot break free. The law has no power to create anew; it threatens us with destruction, the opposite of life. It causes us, says Calvin, "to die to itself"; it leads us to despair of itself so that we will not place our trust in it.[27] With Luther, Calvin writes, "The law bears within itself the curse which slays us."[28] The death imposed by the law is "truly deadly." Opposite this death, Calvin continues, is "death, in the life-giving fellowship of the cross of Christ."[29] Calvin argues the punctuation of this verse—"I through the law am dead to the law, that I may live to God"—"obscures its meaning." He proposes that the context affords a smooth reading of this, thus: "That I might live to God I am crucified with Christ." This rendering means it is by being nailed to the cross along with Christ that we live to God.[30] "To live to God" means more than to abide by his will, but rather to live "the life of God." This reading, Calvin argues, coincides with the antithesis: "For whatever sense we are said to die to sin, in the same sense we live to God."[31] It is by living the autonomous self that we are dead to God; in Calvin's phrase, "like the rotten, corrupt corpses."[32] Conversely, it is by dying to it that we live to God. This death we participate in with Christ, says Calvin, is "the origin of a better life. For God rescues us from the shipwreck of the law and by His grace restores us to eternal life."[33] Through union with Christ's death, we are freed from the

26. *LW* 26:165; WA 40.1:281.
27. *Comm. Gal.* 2:19, in *CNTC* 11:41.
28. *Comm. Gal.* 2:19, in *CNTC* 11:42.
29. *Comm. Gal.* 2:19, in *CNTC* 11:42.
30. *Comm. Gal.* 2:19, in *CNTC* 11:42.
31. *Comm. Gal.* 2:19, in *CNTC* 11:42.
32. *SG*, 199.
33. *Comm. Gal.* 2:19, in *CNTC* 11:42.

bondage of the law; we draw from him life and power, as the shoot draws its vitality from its root.[34]

The cross of Christ does the opposite of what the world does. Whatever the world approves of, the cross condemns; as Paul says, "For it is written, 'I will destroy the wisdom of the wise, and the cleverness of the clever I will thwart'" (1 Cor 1:19). The new identity acquired in Christ represents an exhaustive break with "the world" and the creaturely things that claim our allegiance. As Paul said, "The world has been crucified to me; I to the world" (Gal 6:14). Calvin contrasts the world "to regeneration, as nature to grace or the flesh to the Spirit."[35] The world is set opposite the new creature so that those who die to the world are saved and live to God. The world denotes anything that is hostile to Christ's kingdom, as it falls under the domain of the old creature. Calvin writes, "The world is as it were the object and aim of the old man."[36] The old man must be buried with Christ in order that he might despise the world. Both the world and flesh are rendered as nothing, as Calvin says, "because nothingness belongs to the dead."[37] Neither Paul nor the world affect each other, as both are dead. Things Paul formerly reckoned precious he now considers them repugnant and thus an abomination to God (Phil 3:8). Creaturely righteousness and wisdom do not move us, as they are no valid basis of our assurance. Christ has crucified the flesh and its fruits, and all the things of the world pale in their significance. The flesh and the world as concomitants are dead to the believer through Christ's cross; of this, Luther writes:

> The world, not Christ, lives in men; that the world has the flesh flourishing with its vices and dominating in its sins; that with the apostle it has no taste for the things that are above but glories in having abundance in this life and in acquiring riches and putting its hope in man. Accordingly, Paul does not do, or have a taste for, the things that please the world; nor does the world do, or have a taste for, the things that please Paul. To the one the other is dead, crucified, despised, and detested.[38]

---

34. *Comm. Gal.* 2:19, in *CNTC* 11:42.
35. *Comm. Gal.* 1:4, in *CNTC* 11:12.
36. *Comm. Gal.* 6:14, in *CNTC* 11:117.
37. *Comm. Gal.* 6:14, in *CNTC* 11:117.
38. *LW* 27:405; *WA* 2:614.

Flesh and Spirit in Opposition:
The Old and New Natures

The "spirit" refers to "the renewed nature or the grace of regeneration."[39] The "flesh" is equivalent to the "old man," whose "whole nature" is hostile to God.[40] As support, Calvin quotes Rom 8:7, "All the thoughts of the flesh are enmity against God."[41] The "old man" of Rom 6:6 is a reference to the "person," Luther contends, "not according to his [created] nature but according to the defect of his nature."[42] It describes the self as "curved in on itself."[43] The old man, Calvin avers, is "incapable of receiving the kingdom of God" unless it is slain by the cross of Christ and renewed into true life.[44] He continues, "The 'old' man . . . begins to be old when his regeneration is begun, and his old nature is gradually put to death."[45] The world is opposed to God, as is the old man. Calvin writes, "The world is as it were the object and aim of the old man."[46] The old Adam, says Luther, must "be brought low by the cross in order to be annihilated all the more."[47] Nailed to the cross, the flesh is not allowed free rein over us; it must give way to the Spirit. Sanctification for Calvin consists in this: "The death of the flesh is the life of the Spirit."[48] No correspondence occurs between the lust of the old self and the righteousness of the new self, he continues, just as fire and water do not mix.[49] The depraved nature of the old is opposed to the new life of Spirit. The opposition of flesh and spirit impedes us to do whatever we will; as Paul says in Rom 7:14, "But I am carnal, sold under sin. The good that I want I do not do. The evil that I do not want, this I do." No remnant of goodness is found in free will, which may cause us to turn toward God. The old nature is inclined toward evil; neither does it feel any conflict with its depraved lusts nor possess any true desire for godliness. The cognition

39. *Comm. Gal.* 5:17, in *CNTC* 11:102.
40. *Comm. Gal.* 5:17, in *CNTC* 11:103.
41. *Comm. Gal.* 5:17, in *CNTC* 11:102; *Comm. Rom.* 8:7, in *CNTC* 8:162.
42. *LW* 25:313; WA 56:325.
43. *LW* 25:291; WA 56:305.
44. *Comm. Rom.* 6:6, in *CNTC* 8:125.
45. *Comm. Rom.* 6:6, in *CNTC* 8:124–25.
46. *Comm. Gal.* 6:14, in *CNTC* 11:117.
47. *LW* 31:55.
48. *Comm. Gal.* 5:25, in *CNTC* 11:106.
49. *Comm. Gal.* 5:17, in *CNTC* 11:102.

of the conquest between the old life and new life is a sign of a life already seized by faith. The Christian's struggle, real as it is, is not one of despair and deprived of joy, since God's grace reigns, not sin. Sin remains after faith but no longer "dominates" us; as Luther says, "The Spirit . . . dominates them so that they do not rule."[50] Mannermaa writes appropriately, "It is true that in faith these [carnal desires] no longer dominate; however, they do not die, either, but are still there, smoldering."[51] Luther describes the believer's two modes of existence, placing the Spirit above our flesh, and righteousness above sin: "the Spirit rules and the flesh is subordinate, . . . righteousness is supreme and sin is a servant."[52] The believer "feels" the lust of the flesh but does not "follow" or "gratify" it.[53] The battle with the flesh is not fatal but salutary, as it causes us to draw nigh to Christ for aid. This is borne out in Luther's commentary on Gal 5:17, where he writes:

> For when his flesh impels him to sin, [the believer] is aroused and incited to seek forgiveness of sins through Christ and to embrace the righteousness of faith, which he would otherwise not have regarded as so important or yearned for with such intensity. . . . Through such an opportunity a Christian becomes a skillful artisan and a wonderful creator, who can make joy out of sadness, comfort out of terror, righteousness out of sin, and life out of death, when he restrains his flesh for this purpose, brings it into submission, and subjects it to the Spirit.[54]

Though believers still suffer under the assaults of the flesh, they are no longer under its enslavement. Having been granted liberty in Christ, they are no longer the subjects or slaves of the flesh but of the Spirit, endowed with a new inclination toward God. Calvin writes, "Not that the flesh is entirely destroyed, but it ought not to exercise dominion but should yield to the Spirit."[55] By the agency of the Spirit of regeneration (Gal 5:25), the renewed self strives to resist the works of the flesh. "When once we have tasted the inestimable love of our God, and known the Lord Jesus Christ," Calvin writes, "we become so affected by the Holy Spirit that we condemn evil and

---

50. *LW* 26:189; WA 40.1:312.

51. Mannermaa, *Christ Present in Faith*, 70.

52. *LW* 27:74; WA 40.2:93.

53. *LW* 27:81; WA 40.2:102; *LW* 27:70; WA 40.2:88; also quoted in Mannermaa, *Christ Present in Faith*, 69.

54. *LW* 27:74; WA 40.2:93.

55. *Comm. Gal.* 6:24, in *CNTC* 11:106.

seek to draw nearer to God in conformity to God's will."[56] Where the Spirit does not reign over us, our actions remain self-generated and cannot bear worthy fruits. On Gal 5:26, "If we live by the Spirit, let us also walk in the Spirit," Calvin explains that the Spirit of God is "not idle" and "his presence will reveal itself" in our actions.[57] While "life" refers to "inward power," for Calvin, "walk" refers to "outward actions."[58] Walking in newness of life is living proof of the Spirit's presence in our lives. "The reason why [Paul] is crucified to the world and the world to him," Calvin stresses, "is that, in Christ, in whom he is engrafted, only a new creature is of any avail."[59] The new I acquired in Christ has lost interest in what pleases the world; conversely, the world shows no interest in what pleases the new creature. The new creature "in Christ" is made alive to God and renewed by the Spirit, no longer living to herself or the world. Calvin stresses, "Everything else must be discarded, nay, perish."[60] Everything of this world, including the law, sin, the devil, and death, is made nothing, and increasingly so, as they perish under the crushing power of the cross. These enemies of life—law, sin, and death— become "shadows" and no longer terrorize justified saints in Christ, as they now live by the life of Christ, which dominates the life of the flesh, and by the righteousness of faith, which reigns over the lust of the flesh; as Calvin says, "The truth of the Gospel swallows up and negatives all the shadows of the law."[61] As a result, the renewed person can serve God with freedom and joy, knowing that she has found plenary acceptance with God, despite her unworthiness. God's acceptance of our obedience is not grounded in our own merits, but solely on his abundant mercy. Calvin writes, "He shows himself to be so bountiful and kind to us by accepting what we do as if it were fully pleasing to him, although there is no inherent merit or worth in our works at all."[62]

Salvation is accomplished by the perpetual death of the self through faith in Christ; it is not by a gradual forming into Christ's likeness by means of infused grace. Hampson captures Luther's point: "There is no linear progress from being a sinner to being justified. It is not that that which is

56. *SG*, 198.

57. *SG*, 561.

58. *Comm. Gal.* 6:25, in *CNTC* 11:106.

59. *Comm. Gal.* 6:14, in *CNTC* 11:118.

60. *Comm. Gal.* 6:14, in *CNTC* 11:118.

61. *Comm. Gal.* 6:15, in *CNTC* 11:118.

62. *SG*, 202.

given in creation is transformed through grace. It is only through a discontinuity, through repentance and failure, that in response to the good news of the gospel the human being can come to gain a sense of himself through trusting not in himself but in God."[63] Those who are justified by faith are righteous, though they remain sinners. Luther describes the poignant simultaneity of saint and sinner (*simul Justus et peccator*) that is our status:

> Everyone who believes in Christ is righteous, not yet fully in point of fact, but in hope. For he has begun to be justified and healed, like the man who was half-dead (Lk. 10:30). Meanwhile, however, while he is being justified and healed, the sin that is left in his flesh is not imputed to him. This is because Christ, who is entirely without sin, has now become one with His Christian and intercedes for him with the Father.[64]

Those who cling to their worth or merits, Trueman writes, are "outwardly righteous," but "inwardly foul or obnoxious to God"; they are "*simul Justus* (outward) *et peccator* (inward). The Christian, however, is *simul Justus* (inwardly) precisely because of being *peccator* in his or her eyes, . . . and in the eyes of the world."[65] The tension between the righteous identity of the new I and her sinful actions of the old I abides in the Christian life. "The return to a person's true self," Kolb writes, is made possible by a "life driven by fear, love, and trust in God above all that he has created."[66] The recreation of the Christian occurs through, to use Forde's phrase, "the reversal of direction"[67] in trust: from self to Christ, from works of the law to the grace of Christ. Law, sin, and human works must be removed from us, and Christ, righteousness, and faith in Christ implanted.[68] The Christian abandons the former I in exchange for a life in another—namely, Christ's life. We live the life of God, not by a righteousness of our own that we do not have, but rather by the alien righteousness of Christ, "that righteousness by which Christ lives in us."

> Therefore when it is necessary to discuss Christian righteousness, the person must be completely rejected. For if I pay attention to the person or speak of the person, then, whether intentionally or

---

63. Hampson, *Christian Contradictions*, 101.
64. *LW* 27:227; WA 2:495. For further discussion, see Kolb et al., *Simul*.
65. Trueman, "*Simul peccator et justus*," 83.
66. See Kolb, *Luther's Treatise*, 59.
67. Forde, "Luther's Theology of Cross," 49.
68. *LW* 26:168; WA 40.1:283.

unintentionally on my part, the person becomes a doer of works who is subject to the Law. But here Christ and my conscience must become one body, so that nothing remains in my sight but Christ, crucified and risen . . . By paying attention to myself . . . I lose sight of Christ, who alone is my righteousness and life.[69]

In justification, Paul neither pays attention to "[his] own person or substance," signified by the "yet not I," nor separates himself from Christ, for faith unites Christ and us as "one person."[70] Where our person is severed from Christ, Luther avers, we fall back into the law and live in ourselves.[71] As a result, we incur God's judgment and damnation by the law. Paul-life is dead; Christ-life lives. The shift from the former to the latter has occurred in Christ to whom we are united. But where our person is joined to Christ, the apostle can extol the joy of being found in him and living an "alien life" of Christ in exchange for our "natural or animate" life. Luther elaborates:

> "I am not living as Paul now, for Paul is dead." Who then is living? "The Christian." Paul, living in himself, is utterly dead through the Law but living in Christ, or rather with Christ living in him, he lives an alien life. Christ is speaking, acting, and performing all actions in him; these belong not to the Paul-life, but to the Christ-life . . . "By my own life I am not living, for if I were, the Law would have dominion over me and hold me captive. To keep it from holding me, I am dead to it by another Law. And this death acquires an alien life for me, namely, the life of Christ, which is not inborn in me but is granted to me in faith through Christ."[72]

For Paul, life is located not in his own person but in Christ. To look only at ourselves, our own condition and achievement is to lose sight of Christ, our sole righteousness. Paul must abandon his Paul-life, for to remain in it is despair and death. He must abandon himself and every creaturely thing, including the law, that causes him to be self-focused, and embrace the Christ-life, which is hope and life. He draws from union with Christ the power to live an alien life, a life lived outside himself and in Christ. Self-preoccupation is the fruit of the fallen I. The recreation of our person, Luther writes, occurs by "leaving ourselves behind," including all

69. *LW* 26:166; WA 40.1:282.
70. *LW* 26:168; WA 40.1:285.
71. *LW* 26:168; WA 40.1:285.
72. *LW* 26:170; WA 40.1:281.

that might divert our attention from Christ and his benefits.[73] To borrow Jüngel's phrase, "self-forgetfulness" is how one may attain a "yet not I" life.[74] Chester expresses it aptly: "The Christian must come out of him- or herself in order to come to him- or herself."[75] Neither the world nor human piety is the center; Christ is. Barclay puts it well, writing that "the believer is reconstituted *relationally* by becoming, we might say, 're-centered' in Christ."[76] The Gospel re-centers us, steering us "away from ourselves," placing us "outside ourselves" and "in Christ" so that we yield all self-reliance and trust only in the promise of God.[77]

Galatians 2:20, "Therefore, whatever this life is that I now live in the flesh, I live by faith in the Son of God,"[78] points out the believer's two modes of living: in the flesh, and by faith in God's Son. The former is the condition, universal to all humans; the latter is the privilege, particular to believers. The life the new I lives is "in" the flesh. The life Paul lives in the flesh is no different from that of any other human being. The physical life is nurtured by things of this world such as physical food and clothing. The discontinuity between his own life and life in Christ may be open to dispute, as it is not always transparent or apparent before others.[79] Paul may appear the same as before his conversion, but the change is concealed in Christ. Luther summarizes, in brief, that "this life is not the life of the flesh, although it is a life in the flesh; but it is the life of Christ, the Son of God, whom the Christian possesses by faith."[80] The life Paul lives in his flesh, says Luther, is "not a true life but only a mask of life, under which there lives another, namely, Christ, who is truly my life."[81] The break with the mask (Paul's life) and the movement to true life (Christ's life) reflects the very source from which the converted Paul now lives, that is, either by his own flesh or by faith in Christ. A change has already occurred: pre-conversion, Paul spoke

---

73. *LW* 26:166; WA 40.1:287.

74. Jüngel, *Justification*, 243.

75. Chester, "No Longer I," 329.

76. Barclay, *Paul and the Gift*, 112.

77. *LW* 31:371; WA 7:69.

78. "Faith in the Son of God" is Luther's translation; "faith of God's Son" is Calvin's. As demonstrated before, the two are one. For our purpose, I will use the objective genitive "faith in God's Son."

79. See Chester, *Reading Paul with Reformers*, 192–93.

80. *LW* 26:172; WA 40.1:290.

81. *LW* 26:170; WA 40.1:288.

blasphemous words; post-conversion, he spoke spiritual words. In both instances, the instruments—voice and tongue—are the same, but the effect proceeds from a different source; activities such as his speaking "do not come from the flesh and do not originate there; they are given and revealed divinely from heaven."[82] The instrument of the flesh becomes the instrument of God's power. Hearing God's voice, for example, does not originate "from" the flesh; it is "in" the flesh but "from" God.[83] Commenting on the phrase "I live by faith in the Son of God," Luther links Christ and the Spirit to speak of the source from which the action emerges; "it is," he writes, "in and from the Holy Spirit."[84] To rephrase, to live by faith in the Son is to live the Christ-life by the Spirit.

The paradox here consists in the fact that the life the Christian lives in his flesh is not his but God's, as Calvin acknowledges.[85] The Christian, Calvin continues, "bids reason give way to, submit and subject [himself] to, the Holy Spirit so that the man himself may no longer live but hear Christ living and reigning within him."[86] We who are crucified with Christ, says Calvin, do not live by our own resources, which we do not have, but by the "secret energy"[87] of the Christ who lives in us. Calvin speaks of the "true and genuine communication" of Christ's life to the sinners who "live outside themselves (*fideles extra se vivere*) . . . [and] in Christ."[88] The transference of gifts occurs in Christ, not apart from him. We live not by ourselves but by the twofold benefits—regeneration and justification—of union with Christ.[89] Union with Christ confers on us the blessing of the gospel, which conquers the oppression of the law. The more Christ's life is imparted to us, the more we are made alive and grow in him. We do not turn inward for soteriological resources to constitute ourselves, for there are none in us; rather, we are to turn outward to Christ, who, Calvin writes, is not "standing far off" but rather "dwelling in us," communicating the benefits he has acquired for us.[90] Thus, Calvin asserts, "we are not to separate Christ from

---

82. *LW* 26:171; *WA* 40.1:290.

83. *LW* 26:171; *WA* 40.1:290.

84. *LW* 26:171; *WA* 40.1:289.

85. *Comm. Gal.* 2:20, in *CNTC* 11:43.

86. *Inst.* 3.7.1.

87. *Comm. Gal.* 2:19, in *CNTC* 11:42.

88. *Comm. Gal.* 2:20, in *CNTC* 11:42–43.

89. *Comm. Gal.* 2:20, in *CNTC* 11:42–43.

90. *Inst.* 3.2.24.

ourselves or ourselves from him. Rather, we ought to hold fast bravely with both arms to that fellowship by which he has bound himself to us."[91]

Believers, through the "secret union" with Christ, as members united to their head, already possess all heavenly blessings.[92] This heavenly life of Christ, Calvin avers, is a "secret hidden" from human senses but revealed to the eyes of faith. He continues, "The life therefore we obtain by faith is not visible to the eye, but is inwardly perceived in the conscience in the power of the Spirit."[93] By faith, we possess all of Christ's benefits now, as if we dwell in heaven. As support, Calvin quotes Paul, who writes that "our citizenship is in heaven" (Phil 3:20), and that God "has made us sit together in heavenly places in Christ" (Eph 2:6).[94] We know for sure that we already possess everything we hope for, not on account of "chance," but on account of "the pledge and guarantee of our inheritance in the Lord Christ."[95] Likewise, for Luther, believers who are united to Christ as one person grasp in this life only a tiny portion of the immeasurable inheritance that is yet to come at the end. Luther explains, "He does not see that revealed but it is kept for him in faith, for this life could not bear the revelation of such blessings."[96] Neither is our righteousness "visible" nor "conscious"; "the hoped-for righteousness" awaits its full revelation in due course.[97] The certainty of faith is not furnished by the law, which condemns us for the sins it reveals and causes us to wallow in despair; rather, it is grounded in "the promise," which arouses in us the "feeling of hope" that Christ is indeed our "perfect and eternal righteousness."[98] We now "through the Spirit wait for the hope of righteousness" (Gal 5:5), though this gift is not perceptible by the physical eyes.

---

91. *Inst.* 3.2.24.
92. *Comm. John* 5:24, in *CNTC* 4:129.
93. *Comm. Gal.* 2:20, in *CNTC* 11:43.
94. *Comm. Gal.* 2:20, in *CNTC* 11:43.
95. *SG*, 218.
96. *LW* 75:395; *WA* 40.1.1:377.
97. *LW* 27:21; *WA* 40.2:25.
98. *LW* 27:21; *WA* 40.2:25.

The Pronoun "Me":
Applying It to the Self

Luther's and Calvin's theologies are about God's ways with us, so they particularly focus on the "for us" (*pro nobis*) aspects of Christ's person. "The '*pro me*,'" Ebeling notes, "the sign of the love of the crucified Christ," applies to those who are what they are, that is, sinners terrified by the law. He continues, "By virtue of the love in which the Son of God sacrificed himself, those for whom this took place are already included."[99] The cross was not merely an event of the past, which has no bearing upon the present. Rather, it happened "for us," as an event that draws us into the fatherly love of the Son, from whom we derive the efficacy of faith. Elert writes, "The hearer who is really a hearer hears the Gospel as meant for him."[100] The sophists teach otherwise, that human beings are endowed with the natural ability to love God above all else and earn a congruent merit as a result.[101] In so doing, Luther argues, they have inverted the meaning of Paul's words ("He loved me and gave himself for me") and thus subverted the gospel.[102] Those who brag about their performance would never say "Christ was given for me." While they hold that we draw God to us by our love, or "by doing what lies within us,"[103] the Reformers hold that God draws us by his love, causing him to give himself for us. The antithesis between the corrupted I full of vices and the consoling "Christ" full of love reflects the distinction between death, the fruit of sin, and life, the gift of grace. The fallen I boasts of a person's natural ability: It was I who loved God and gave myself for him, resulting in damnation. However, the gospel declares God's salvific action: It was "Christ" who "loved me and gave Himself for us," offering me salvation. "For to preach the Gospel," says Luther, "is nothing else than Christ's coming to us or bringing us to Him."[104] The Christian applies to himself all that Christ has accomplished for him; as Elert puts it, "Without the application to the 'I' there can be no evangelical faith."[105] The renewed I acknowledges that it is I, the miserable and damnable sinner, unworthy in himself, who is

---

99. Ebeling, *Truth of the Gospel*, 145.

100. Elert, *Structure of Lutheranism*, 68.

101. *LW* 26:172; *WA* 40.1:291. The medieval phrase "merit of congruity" occurs.

102. *LW* 26:172; *WA* 40.1:291.

103. *LW* 31:10, 50.

104. *WA* 10 1.1:14, 22, as quoted in Elert, *Structure of Lutheranism*, 68.

105. Elert, *Structure of Lutheranism*, 69.

deemed the object of the love of the cross. Cary writes, "The grammar itself ['for me'] illustrates how Luther's faith is about being the *object* of divine forgiveness and grace, the one whom God loves and addresses and justifies, rather than the *subject* of faith, the one who believes."[106] Assurance of faith rests on the strength of "Christ for us," that is, his grip on us rather than our grip on him.

The life we live is God's, Barclay notes, bestowed by "the incongruity of gift"; it is "a perfect gift," totally independent of any prior action or worth of the recipient.[107] The value formerly attached to circumcision ceases, since Christ has already fulfilled the promise of the covenant. The Papists substitute circumcision by external forms of piety, making them count as congruous merit before God. The Papists' error, Calvin argues, is no different from the Galatians'. To attribute salvation both to Christ and to human actions, as the Papists did, is to divide Christ so that he only achieves "half of salvation."[108] In so doing, they have corrupted the gospel and "not embraced Him in His wholeness."[109] Calvin declares, "Whoever wants to have a half-Christ loses the whole."[110] For Paul, such a half-Christ is inconceivable; as Hendriksen writes, "A supplemented Christ is a supplanted Christ."[111] The cross reduces to nothingness all worldly and fleshly things in us so that nothing, not even the tiniest drop of congruous merit, remains—nothing, that is, except Christ. As Paul declares in Gal 2:21, "If righteousness is through the law, then Christ died for nought."

No human preparations, no quality of our piety, even when wrought by the Holy Spirit, can produce the justified self. The new identity is a gift of grace, not a human achievement. The new I lives by these consoling words: the "whole" Christ is given "for me," through whom the old I dies. These words of God annihilate the old I in order that they might animate the new I. The entrapped, old self cannot free itself unless Christ works it in us. Christ is that gift, given to help us to live out his life in us. He is the dynamism of everything that is good in us. "Christ is speaking, acting, and performing all actions" in us.[112] In his commentary on Gal 4:19, "until

106. Cary, *Meaning of Protestant Theology*, 156.

107. Barclay, *Paul and the Gift*, 73.

108. *Comm. Gal.* 5:2, in *CNTC* 11:93.

109. *Comm. Gal.* 5:2, in *CNTC* 11:93.

110. *Comm. Gal.* 5:2, in *CNTC* 11:93.

111. Hendriksen, *Exposition of Galatians*, 112.

112. *LW* 26:170; *WA* 40.1:287.

Christ be formed in you," Luther describes how Christ's life is formed in us passively:

> Note Paul's careful choice of words. He does not say: "Until I form Christ in you" but "until He be formed," as he ascribes more to the grace of God than to his own works. . . . Neither did he say "until you are formed in Christ." No, his words are "until Christ be formed in you," because the Christian's life is not his own; it is Christ's, who lives in him.[113]

The passive sense of being formed heightens the fact that Christ is formed in our hearts purely by grace, like a child is formed in a mother's womb.[114] "Formless" means without anything of our own, either inherited or acquired, or any other creaturely things except "faith, the trust of the heart," says Luther, "the true form of Christ."[115] For Christ to be formed in us, we must strip away all other forms, including circumcision and other observances of the law, so that faith in Christ remains the only one. The "formless" heart, Luther intimates, is where "Christ can be formed and be alone" in it, just as an empty heart is where Christ would reside.[116] The old self must undergo destruction or formlessness under the law; it must, in Luther's phrase, "be destroyed and rendered formless"[117] so the heart is made ready for the construction of self and of Christ's formation within it.

On the same text, Calvin considers the word "form" as equivalent to "born": "For we are born that we may be new creatures in Him. And He, on the other hand, is born in us so that we may live His life."[118] In a passive sense, both births—Christ's in us and ours in him—are brought about by the word through the ministers whom God designed as the instruments for that purpose.[119] God's word is primarily oral, says Pelikan; it is "the speech of God."[120] In Luther's words, "In the case of God to speak is to do, and . . . the word [of God] is the deed."[121] For Calvin, as for Luther, God's word is God's action; it is creative, bringing about a reality that corresponds to

113. *LW* 27:308; WA 40.2:548.
114. *LW* 27:308; WA 40.2:548.
115. *LW* 26:430; WA 40.1:649.
116. *LW* 27:308; WA 40.2:548.
117. *LW* 27:308; WA 40.2:548.
118. *Comm. Gal.* 4:19, in *CNTC* 11:82.
119. *Comm. Gal.* 4:19, in *CNTC* 11:83.
120. Pelikan, *Luther the Expositor*, 50.
121. *LW* 12:33.

itself. Commenting on Rom 3:4, "But let God be true," Calvin expands, "He calls God true, not only because He is prepared to stand faithfully to His promises, but also because He also really fulfills whatever he declares; for he so speaks, that his command becomes a reality."[122] The word truly delivers what it says. Through the word, Paul labored painstakingly throughout the course of his ministry to form Christ in his people, not in himself; he suffered in travail to restore "the true image of Christ," which had suffered deformity through the false teachers who formed images other than Christ in the heart.[123] The goal of his ministry was to reverse their trust: from the false form, that of works of the law from which they were formerly delivered, to faith in Christ, the true form from which they have defected. The minister by himself cannot achieve anything, Calvin says, for "he is nothing and can do nothing but is a useless instrument."[124] But when the Holy Spirit is present, the ministry of preaching is fused with power and is effectual. Calvin writes, "He ascribes to them what is His, so joining the power of His Spirit to the activity of man."[125] With Calvin, Luther concurs: "For the Word proceeds from the mouth of the apostle and reaches the heart of the hearer; there the Holy Spirit is present and impresses that Word on the heart, so that it is heard."[126] Luther extols the Holy Spirit as the effective agent who causes the preached word to enter the human heart, allowing "the true form of Christ" to shine so brightly in the Galatians that they glory in God rather than in their flesh (Gal 6:13).[127]

The word of God by which the self is justified is precisely that by which it relinquishes itself and relies on the alien life of Christ. The word of God is creative, resulting in new realities corresponding to it; it is causative of the true image of Christ in us. Believers apply the words of the gospel ("he was given for me") individually to themselves and rests solely on the "whole" Christ as the basis and source of self-constitution. The sinful self has no means of deliverance except for the self-sacrificial love of God, the ground of Christ's death for sinners. Salvation is wholly accomplished in Christ, not in need of anything else. Hence, the new I acknowledges its total lack and seeks Christ alone as the remedy, without any conjunction. The self seized

---

122. *Comm. Rom.* 3:4, in CTS 19:116.

123. *Comm. Gal.* 4:19, in CNTC 11:83.

124. *Comm. Gal.* 4:19, in CNTC 11:83.

125. *Comm. Gal.* 4:19, in CNTC 11:83.

126. *LW* 26:430–31; WA 40.1:649.

127. *LW* 26:430; WA 40.1:649.

by the "whole" Christ finds its vitality and wholeness in the words "who loved me," from which we receive "the power of faith."[128] Calvin exhorts us to meditate on the efficacy of the death and passion of Christ to reap from it these salutary fruits for the recreation of the new I. He specifies four atoning fruits that nourish the true self:[129] Christ's "sacrifice" averts God's wrath, his "payment" erases our debts, his "obedience" rectifies our disobedience, and his "cleansing" removes all vices. These fruits flow from the word of the cross, not from any of our own exertions. Whoever transfers the fruits of the cross to human works, Calvin asserts, vitiates the cross of Christ.[130] As a result, the I remains trapped in the old I, separated from the source of self-constitution. To turn to the self for help where there is none is to sink into sheer despair from which there is no respite. It is to fall back to the old life of sin, wrath, and death, and to lose all goods brought about by the gospel.

To apply the pronoun "me" to the self is to renounce all forms of allegiance, move outside the self, and live in another. Luther's dogmatic statement about the identity of the justified person, the new I, is clearly stated in Luther's *The Freedom of the Christian* (1520). The Christian lives "not in himself, but in Christ and in his neighbor . . . By faith he is caught up beyond himself into God. By love, he descends beneath himself into his neighbor."[131] The christological phrase "in Christ Jesus" underscores the new relationship with God under which believers are placed, one that is no longer ruled by the old self. In this case, the relational rather than the localized nature of "in" is in view; it means "next to" or "in close relationship to" Christ. Hampson writes, "The Christian lives by something which is not at his or her disposal. That is, the Christian lives 'from' another reality. To be a Christian is to have faith, trusting in something beyond ourselves which we cannot control."[132] The Christian lives "in Christ Jesus," and from that reality, she acquires a new self; not one that stands by itself, but an excentric self, standing outside itself and under God's word. This is contrary to Biel, a scholastic theologian, according to whom the self lives out of that which lies within—namely, residual power or salvific resources.[133] The Bielian premise "doing what lies within" calls for an inward turn to the self as a

128. *Comm. Gal.* 2:20, in *CNTC* 11:43.

129. *SG*, 212.

130. *Comm. Gal.* 2:21, in *CNTC* 11:44.

131. *LW* 31:371.

132. Hampson, *Christian Contradictions*, 225.

133. *LW* 31:30.

basis of justification. That for Luther is another form of magnifying the self as lord. It is tantamount to fostering the autonomous self, which is the sinful self. Yet "the sinful shape," says Allen, "is no longer self-determining."[134] A true self is one who has lost the sense of self-governing identity. It dies to everything within, including its natural endowments, but "lives excentrically to himself"[135] by an alien righteousness of Christ, not by circumcision or any special status (Gal 6:15).

The Word and Baptism: God's Attack on the Old Self

For the Reformers, baptism is neither a "bare" sign[136] nor a "small and empty sign"[137] devoid of the promise of his presence. For both, it is an "effective" sign;[138] it truly conveys righteousness. Through baptism, believers put on Christ, the "new garment" of righteousness (Gal 3:27),[139] which, as Calvin puts it, "covers up all that would cause the Father to reject us."[140] Just as in justification, we work nothing but receive his righteousness, so in both baptism and the Lord's Supper, we "do nothing" but simply come to "receive" his grace offered there.[141] "Baptism, from our side," Calvin stresses, "is a passive work (*respectu nostri est opus passivum*). We bring nothing to it but faith, which has all things laid up in Christ."[142] We are justified not by baptism, but, as Luther says, "it is faith in that word of promise to which baptism is added. This faith justifies, and fulfills that which baptism signifies."[143] With the emphasis on faith, both Reformers reject the medieval doctrine of *opus operatum*, that is, the doctrine that grace is merited through the work of the administrant.[144] The creative word spoken in baptism performs two functions; in Luther's phrase, "the submersion of the old and emerging

134. Allen, *Justification and the Gospel*, 104.

135. Hampson, *Christian Contradictions*, 12.

136. *Comm. Gal.* 3:27, in *CNTC* 11:68.

137. *LW* 26:353; *WA* 40.1:541.

138. *LW* 26:353; *WA* 40.1:541.

139. *LW* 26:353; *WA* 40.1:541.

140. *SG*, 344.

141. *LW* 26:5; *WA* 40.1:41; *Comm. Gal.* 3:27, in *CNTC* 11:68.

142. *Comm. Gal.* 5:3, in *CNTC* 11:95.

143. *LW* 36:66.

144. *Comm. Gal.* 5:3, in *CNTC* 11:95.

of the new."[145] In his *Babylonian Captivity of the Church*, Luther highly regards baptism as "full and complete justification . . . This should not be understood allegorically as the death of sin and the life of grace, as many understood it, but as actual death and resurrection. For baptism is not a false sign."[146] Baptism is effective, says Luther, in transposing us "beyond the Law into a new birth."[147] It has placed us outside the law and its jurisdiction; it also placed us in Christ and his grace. To live a baptized life is to live a repentant life, marked by passing through the cross where sin is removed from the old existence to resurrection where righteousness is restored in the new. Baptism, Paulson writes, "is not a human act of obedience to a law, it is God's attack on sin by attacking the actual sinner; it is death."[148] Because sin remains in the life of the justified, Luther teaches, a continual return to baptism is necessary, as we daily suffer "an earnest attack" on the old self so that we may come forth in newness of life.[149] A Christian might fall into sin, but this does not invalidate baptism, because it is "God's ordinance," says Luther, not ours.[150]

Calvin also makes use of Rom 6:4 to assert that baptism not only effects the remission of sins but also the mortification of the old man.[151] What is Christ's is communicated to those who "put on Christ" in baptism (Gal 3:27), as one would put on a garment. Believers "are united to Christ in such a way that, in the sight of God, they bear the name and person of Christ and are viewed in Him rather in themselves."[152] The death of the old self via Christ's death, Calvin intimates, "is the focal centre of baptism," but it is not to be separated from the life of the new self via Christ's resurrection.[153] The reconstitution of the new self entails a movement of grace from death to life, as it presupposes the antithetical unity of Christ's death, says Calvin, which mortifies our old nature, and his resurrection, which fortifies our new nature.[154] Baptism admits believers "into participation in

145. *LW* 36:66.

146. *LW* 36:67.

147. *LW* 26:353; *WA* 40.1:541.

148. Paulson, *Lutheran Theology*, 155.

149. "The Large Catechism," in *BC*, 466.

150. "The Large Catechism," in *BC*, 464.

151. *Comm. Rom.* 6:3, in *CNTC* 11:122.

152. *Comm. Gal.* 3:27, in *CNTC* 11:68.

153. *Comm. Rom.* 6:3, in *CNTC* 11:122.

154. *Comm. Rom.* 6:4, in *CNTC* 8:123.

this grace."[155] "In spiritual engrafting," Calvin writes, "we not only derive the strength and sap of the life which flows from Christ, but we also pass from our nature into His."[156] He expands this in his *Sermons on Galatians*; there he makes full use of the Pauline imagery of planting in Rom 6:5 to explain the continuing effect of baptism.

> This image of being planted or grafted in is just as appropriate as that of the "putting on" of Christ. You take a cutting from a tree; then you make a cut in the trunk or branch of another tree, and bind on to it the cutting you took from the first tree. They will grow together and become one, because the roots will provide sap to make the sprig grow. In the same way, says Paul, we have been grafted into the Lord Jesus Christ; our old man has been crucified with him and raised in newness of life.[157]

The baptismal word transitions a person, says Calvin, "from the fellowship of Christ's death to the sharing of His life."[158] We are changed from Adam to Christ and have become new creatures. But sin continues to cling to the old Adam. God's baptismal word of promise continues to assure us, says Calvin, that "God does not see us as we are in ourselves, nor what we have deserved. He sees us as if Jesus Christ were with us, for indeed, we cannot be separated from him."[159] Baptism negates all attempts at self-constitution and kills the autonomous self; it, too, renews the self and causes it to live to God. Calvin writes, "We truly grow up into the body of Christ only when His death produces its fruits in us."[160] Through union with the Son, everything that is God's is communicated to us for our enjoyment. By repentance and faith, we make full use of baptism in our battle against the sin that robs us of the joy of salvation, the trials of life that deprive us of certainty, and the voices of conscience that send us into despair.

God hides in the earthy elements to meet us; yet he remains distinct from them. The word in the forms of preaching and sacraments truly accomplishes what it says, despite appearances sometimes, due to the mystery of the remnant of sin and evil in the lives of the faithful. Word and sacraments are God's accommodated mode of his stooping down to reach

155. *Comm. Rom.* 6:4, in *CNTC* 8:122–23.

156. *Comm. Rom.* 6:5, in *CNTC* 8:124.

157. *SG*, 347.

158. *Comm. Rom.* 6:5, in *CNTC* 8:122.

159. *SG*, 350.

160. *Comm. Rom.* 6:3, in *CNTC* 8:122.

us with his heavenly goods. The created forms of God's word are not inherently causative of grace; rather, they are consecrated by God as the instrumental causality of his grace. Glory belongs to God who manifests his power efficaciously through created forms, which for the Reformers are the perfecting cause of the saint's faith, not its efficient cause. "In this way," says Calvin, "what is proper to God is not transferred to the sign and yet the sacraments keep their power, so that they cannot be regarded as empty and cold spectacles."[161] Christ and all his gifts do not profit anyone unless received by faith; as Calvin notes, "The believers receive what is offered."[162] The promise is valid because God speaks it, quite apart from faith. Those who disbelieve or lack faith fail to benefit from it, but the promise remains God's. Both Reformers stress the intrinsic link between promise and faith: God's promise is made ours by faith, its means; faith is vacuous apart from God's promise, its substance. The new I lives not by his natural life and its resources, but by the alien life of Christ and his word, and by the forms that word assumes. Therefore, the believer neither arrogates growth to her own efforts nor reaches a point where she exceeds the need for the sacramental word of promise. Calvin acknowledges this discrepancy that not all baptized members manifest the fruits of the word attached to the outward sign.[163] They may fall, but they do not fall outside the promise God has attached to their baptisms, just as he promised with the Lord's Supper. For God does not lie and we can trust him. Our failure or unbelief, says Calvin, does not "destroy the faithfulness of God" offered in baptism.[164]

Concluding Reflections

The gospel creates our new identity; it equips us with everything we need for our identity formation against the ongoing threats of our existence. Any attempt to construct one's own identity by works of the law magnifies oneself as lord and thus constitutes sin against the God of the first commandment. Luther writes, "Whoever holds that our works shape and create us, or that we are the creature of our own work, blasphemes. For it is as blasphemous as saying: I am my own god and I created myself . . . Likewise,

161. *Comm. Gal.* 3:27, in *CNTC* 11:69.
162. *Comm. Gal.* 3:27, in *CNTC* 11:68.
163. *Comm. Rom.* 6:4, in *CNTC* 8:123.
164. *Comm. Gal.* 3:27, in *CNTC* 11:68.

it is blasphemous to seek one's own justification in works."[165] No human deeds can create the true self. Iwand captures Luther's point, writing that "our work could never bring a person to the expression of who he is but seeks to present to a person who he would like to be!"[166] "Act and being," says Lage, "are inextricably intertwined."[167] Luther places the priority on being, which constitutes the act and determines its value; in his words, "The deed does not make the person, but the person does the deed; the law does not create the deed, but merely informs of it."[168] Human actions are incapable of making the movement from the old I to the new I, from death to life, except by new birth; "that is," Luther writes, "just his being born, not his producing or working or worrying, makes him an heir. He does not do anything toward his being born but merely lets it happen."[169] The reconstituted self lives the life of Christ and partakes of the blessings of God passively, not actively. Chester's words are appropriate: "To grasp the permanently alien nature of new life in Christ involves rejection born of any temptation to superiority in which 'the religious person sees himself as an exception to sinful human possibilities, claiming a perceivable nearness to God,' and of any claim to autonomy or the capacity for the self to remake identity according to personal preferences."[170]

Calvin acknowledges that remnant sparks of light glimmer in the depraved nature. "Yet," he avers, "this light [is] choked with dense ignorance, so that it cannot come forth effectively."[171] Even though sinners retain some residual understanding and judgment, the mind is distorted; the will is bent toward evil and wills only the opposite of right. The natural self is held captive to, in Calvin's phrase, "the disease of his lusts."[172] Apart from God's grace, it cannot apprehend the true piety of the first table of the law, nor can it rightly appropriate the truth in the second table.[173] "In any event,"

165. WA 39.1:283.9, as quoted in Iwand, *Righteousness of Faith*, 61–62.

166. Iwand, *Righteousness of Faith*, 61–62.

167. Lage, *Martin Luther's Christology*, 152.

168. See WA 39.1:283.9, as cited in Iwand, *Righteousness of Faith*, 98n140.

169. *LW* 26:392; WA 40.1:597.

170. Chester, *Reading Paul with Reformers*, 370n15, where he cites Eberhard Busch, *Karl Barth and the Pietists: The Young Karl Barth's Critique of Pietism and Its Response*, translated by Daniel W. Bloesch (Downers Grove, IL: IVP, 2004), 84.

171. *Inst.* 2.2.12.

172. *Inst.* 2.2.24.

173. *Inst.* 2.2.24.

Niesel comments, "the natural man is unable to realize that his covetous desires point to the rottenness of his condition."[174] The insights and voice of conscience cannot be treated as a basis for the acquisition of a righteous identity. All human goodness is predicated upon God's prior action, for good works in themselves do not possess any causal power to turn toward God. Only the grace of the Holy Spirit can create anew and transform an unrighteous person to a righteous one. We who were once slaves are now sons and heirs of God. The new identity is bestowed by grace, not merited by works. We receive our identity passively, and we are grasped by God and do not actively grasp him (Gal 4:8–9).

For Luther, faith permits the word to be the "divine womb in which we are conceived, carried, born, reared etc."[175] Likewise, in his *Sermons on Galatians*, Calvin avers, "We must . . . allow ourselves to be governed only by his Word and by the Holy Spirit . . . [Believers] must deny themselves and all that proceeds from man, and tread it underfoot, seeking to cleave to the pure and simple truth of God."[176] Our works are futile and cannot constitute ourselves; faith created by God's word is fertile and can create anew. "Faith," Luther stresses, "is a divine work in us which changes us"[177] into a new person. "Faith," Linebaugh elucidates, "is not a predicate of a self-defined person; it is, rather, a name for the relation with Christ that creates and carries the person—it is *being* grounded in gift."[178] The person recreated by the gospel is enabled to receive God's kingdom. She lives by faith in Christ who by his death procures for us the benefits through which the new self may develop. Both Reformers stress the importance of the Word by which the self is formed in Christ's image, dies to itself and the world, and lives to God; conversely, Christ, who is the causative agency of everything good in us, is formed in us. For Luther, to hear the pronoun "me" pronounced upon us is to be revived by the gospel—namely, the "giving" of God's Son—and to live on God's justifying verdict, that "God's grace is superabundant when sin was abundant."[179] Whenever the gospel, that Christ through his death and passion has banished curse and damnation for us, is "preached," Calvin avers, we receive "an invitation" from God, calling us to forsake all things

174. Niesel, *Theology of Calvin*, 103.

175. *LW* 26:392; *WA* 40.1:597.

176. *SG*, 388.

177. *LW* 35:370.

178. Linebaugh, "Speech of the Dead," 101.

179. *LW* 26:169; *WA* 40.1:286.

and trust only in him, or else the cross is emptied of its efficacy.[180] "Since this is the case," Calvin notes, "we must not 'frustrate' the grace of God" (Gal 2:21).[181] The natural self, that which lives out of itself, cannot turn toward God but turns inward to itself, thereby placing itself under sin and death. Only the regenerated self, that which stems from the creative word of God, can turn toward God, thereby placing itself under grace and life. Grace, the fountain of faith, works in us a change of being, from the old I (to which we die) to the new I (to which we live). We cannot free ourselves except by hearing *extra nos* the external Word "he gave himself for me." Whoever is rooted in Christ will be shaped and sustained by the fruits of Christ's passion; he will grow the Christ-life in him and shine forth vigorously from Christ. His vision, says Calvin, is no longer bound to the "natural state"; he is able to "look beyond it to the glory which awaits" him.[182] He is enabled to live independently of himself and, to use Calvin's phrase, "live by faith in the gospel."[183] The new self knows for sure he will not be forsaken because his "trust" is not in anything creaturely and fleshly, but in the "promises contained in the gospel."[184] The Christ-life we now live is alien to us, just as is the righteousness of faith. So, we do not turn inward for the recreation of the self; rather, we turn outward to Christ, placing our trust in the gospel and the baptismal word of promise. Luther stresses, "This is the reason why our theology is so certain: it snatches us away from ourselves and places us outside ourselves, so that we do not depend on our own strength, conscience, experience, person, or works but depend on that which is outside ourselves, that is, on the promise and truth of God, which cannot deceive."[185] Not the quality of our spiritual life but the efficacy of God's promise is the ground of the assurance of faith. Its experiential aspect has validity outside us apart from what we do without, and against what we subjectively feel within.

The tension in Paul's antithetical phrase "it is no longer I but Christ" is resolved for those who believe. Faith removes sin from us and adorns us with his righteousness. Both Luther and Calvin affirm faith as the operational agency of the transition from the old to the new via a real communication

180. *SG*, 214.
181. *SG*, 214.
182. *SG*, 212.
183. *SG*, 212.
184. *SG*, 212.
185. *LW* 26:387; *WA* 10.1:589.

of attributes between Christ and the justified self. The new self is given to participate in Christ's righteousness, life, and heaven in exchange for sin, death, and hell, which are of the old self. The works of Christ reveal who we are: the old I and his miserable and helpless state—in bondage, in debt, in guilt and filth. As Calvin writes, "If the death of Christ is redemption, then we were captives; if it is payment, we were debtors; if it is atonement, we were guilty; if it were cleansing, we were unclean."[186] The cross discloses the opposites of what the gospel seeks to cure and makes a new creature out of the old nature. Whoever attributes these fruits of the cross (redemption, payment, atonement, and cleansing) to human works magnifies the old Adam, which is an occasion of fulfilling the flesh and its lusts. Where the old I reigns, says Luther, the contraries of sin, death, and hell oppose us; where Christ reigns, they are deposed.[187] The old Adam loses its grip on us, as it comes under the law's crushing power of Christ's death. It feels the effect of "participation in the death of Christ," Calvin avers, "the only source of mortification" through which the renewed nature flourishes in true life.[188] Neither can the old I predispose itself to the kingdom of God nor prepare itself for a reception of God's grace, unless she is united to Christ through baptism and renewed into the Christ-life in which she now lives. The old self is annihilated, as is the world; both are crucified through the cross so that Christ alone remains Lord of all. We are most truly ourselves when we have Christ as Lord; we falsify our identity when we have the world or ourselves as the lord instead. To live out of the old I is death; to live out of the new I is life. The Christian life is one of paradox: we must die by the annihilating power of the law in order to live by the animating power of the gospel. We are most crucified when our old Adam is most crucified; conversely, our old Adam is most dead when we are most edified. The gospel by which we live recreates us by the fruits of the cross so that the old Adam and his works are subdued. The new I lives in our flesh, but the new I lives her life by relying not on the flesh and works of the law, but on the Christ who lives in her by his righteousness and holiness. Linebaugh writes aptly, "In this sense, the no longer and now living selves are not identical: the 'I' *is* in another as a gift. And yet, the 'I' who lives by grace is also the 'I' who was, is, and will be loved by 'the Son of God who loved me and gave

186. *Comm. Gal.* 2:21, in *CNTC* 11:44.

187. *LW* 26:282; *WA* 40.1:440.

188. *Comm. Rom.* 6:6, in *CNTC* 8:125.

himself for me.'"[189] The I of the renewed self in Christ is identical to the I of the pristine self of the original creation. Apart from human actions or merits, Christ's justifying action effects a return of the renewed I to Eden, to partake of the eternal bliss of communion with God, the very purpose for which humanity had originally been created.

189. Linebaugh, "Speech of the Dead," 87. Linebaugh's insight is drawn from his reading of Luther, but it applies to Calvin as well.

Bibliography

Allen, R. Michael. *Justification and the Gospel: Understanding the Contexts and Controversies.* Grand Rapids: Baker Academic, 2013.

———, and Jonathan A. Linebaugh, eds. *Reformation Readings of Paul: Explorations in History and Exegesis.* Downers Grove, IL: IVP Academic, 2015.

Althaus, Paul. *The Theology of Martin Luther.* Philadelphia: Fortress, 1966.

Aquinas, Thomas. *Commentary on Saint Paul's Epistle to the Galatians.* Translated by Fabian R. Larcher. Albany, NY: Magi, 1966.

Augustine. "The Grace of Christ and Original Sin." In *Basic Writings of St. Augustine,* edtied by Whitney J. Oates, 1:583–654. New York: Random House, 1948.

———. *The Trinity (De Trinitate).* Edited and translated by Edmund Hill. Vol. 5 of *The Works of St. Augustine: A Translation for the 21st Century.* Hyde Park, NY: New City, 1991.

Barclay, John M. G. *Obeying the Truth: Paul's Ethics in Galatians.* Minneapolis: Fortress, 1988.

———. *Paul and the Gift.* Grand Rapids: Eerdmans, 2017.

———. "The Text of Galatians and the Theology of Luther." In *Reformation Readings of Paul: Explorations in History and Exegesis,* edited by Michael R. Allen and Jonathan A. Linebaugh, 49–69. Downers Grove, IL: IVP Academic, 2015.

Barrett, C. K. *The Second Epistle to the Corinthians.* London: Harper & Row, 1957.

Bayer, Oswald. "The Ethics of Gift." *Lutheran Quarterly* 24 (2010) 447–68.

———. *Martin Luther's Theology: A Contemporary Interpretation.* Translated by Thomas H. Trapp. Grand Rapids: Eerdmans, 2008.

Bertram, Robert W. "Luther on the Unique Mediatorship of Christ." In *The One Mediator, The Saints, and Mary: Lutherans and Catholics in Dialogue VIII,* edited by H. George Anderson et al., 249–62. Minneapolis: Augsburg, 1992.

———. "The Radical Dialectic between Faith and Works in Luther's Lectures on Galatians (1535)." In *Luther for an Ecumenical Age: Essays in Commemoration of the 450th Anniversary of the Reformation,* edited by Carl S. Meyer, 219–41. St. Louis: Concordia, 1967.

Beveridge, Henry, and Jules Bonner, eds. *Select Works of John Calvin.* Vol. 3. Grand Rapids: Baker, 1983.

Billings, J. Todd. *Calvin, Participation, and the Gift: The Activity of Believers in Union with Christ.* Oxford: Oxford University Press, 2007.

Bluhm, Heinz S. *Luther, Translator of Paul: Studies in Romans and Galatians.* New York: Lang, 1985.

Braaten, Carl E. "The Person of Jesus Christ." In *Christian Dogmatics*, edited by Carl E. Braaten and Robert W. Jenson, 1:465–569. Minneapolis: Fortress, 1984.

―――, and Robert Jenson, eds. *Christian Dogmatics*. 2 vols. Minneapolis: Fortress, 1984.

Bray, Gerald L., ed. *Galatians, Ephesians*. Reformation Commentary on Scripture, NT 10. Downers Grove, IL: IVP Academic, 2011.

Butin, Philip W. *Revelation, Redemption, and Response: Calvin's Trinitarian Understanding of the Divine-Human Relationship*. New York: Oxford University Press, 1995.

Butler, Geoffrey. "Appeasement of a Monster God? A Biblical and Historical Analysis of Penal Substitutionary Atonement." *Themelios* 46 (2021) 130–44.

―――. "Theologian of the Holy Spirit: A Pentecostal Analysis of John Calvin's Pneumatology." *McMaster Journal of Theology and Ministry* 22 (2020–2021) 3–30.

Calvin, John. "Acts of the Council of Trent with the Antidote." In *Select Works of John Calvin*, edited by Henry Beveridge and Jules Bonnet, 3:17–188. Grand Rapids: Baker, 1983.

―――. *Calvin's Commentaries*. 46 vols. Edinburgh: Calvin Translation Society, 1844–1855. Reprint, 22 vols. Grand Rapids: Baker, 1979.

―――. *Calvin's New Testament Commentaries*. 12 vols. Edited by David W. Torrance and Thomas F. Torrance. Grand Rapids: Eerdmans, 1959–1972.

―――. *Institutes of the Christian Religion*. 3 vols. Translated by Henry Beveridge. Edinburgh: Calvin Translation Society, 1845.

―――. *Institutes of the Christian Religion*. Edited by John T. McNeil. Translated by Ford Lewis Battles. Library of Christian Classics 20–21. Philadelphia: Westminster, 1960.

―――. *Sermons on Galatians*. Translated by Kathy Childress. Edinburgh: Banner of Truth, 1997.

Camden, Vera J. "'Most Fit for a Wounded Conscience': The Place of Luther's 'Commentary on Galatians' in Grace Abounding." *Renaissance Quarterly* 50 (1997) 819–49.

―――. "'Most Fit for a Wounded Conscience': The Place of Luther's 'Commentary on Galatians' in Grace Abounding." In *Literature Criticism from 1400 to 1800*, edited by Thomas J. Schoenberg and Lawrence J. Trudeau, 150:215–29. Farmington Hills, MI: Gale, 2008.

Campbell, Douglas A. *The Quest for Paul's Gospel*. London: T. & T. Clark, 2005.

Canlis, Julie. *Calvin's Ladder: A Spiritual Theology of Ascent and Ascension*. Grand Rapids: Eerdmans, 2010.

Carlson, Arnold E. "Luther and the Doctrine of the Holy Spirit." *Lutheran Quarterly* 11 (May 1958) 135–46.

Carson, Donald A., ed. *The Enduring Authority of the Christian Scriptures*. Grand Rapids: Eerdmans, 2016.

―――, et al., eds. *The Paradoxes of Paul*. Vol. 2 of *Justification and Variegated Nomism*. Grand Rapids: Baker Academic, 2004.

Cary, Philip. *The Meaning of Protestant Theology: Luther, Augustine, and the Gospel That Gives Us Christ*. Grand Rapids: Baker Academic, 2019.

Chalmers, Thomas. *The Expulsive Power of a New Affection*. Wheaton, IL: Crossway, 2020.

Chester, Stephen. "'Abba! Father!' (Gal. 4:6): Justification and Assurance in Martin Luther's Lectures on Galatians (1535)." *Biblical Research* 63 (2018) 15–22.

―――. "Faith Working through Love (Galatians 5:6): The Role of Human Deeds in Salvation in Luther and Calvin's Exegesis." *Covenant Quarterly* 72 (2014) 41–54.

―――. "It Is No Longer I Who Live: Justification by Faith and Participation in Christ in Martin Luther's Exegesis of Galatians." *New Testament Studies* 55 (2009) 315–37.

———. *Reading Paul with the Reformers: Reconciling Old and New Perspectives*. Grand Rapids: Eerdmans, 2017.

———. "When the Old Was New: Reformation Perspectives on Galatians 2:16." *Expository Times* 119 (2008) 320–29.

Clark, Scott R. "'Subtle Sacramentarian' or Son? John Calvin's Relationship to Martin Luther." *Southern Baptist Journal of Theology* 21 (2017) 35–60.

Congar, Yves. *Dialogue between Christians: Catholic Contributions to Ecumenism*. London: Chapman, 1966.

Cortez, Marc. *Christological Anthropology in Historical Perspective: Ancient and Contemporary Approaches to Theological Anthropology*. Grand Rapids: Zondervan, 2016.

Cross, Richard. *Communicatio Idiomatum: Reformation Christological Debates*. Oxford: Oxford University Press, 2019.

De Boer, Martinus C. *Galatians*. New Testament Library. Louisville: Westminster John Knox, 2011.

Dewdney, A. S. "Agape and Eros: A Critique of Ander Nygren." *Canadian Journal of Theology* 1 (1955) 19–27.

Dowey, Edward A., Jr. *The Knowledge of God in Calvin's Theology*. Grand Rapids: Eerdmans, 1994.

———. "Law in Luther and Calvin." *Theology Today* 41 (1984) 146–53.

Dubbelman, Samuel J. "The Darkness of Faith: A Study in Martin Luther's 1535 Galatians Commentary." *Trinity Journal* 37 (2016) 213–32.

Eastman, Susan Grove. *Paul and the Person: Reframing Paul's Anthropology*. Grand Rapids: Eerdmans, 2017.

Ebeling, Gerhard. *The Truth of the Gospel: An Exposition of Galatians*. Translated by David Green. Minneapolis: Fortress, 1985.

———. *Word and Faith*. Translated by James W. Leitch. Philadelphia: Fortress, 1963.

Edmondson, Stephen. *Calvin's Christology*. Cambridge: Cambridge University Press, 2004.

Elert, Werner. *The Structure of Lutheranism*. Translated by Walter A. Hansen. Vol. 1. St. Louis: Concordia, 1962.

Elliot, Mark W., et al., eds. *Galatians and Christian Theology: Justification, the Gospel, and Ethics in Paul's Letters*. Grand Rapids: Baker Academic, 2014.

Evans, Eifion. "John Calvin: Theologian of the Holy Spirit." *Reformation & Revival* 10 (2001) 82–105.

Femiano, S. "The Holy Spirit in Luther's Commentary on Galatians." *Canadian Journal of Theology* 8 (1962) 43–48.

Fink, David C. "Martin Luther's Reading of Galatians." In *Reformation Readings of Paul: Explorations in History and Exegesis*, edited by Michael R. Allen and Jonathan A. Linebaugh, 23–48. Downers Grove, IL: IVP Academic, 2015.

Forde, Gerhard O. "Caught in the Act: Reflections on the Work of Christ." *Word & World* 3 (1983) 22–31.

———. *Justification by Faith*. Philadelphia: Fortress, 1982.

———. "Luther's Theology of the Cross." In *Christian Dogmatics*, edited by Carl E. Braaten and Robert W. Jenson, 2:47–64. Minneapolis: Fortress, 1984.

———. *Theology Is for Proclamation*. Minneapolis: Fortress, 1990.

Garcia, Javier A. "A Critique of Mannermaa on Luther and Galatians." *Lutheran Quarterly* 27 (2013) 33–55.

George, Timothy. "Afterword: What Evangelicals Can Learn from the Reformation." In *The Reformation and the Irrepressible Word of God: Interpretation, Theology, and Practice*, edited by Scott M. Manetsch, 191–212. Grand Rapids: IVP Academic, 2019.

———. *Galatians*. Christian Standard Commentary. Nashville: Holman Reference, 2020.

Gerrish, Brian A. *The Old Protestantism and the New: Essays on the Reformation Heritage*. Chicago: University of Chicago Press, 1982.

Godfrey, W. Robert. "Calvin and the Council of Trent." In *Christ the Lord: The Reformation and Lordship Salvation*, edited by Michael Horton, 119–28. Grand Rapids: Baker, 1991.

Gorman, Michael J. *Inhabiting the Cruciform God: Kenosis, Justification, and Theosis in Paul's Narrative Soteriology*. Grand Rapids: Eerdmans, 2009.

Green, Lowell C. *How Melanchthon Helped Luther Discover the Gospel: The Doctrine of Justification in the Reformation*. Fallbrook, CA: Verdict, 1980.

Gritsch, Eric W. "Martin Luther's Commentary on Gal 5,2–24, 1519 (WA 2,574–597) and Sermon on Gal 4,1–7, 1522 (WA 10 I 1,325–378)." In *Freiheit als Liebe bei Martin Luther (Freedom as Love in Martin Luther)*, edited by Dennis D. Bielfeldt and Klaus Schwarzwäller, 105–11. Frankfurt: Lang, 1995.

Hagen, Kenneth. "Did Peter Err? The Text Is the Best Judge: Luther on Gal 2:11." In *Augustine, the Harvest, and Theology (1300–1650): Essays Dedicated to Heiko Augustinus Oberman in Honor of His Sixtieth Birthday*, edited by Kenneth Hagen, 110–26. Leiden, Neth.: Brill, 1990.

———. *Luther's Approach to Scripture as Seen in His "Commentaries" on Galatians, 1519–1538*. Tübingen: Mohr Siebeck, 1993.

Hamm, Berndt. *The Early Luther: Stages in a Reformation Reorientation*. Translated by Martin J. Lohrmann. Minneapolis: Fortress, 2017.

———. "Martin Luther's Revolutionary Theology of Pure Gift without Reciprocation." *Lutheran Quarterly* 29 (2015) 125–61.

Hampson, Daphne. *Christian Contradictions: The Structures of Lutheran and Catholic Thought*. Cambridge: Cambridge University Press, 2001.

Hays, Richard B. "Christ Died for the Ungodly: Narrative Soteriology in Paul." *Horizons in Biblical Theology* 26 (2004) 48–68.

———. *The Faith of Jesus Christ: The Narrative Substructure of Galatians 3:1—4:11*. Rev. ed. Grand Rapids: Eerdmans, 2002.

Hendriksen, William. *Exposition of Galatians*. New Testament Commentary. Grand Rapids: Baker, 1968.

Hesselink, I. John. *Calvin's Concept of the Law*. Princeton Theological Monograph. Allison Park, PA: Pickwick, 1992.

———. "Law and Gospel or Gospel and Law? Karl Barth, Martin Luther, and John Calvin." *Reformation & Revival* 14 (2005) 139–71.

———. "Luther and Calvin on Law and Gospel in Their Galatians Commentaries." *Western Theological Seminary* 37 (1984) 69–82.

Hick, John. *Evil and the God of Love*. Glasgow: Collins, 1979.

Holder, R. Ward, ed. *Calvin and Luther: The Continuing Relationship*. Göttingen: Vandenhoeck & Ruprecht, 2013.

Horrell, David G. *An Introduction to the Study of Paul*. 3rd ed. New York: Bloomsbury T. &. T Clark, 2015.

Horton, Michael. *Calvin and the Christian Life*. Wheaton, IL: Crossway, 2014.

————, ed. *Christ the Lord: The Reformation and Lordship Salvation*. Grand Rapids: Baker, 1991.

Hultgren, Arland J. "Luther on Galatians." *Word & World* 20 (2000) 232–38.

Iwand, Hans J. *The Righteousness of Faith According to Luther*. Edited by V. F. Thompson. Translated by R. H. Lundell. Eugene, OR: Wipf & Stock, 2008.

Jensen, Gordon A. "The Christology of Luther's Theology of the Cross." *Consensus* 23 (1997) 11–25.

Jenson, Robert. *Systematic Theology*. 2 vols. Oxford: Oxford University Press, 1997, 1999.

Johnson, Marcus Peter. "Luther and Calvin on Union with Christ." *Fides et Historia* 39, (2007) 59–77.

Jüngel, Eberhard. *The Freedom of a Christian: Luther's Significance for Contemporary Theology*. Translated by Roy A. Harrisville. Minneapolis: Augsburg, 1988.

————. *God as the Mystery of the World: On the Foundation of the Theology of the Crucified God in between Theism and Atheism*. Translated by Darrell L. Gruder. Grand Rapids: Eerdmans, 1983.

————. *Justification: The Heart of the Christian Faith*. Edinburgh: T. & T. Clark, 2001.

Just, Arthur A., Jr. "The Faith of Christ: A Lutheran Appropriation of Richard Hays's Proposal." *Concordia Theological Quarterly* 70 (2006) 3–15.

Kamell, Mariam J. "Life in the Spirit and Life in Wisdom: Reading Galatians and James as a Dialogue." In *Galatians and Christian Theology: Justification, the Gospel, and Ethics in Paul's Letter*, edited by Mark W. Elliot et al., 353–63. Grand Rapids: Baker Academic, 2014.

Kärkkäinen, Veli-Matti. "'Evil, Love and the Left Hand of God': The Contribution of Luther's Theology of the Cross to an Evangelical Theology of Evil." *Evangelical Quarterly* 74 (2002) 215–34.

Kim, Sun-young. *Luther on Faith and Love: Christ and the Law in the 1535 Galatians Commentary*. Minneapolis: Fortress, 2014.

Kolb, Robert. "The Influence of Luther's Galatians Commentary of 1535 on Later Sixteenth-Century Lutheran Commentaries on Galatians." *Archiv für Reformationsgeschichte* 84 (1993) 156–84.

————. "Luther on the Two Kinds of Righteousness: Reflections on His Two-Dimensional Definition of Humanity at the Heart of His Theology." *Lutheran Quarterly* 13 (1999) 449–66.

————. *Luther's Treatise on Christian Freedom and Its Legacy*. Lanham, MD: Lexington/ Fortress Academic, 2020.

————. *Martin Luther: Confessor of the Faith*. Christian Theology in Context. Oxford: Oxford University Press, 2009.

Kolb, Robert, and Charles Arand. *The Genius of Luther's Theology: A Wittenberg Way of Thinking for the Contemporary Church*. Grand Rapids: Baker Academic, 2008.

Kolb, Robert, and Timothy J. Wengert, eds. *The Book of Concord: The Confessions of the Evangelical Lutheran Church*. Minneapolis: Fortress, 2000.

Kolb, Robert, et al., eds. *The Oxford Handbook of Martin Luther's Theology*. Oxford: Oxford University Press, 2014.

————. *Simul: Inquiries into Luther's Experience of the Christian Life*. Refo500 Academic Studies 80. Göttingen: Vandenhoeck & Ruprecht, 2021.

Lage, Dietmar. *Martin Luther's Christology and Ethics*. Texts and Studies in Religion 45. Lewiston, NY: Mellen, 1990.

Leith, John H. "Calvin's Doctrine of the Proclamation of the Word and Its Significance for Today in the Light of Recent Research." *Review & Expositor* 86 (1989) 29–44.

Lienhard, Marc. *Luther: Witness to Jesus Christ; Stages and Themes of the Reformer's Christology.* Translated by Edwin H. Robertson. Minneapolis: Augsburg, 1982.

Linebaugh, Jonathan A. "The Christo-Centrism of Faith in Christ: Martin Luther's Reading of Galatians 2.16, 19–20." *New Testament Studies* 59 (2013) 535–44.

———, ed. *God's Two Words: Law and Gospel in the Lutheran and Reformed Traditions.* Grand Rapids: Eerdmans, 2018.

———. "The Grammar of the Gospel: Justification as a Theological Criterion in the Reformation and Paul's Letter to the Galatians." *Scottish Journal of Theology* 71 (2018) 287–307.

———. "'The Speech of the Dead': Identifying the No Longer and Now Living 'I' of Galatians 2.20." *New Testament Studies* 66 (2020) 87–105.

Lohse, Bernhard. *Martin Luther's Theology: Its Historical and Systematic Development.* Translated by Roy A. Harrisville. Minneapolis: Fortress, 1999.

Luther, Martin. *The Bondage of the Will.* Translated by J. I. Packer and O. R. Johnston. Grand Rapids: Baker Academic, 2012.

———. *D. Martin Luthers Werke: Kritische Gesamtausgabe.* Part 1, *Schriften*: Vols. 1–56. Weimar: Böhlau, 1883–1929.

———. *D. Martin Luthers Werke: Kritische Gesamtausgabe.* Part 2, *Tischreden*: Vols. 1–6. Weimar: Böhlau, 1883–1929.

———. *D. Martin Luthers Werke: Kritische Gesamtausgabe.* Part 3, *Die Deutsche Bibel*: Vols. 1–12. Weimar: Böhlau, 1883–1929.

———. *Luther's Works.* Edited by Jaroslav Pelikan. Vols. 1–30. American ed. St. Louis: Concordia, 1955–1973.

———. *Luther's Works.* Edited by Helmut T. Lehman. Vols. 31–55. American ed. Philadelphia: Fortress, 1957–1986.

———. *Luther's Works.* Edited by Christopher Boyd et al. Vols. 56–82. American ed. New series. St. Louis: Concordia, 2009–

———. *Sermons of Martin Luther.* Vol. 1. Edited and translated by Eugene F. A. Klug et al. Grand Rapids: Baker, 1996.

Małysz, Piotr J. "Luther and Dionysius: Beyond Mere Negations." In *Re-thinking Dionysius the Areopagite*, edited by Sarah Coakley and Charles Stang, 49–62. Malden, MA: Wiley-Blackwell, 2009.

Mannermaa, Tuomo. *Christ Present in Faith: Luther's View of Justification.* Minneapolis: Fortress. 2005.

———. *Two Kinds of Love: Martin Luther's Religious World.* Minneapolis: Fortress, 2010.

Manns, Peter. "Absolute and Incarnate Faith—Luther on Justification in the Galatians' Commentary of 1531–1535." In *Catholic Scholars Dialogue with Luther*, edited by Jared Wicks, 121–56. Chicago: Loyola University Press, 1970.

Maschke, Timothy. "The Authority of Scripture: Luther's Approach to Allegory in Galatians." *Logia* 4 (1995) 25–31.

———, et al., eds. *Ad Fontes Lutheri: Toward the Recovery of the Real Luther; Essays in Honor of Kenneth Hagen's Sixty-Fifth Birthday.* Milwaukee: Marquette University Press, 2001.

Mattes, Mark C. *Martin Luther's Theology of Beauty: A Reappraisal.* Grand Rapids: Baker Academic, 2017.

McDonough, Thomas M. *The Law and the Gospel in Luther: A Study of Luther's Confessional Writings*. Oxford: Oxford University Press, 1963.

McGrath, Alister E. *Iustitia Dei: A History of the Christian Doctrine of Justification*. 4th ed. Cambridge: Cambridge University Press, 2020.

———. *Luther's Theology of the Cross: Martin Luther's Theological Breakthrough*. Oxford: Blackwell, 1985.

McKim, Donald K., ed. *The Cambridge Companion to Martin Luther*. Cambridge: Cambridge University Press, 2006.

Mikkonen, Juha. *Luther and Calvin on Paul's Epistle to the Galatians: An Analysis and Comparison of Substantial Concepts in Luther's 1531/35 and Calvin's 1546/48 Commentaries on Galatians*. Turku: Åbo Akademi University Press, 2007.

Muller, Richard A. *Calvin and the Reformed Tradition*. Grand Rapids: Baker Academic, 2012.

Nagel, Norman E. "Martinus: 'Heresy, Doctor Luther, Heresy!' The Person and Work of Christ." In *Seven-Headed Luther: Essays in Commemoration of a Quincentenary, 1483–1983*, edited by Peter Newman Brooks, 25–49. Oxford: Clarendon, 1983.

———. "*Sacramentum et Exemplum* in Luther's Understanding of Christ." In *Luther for an Ecumenical Age: Essays in Commemoration of the 450th Anniversary of the Reformation*, edited by Carl S. Meyer, 172–99. St. Louis: Concordia, 1967.

Niesel, Wilhelm. *The Theology of Calvin*. Translated by Harold Knight. Philadelphia: Westminster, 1956.

Oates, Whitney J., ed. *Basic Writings of St. Augustine*. Vol. 1. New York: Random House, 1948.

Pannenberg, Wolfhart. "God of the Philosophers." *First Things* 174 (2007) 31–34.

———. "A Theology of the Cross." *Word & World* 8 (1988) 162–72.

Parker, T. H. L. *John Calvin: A Biography*. Philadelphia: Westminster, 1976.

Parker, Thomas D. "The Interpretation of Scripture I: A Comparison of Calvin and Luther on Galatians." *Interpretation* 17 (1963) 61–75.

Parsons, Michael, ed. *Since We Are Justified by Faith: Justification in the Theologies of the Protestant Reformation*. Bletchley, UK: Paternoster, 2012.

Partee, Charles. *The Theology of John Calvin*. Louisville: Westminster John Knox, 2008.

Paul, Robert S. "The Atonement: Sacrifice and Penalty." In *Readings in Calvin's Theology*, edited by Donald K. McKim, 142–52. Grand Rapids: Baker, 1984.

Paulson, Steven. *Lutheran Theology*. London: T. & T. Clark, 2011.

Pelikan, Jaroslav. *Luther the Expositor: Introduction to the Reformer's Exegetical Writings*. *Luther's Works* Companion. St. Louis: Concordia, 1959.

Peters, Ted. *God—The World's Future: Systematic Theology for a Postmodern Era*. Minneapolis: Fortress, 1992.

Prenter, Regin. *Spiritus Creator*. Philadelphia: Fortress, 1953.

Rabens, Volker. "'Indicative and Imperative' as the Substructure of Paul's Theology-and-Ethics in Galatians? A Discussion of Divine and Human Agency in Paul." In *Galatians and Christian Theology: Justification, the Gospel, and Ethics in Paul's Letter*, edited by Mark W. Elliot et al., 285–305. Grand Rapids: Baker Academic, 2014.

Riches, John. *Galatians through the Centuries*. Blackwell Bible Commentaries. Oxford: Blackwell, 2008.

Ritskes, Cheryl. "A Defence of Substitutionary Atonement and Divine Justice." *Churchman* 132 (2018) 311–18.

Schaff, Philip. *The Greek and Latin Creeds*. Vol. 2 of *The Creeds of Christendom*. Grand Rapids: Baker, 1977.

Schreiner, Thomas R. *Faith Alone: The Doctrine of Justification*. Grand Rapids: Zondervan, 2015.

———. *Galatians*. Zondervan Exegetical Commentary on the New Testament. Grand Rapids: Zondervan, 2010.

Seifrid, Mark A. *Christ, Our Righteousness: Paul's Theology of Justification*. Downers Grove, IL: IVP Academic, 2000.

———. "Paul, Luther, and Justification in Gal 2:15–21." *Westminster Theological Journal* 65 (2003) 215–30.

———. "Rightly Dividing the Word of Truth: An Introduction to the Distinction between Law and Gospel." *Southern Baptist Journal of Theology* 10 (Summer 2006) 56–68.

Siggins, Ian D. K. *Martin Luther's Doctrine of Christ*. New Haven, CT: Yale University Press, 1970.

Sundquist, Ralph R., Jr. *The Third Use of the Law in the Thought of John Calvin: An Interpretation and Evaluation*. New York: Columbia University, 1970.

Swain, Scott R. "Heirs through God: Galatians 4:4–7 and the Doctrine of the Trinity." In *Galatians and Christian Theology: Justification, the Gospel, and Ethics in Paul's Letter*, edited by Mark W. Elliot et al., 258–67. Grand Rapids: Baker Academic, 2014.

Tappert, Theodore G., ed. and trans. *The Book of Concord: The Confessions of the Evangelical Lutheran Church*. Minneapolis: Fortress, 1959.

Trueman, Carl R. "Is the Finnish Line a New Beginning? A Critical Assessment of the Reading of Luther Offered by the Helsinki Circle." *Westminster Theological Journal* 65 (2003) 213–44.

———. "*Simul peccator et justus*: Martin Luther and Justification." In *Justification in Perspective: Historical Development and Contemporary Challenges*, edited by Bruce L. McCormack, 73–97. Grand Rapids: Baker Academic, 2006.

Tylenda, Joseph N. "Calvin's Understanding of the Communication of Properties." *Westminster Theological Journal* 38 (1975–1976) 54–65.

———. "Christ the Mediator: Calvin versus Stancaro." *Calvin Theological Journal* 8 (1973) 5–16.

Wannenwetsch, Bernd. "Luther's Moral Theology." In *The Cambridge Companion to Martin Luther*, edited by Donald K. McKim, 120–35. Cambridge: Cambridge University Press, 2003.

Warfield, Benjamin B. *Calvin and Augustine*. Phillipsburg, NJ: P&R, 1980.

Watson, Francis. "By Faith (of Christ): An Exegetical Dilemma and its Scriptural Solution." In *The Faith of Jesus Christ: Exegetical, Biblical, and Theological Studies*, edited by Michael F. Bird and Preston M. Sprinkle, 147–63. Milton Keynes, UK: Paternoster, 2009.

Watson, Philip. *Let God Be God: An Interpretation of the Theology of Martin Luther*. Philadelphia: Muhlenberg, 1948.

Webster, John. *Holy Scripture: A Dogmatic Sketch*. Cambridge: Cambridge University Press, 2003.

Wendel, François. *Calvin: Origins and Development of His Religious Thought*. New York: Harper & Row, 1963.

Wengert, Timothy. "Martin Luther on Galatians 3:6–14: Justification by Curses and Blessings." In *Galatians and Christian Theology: Justification, the Gospel, and Ethics in*

Paul's Letter, edited by Mark W. Elliot et al., 91–116. Grand Rapids: Baker Academic, 2014.

Westerholm, Stephen. *Justification Reconsidered: Rethinking a Pauline Theme*. Grand Rapids: Eerdmans, 2013.

Willis, Edward David. *Calvin's Catholic Christology: The Principle of the So-Called Extra-Calvinisticum in Calvin's Theology*. Leiden: Brill, 1966.

Wright, N. T. *Paul and the Faithfulness of God*. Minneapolis: Fortress, 2013.

Zachhuber, Johannes. *Luther's Christological Legacy: Christocentrism and the Chalcedonian Tradition*. Milwaukee: Marquette University Press, 2017.

Zachman, Randall C. *The Assurance of Faith*. Minneapolis: Augsburg Fortress, 1993.

———. "Did the Death of Christ Appease the Wrath of God? Luther and Calvin on the Purpose of the Death of Christ." In *The Interface of Science, Theology, and Religion: Essays in Honor of Alister E. McGrath*, edited by Dennis Ngien, 66–85. Eugene, OR: Pickwick, 2019.

Zheng, Luke Ai-He. *Law and Gospel in Luther's Pastoral Teachings as Seen in His Lecture Notes: Finding Guidance in Genesis and Galatians to Serve the Household of God*. Bern: Lang, 2016.

Index

Index

INDEX